"In *Speak Up, Sister!* Jamie Dandar ___ ___ said ___ ___ to hear, in words that are seasoned with s___ ___ ___ so ___ ___ ___ with our shoulders back, our heads held high ___ and our fee___ ___ ___ standing straight with no excuses, no apologies. If you are ready to be all you were created to be in the Army of Life, this book will set you on a path to greatness such as you have never experienced before."

— **Beatrice Bruno,** The Drill Sergeant of Life

"Wonderful and thought-provoking guide for those just starting out their careers and those at any point in their career progression - especially those in a male dominated industry. *Speak Up, Sister!* feels as if you are having a conversation with your best friend and receiving down to earth yet honest advice."

— **Josie Semmes,** Finance Executive

"Reading *Speak Up, Sister!* is like jumping into a conversation with your closest girl-friend. Jamie's engaging writing style makes you feel as though you have a personal cheer-leader and mentor in your pocket, providing clear steps to help you build and navigate the professional world with confidence and become the best SHERO you can be."

— **Margaret Shaw,** CLC (State Public Health Nutrition Counselor)

"My daughter is an educational professional. After reading Jamie's book I see the positive influence it's had on her. She stands up better, more powerfully, more confident in both her professional and personal life. She's made big waves at work!"

— **Mary Laney,** Mother of a young professional who read this book

"Shortly after reading the chapter about not taking things personally, I was on a Zoom call where the presenter directed a comment at me that could have been interpreted as rude. Rather than let it affect my whole day, I figured that's his problem, not mine and didn't spend another second dwelling on it! It was so liberating!"

— **Colleen Tankoos,** Assistant Director

"*Speak Up, Sister!* is a book that will take you on a personal journey, guiding you as a professional. The author, Jamie Dandar McKinney uses quick wit in her conversations with the reader, making the rhythm of the text so relatable. Each page provoked thought- but not in the exhaustive way that some non-fiction writing does. There are several opportunities for purposeful self-reflection throughout the book. I promise you that you will know more about yourself, as well as your professional goals upon completion of *Speak Up, Sister!* The added bonus is the confidence you will feel!"

— **Lauren Tracy,** Student Services Coordinator

"Jamie's words empowered me to give myself grace. She has successfully coached me to shift from a game-over to game-on mindset, to eliminate the word "sorry" from my business vocabulary, and to embrace brave-ah-na in both my personal and professional life. Jamie has successfully conveyed her face-to-face animated personality, presence, poise and voice successfully in the pages of *Speak Up, Sister!*"

— **Kathleen Mann**, Account Manager

Speak Up, Sister!

SPEAK UP, Sister!

The Professional Woman's Guide to Confidence and Success

Jamie Dandar McKinney

KINGDOM
PUBLISHING

Speak Up, Sister!

Published by Kingdom Publishing
PO Box 630443
Highlands Ranch, CO 80163
www.kingdom-publishing.com

Cover Design: Tracy Fagan
Cover Photo: H. Nguyen Photography

Published 2020
Printed in the United States of America

ISBN 978-1-7333078-3-3 (print)
ISBN 978-1-7333078-4-0 (ebook)

Publisher's Cataloging-in-Publication data
Names: McKinney, Jamie Dandar, author.
Title: Speak up, sister! : the professional woman's guide to confidence and success. / by Jamie Dandar McKinney.
Description: Lone Tree [Colorado] : Kingdom Publishing, 2020. Paperback. Originally published in 2010. Also being published as an ebook.
Identifiers: ISBN: 978-1-7333078-3-3
Subjects: LCSH: Businesswomen. | Business communication.
BISAC: BUSINESS & ECONOMICS / Women in Business.
Classification: LCC HF5718 | DDC 658.45 MCKINNEY—dc22

Dedication

To my nieces, Taylor, Lemon, and Katelyn,
may your voices always be the vehicles that take you
wherever you want to go!

With Gratitude

There are many names sprinkled throughout theses pages and each one has earned my gratitude and praise. I am grateful both for those who lifted me up, inspired me and taught me so many useful things, as well as those who challenged or tested me in ways that taught me lessons of what not to do. In addition to thanking all those whose names appear in the prior pages, there are additional members of my tribe without whom this book would have never made it to the finish line. I'd like to acknowledge them here.

First, to Molly Pilkington who was Molly Baker when we first met. For it was she who set this journey in motion. Molly is an incredible woman whose embodiment of confidence and leadership lifts up all who surround her. It was over lunch at Appaloosa Grill in downtown Denver when she offered to connect me with her then boyfriend's mom, a woman whose name appears in the next paragraph. That introduction was a game changer and one for which I'll be forever grateful.

Annette Pilkington, Molly's now mother-in-law, oversees women's leadership programs at the Colorado School of Mines. "Mines" is a prestigious science and engineering school where the student population has grown to comprise approximately 30% women. Upon hearing my message of empowerment, confidence and leadership, it was Annette who was the first person to ask me, "How do I buy your book?" Writing a book, this book, at that point, had never even crossed my mind. Annette planted an important seed and then invited me to come speak to several women's groups at Mines. That seed was then watered each time I spoke when a handful of women came up afterward and asked me the same question. The 'God whispers' were adding up, I listened and decided to act.

As I started to write I wanted to do an early test drive of my material. Enter Susan Dandar who is several years into her professional career. She is intelligent, driven, well-read and well-spoken. I enlisted Susan's feedback on the first several chapters. Initially I asked her to answer just one question. "When you read these pages is it a cure for insomnia or do you want to keep reading?" Her initial response was, "My only regret in reading this now is that I didn't have it sooner! These exact situations are happening at work and I wish I would have had this advice earlier!" Susan went on to apply the advice and has since achieved recognition, credibility and accolades!

Another person deserving of extreme kudos is Tom Farmer. Tom and I had worked together years earlier on a completely unrelated project. It was then that I first saw Tom in action and hoped a future opportunity would present itself for us to reconvene. Per this project we reconnected, and he blessed me with coaching, guiding, challenging, encouraging, protecting, ideating, joking, creating, revising, and intuiting to levels I'd never known. What an honor to work under the hallowed influence of Tom Farmer. My respect and admiration continue to grow. Working with him was incredibly invigorating.

And lastly to my husband, Rob McKinney, whose support of my dreams and of this journey, specifically, is unwavering, patient, encouraging, and implicitly appreciated. He was always a willing sounding board to my thought processes as I worked through concepts and ideas out loud. Sometimes he offered suggestions and other times he just listened intently, so much so that he now humorously boasts about his own top-notch performance as a confident businesswoman. Always one to insert his wit, a big thank you to *Robbie* for loving me, championing me and pushing me when I needed a boost.

There is really nothing we accomplish in isolation. Everything we experience, learn or gain has somehow been catalyzed by someone else, starting with our parents and continuing with the many people whose paths we're blessed to cross.

With much gratitude and many blessings, I commend the men and women mentioned here and the broad spectrum of those on my path - past, present and future. May we all continue to *speak up*, and support each other in our struggles as well as share in our successes.

Table of Contents

Introduction

Just a Girl and Her Steel-Toe Stilettos

"Just don't be wearing them stilettos out here," was all Bob's email said.

I blinked at my laptop screen as the inbound email alert went off while I sat in my cubicle in the downtown Denver office. It was one of my first days on the job, and per my training schedule, I was required to tour an oil rig in Northern Colorado later that week. My manager, Steve, a man much different than this Bob character, called me into his office.

Now, Steve was everything you could want in a manager. He had a servant leadership style. He struck the perfect balance between supporting his team as professionals while demonstrating just the right amount of interest in our personal lives. As he reviewed my training schedule, he grimaced when he reached the part about who'd be running my rig tour. He shared some words of warning with regard to Bob.

"He's a little rough around the edges. Certainly chauvinistic. I wish I had a better option, but I think you can handle him. I'll be here if you need me." And so the plan proceeded accordingly.

A day prior, following protocol, I had emailed Bob to confirm the PPE (Personal Protective Equipment) required to comply with the safety code. My list included a hard hat, coveralls, safety glasses, gloves, and proper footwear. My tone was friendly and excited, and I mentioned that I looked forward to meeting him. His response, brief, sarcastic, and clearly not up to grammatical code, reinforced the cautionary advice given by my manager. I stared at the email and contemplated my response. Recalling a rule I'd learned some time earlier about mirroring people as a way to connect and also as a way to show that I could play Bob's game, I hit reply, "Well, my stilettos ARE steel-toe, so I'm sure that'll be fine." And hit send.

Receiving no additional communication from Bob, I arrived at the rig site bright and early the next day. Bob greeted me with an overly firm handshake and a crooked smile, perhaps an indication that he wasn't quite sure what to do with his newest trainee.

He gave me a look, nodded and said, "Follow me."

There was no direct communication regarding footwear, although I did see him glance to make sure that there were steel-toe BOOTS peeking out from under my baggy coveralls.

Bob's stoicism lasted only so long. As he patiently and thoroughly answered my steady flow of questions, it started to feel more like he was taking me under his wing, rather than begrudgingly following through with the training schedule and throwing superfluous challenges my way. He wound up showing me things not on the original list. Bob went out of his way to ensure my safety, from both moving equipment parts and the other gentlemen, who also were unaccustomed to anyone other than their own kind being on-site.

Upon my return to the office, Steve asked how it went.

"Great!" I exclaimed. I rattled off my new knowledge.

"And Bob was okay?" he questioned.

"Yep, good guy. We had a nice time."

"Huh," Steve said, "Nice work."

Bob was not the first "gentleman" of his caliber whom I'd encountered. Prior to entering the energy industry, I'd spent ten years in automotive where I joined a team of 400 salespeople, 397 of whom were men. Yes, that's less than a 1:100 ratio on a team of people who looked at me as if I were from another planet. Clearly the only possible origin for a woman 20 years their junior, who hadn't been raised around cars and came with ZERO technical training.

"Okay, honey, what the heck are you doing here?" was a question frequently asked out loud and no doubt thought in silence who knows how many times.

Our customer base's gender ratio was no different than our company's, and my gender-neutral name didn't offer much warning in advance of first-time meetings. I covered more than 70 customers spanning Colorado, Nebraska, and Wyoming. On numerous occasions, when I showed up for an appointment arranged over email, it was naturally assumed that my name belonged to a man. One guy actually spilled coffee all over himself when a female "Jamie" walked through his door.

After the initial shock that a woman was now the Territory Sales Manager, another question that often greeted me was, "You Ralph's granddaughter?" Ralph was my predecessor, a man I had met just once, at a Village Inn outside of Ft. Collins. His territory had opened up when he retired.

"Nope," I'd respond. "I'm Mike's granddaughter," referring of course to my own grandfather who lived in Ohio and was likely no acquaintance of theirs. They'd nod their heads and we'd continue.

From a very early starting point, I realized that I'd need to adapt to my surroundings quickly if I wanted to succeed. I had never been one to shy away from opportunities to use my voice, but this was a whole different ball game; I knew I had to level up.

Only later in my career did I finally identify the survival weapon I had been using the entire time. Whenever I walked into a situation where I was challenged on some level, either because I was the only woman, or the newest one, or the one who had to prove herself, or establish credibility in a way that the others didn't; every time, my survival skill boiled down to one thing. That one, incredibly consistent thing was leading with confidence.

Confidence, my secret weapon, allowed me to stand up for myself, speak up for myself, and create the visibility I needed in order for these guys to respect me and work with me. I had no choice, really. If I wanted to thrive, I first had to survive. And in an environment where I had NOTHING in common with my co-workers, I chose confidence as my most efficient tool. One swift shot of confidence, and we got down to business a whole lot faster.

I used confidence not as a confrontational weapon, but more as a strategic tool to help bridge the demographic and personality gaps between us. Confidence fueled the positive self-talk that cheered me on. Confidence was the voice that told me what I could do and what I would say, while affirmatively drowning out the negative self-talk that told me I couldn't.

Being centered in my confidence was also a device for not taking myself too seriously, for laughing at the many jokes which were appropriate, and for responding to those that crossed a line with a quick, firm "Nope." Carrying myself with confidence was the overarching survival skill I repeatedly deployed – first to prove myself, then to navigate typical workplace scenarios such as communicating with customers, expressing an idea that went against the grain, and using criticism to my advantage.

I learned that in all professional environments, there are two skills absolutely critical for success, especially for females who are outnumbered by their male counterparts: voice and visibility.

As women, we especially tend to take on extra work and more projects and assume that others are noticing. But study after study shows it's rarely the hardest worker who receives the recognition and the promotion. It's the one who is heard and seen the most. The most visible. Thankfully for both introverts and extroverts, there are many ways to amp up our confidence game and all the benefits that come with it. With just a little effort, skills can be developed which graduate into habits and habits which turn into noticeable differences.

Women who embrace these strategic improvements wind up with promotions!

Pre-career, I'll tell you what; my world was an Estrogen Empire. I'm one of three daughters; I played softball; I went to an all-girls high school; I was a cheerleader; I joined a sorority in college; I learned my way around a sewing machine; and to this day I prefer to 'Rosé all day' over any sort of microbrewery extravaganza. And yet my entire career has been spent in the Testosterone Towers of the automotive industry, renewable energy, residential construction, oil and gas, and even a stint in roofing. I've been grossly outnumbered since day one yet survived and thrived and lived to tell about it. I picked up a few tips and tricks along the way.

And if I can do it, anybody can do it!

Thankfully, the population of women I've come across in my career has grown. Typically, the more of us there are, the better. There is one exception, though: women who fall into the "catty category." Case in point: a woman named Jill (name changed to protect the guilty). Jill once called my boss and told him that I, on my recent trip to her territory in middle-of-nowhere Nebraska, I had bought rounds for the guys at the local bar, danced on the bar, and shown a little too much skin. The true story, far less interesting, is that I saw a movie in the theater alone that night. Luckily, having earned the respect of my boss, he didn't question me for a second. It was SHE who wound up with the tarnished reputation, whereas mine stayed clean.

I feel blessed to say, however, that Jill is the exception, not the rule. The vast majority of women I've encountered through work, the ones whom I consider friends, are a phenomenal group I like to call my 'Sheroes.' Women who work together with mutual respect.

We see each other as allies, not enemies.
It is a sisterhood of She + hero = Sheroes, where the
'Sherohood,' is an unstoppable force.

Comprised of women who recognize each other's strengths and weaknesses, the Sherohood collaborates for support and professional development. **We choose to be more like birds flying in formation, less like desperate crabs in a bucket.** Birds fly in formation so that the one in front provides uplift to the one behind it, and when a flock travels as a team, the birds increase their range by seventy-one percent! SEVENTY-ONE PERCENT! Crabs, on the other hand, all in a bucket, all trying to escape, continuously pull down the one who's managed to somehow climb her way to the top, on the brink of freedom, and all of a sudden, BAM! Another one of her very own kind pulls her back down into the bucket. I mean, I don't know about you, but I'd much rather fly like a bird than claw like a crab! #lifegoals. Sheesh!

This book is for you, if...

First, please allow me to express gratitude that you're here. I feel honored and privileged that we're able to spend this time together. Since I started writing this book, I'm thrilled to report that there's already a sizable ripple of success stories that I hope will grow into a tidal wave and include my readers' first-hand experiences! It gives me goosebumps just thinking about it!

A quick heads-up. This book was written for my ladies, yet there is something for everyone and all are welcome!

This book is for you, in particular, if:

1. You want to grow your love for yourself and stand firm in your power.

2. You have ever suffered self-doubt or heard that annoying little voice inside your head telling you that "You can't" or "You shouldn't." (Keep reading and it won't be long before you never hear from her again!)

3. You KNOW you have gifts, talents, and ideas that you badly want to share with the world but have kept inside for fear of judgment or that they're not good enough.

4. Anyone who recognizes the value of women and has a compassionate curiosity for offering support and understanding in a workplace environment. Just a small shift in support can make a big difference to indivduals, to groups of women and even to a company's bottom line.

Part I and Part II are very different

Part I covers the fundamentals of confidence, including the science behind it, why having a strong foundation of confidence is critical, how to build that foundation and how to fortify it when challenged. For maximum results, I encourage you to take the time to do the exercises.

Part II is arranged into predominantly stand-alone chapters. The chapters in this section describe common workplace challenges and offer proven solutions for successfully, effectively, and confidently navigating them. When you have a strong foundation of confidence, you are an unstoppable force. You will learn howbe able to break through barriers that tend to hold back women by using both grit and grace! There are stories, studies, checklists, and more!

What's in it for you? The journey to Brave-ah-na!

This book is an authentic collection of my stories, first-hand experiences, and observations culled from over two decades in the working world. It is my truth, and I'm honored to share it with you. My dream and hope for you is that in reading through this book and applying the suggestions, you'll experience an amazing feeling called *Brave-ah-na*.

Brave-ah-na rhymes with nirvana. It's the feeling of euphoria that washes over one after she's confronted and overcome a fear that no longer holds her back. Brave-ah-na, a concept that will surface throughout the book, starts off as fear. Fear is challenged by courage. Courage breeds success. Success manifests as confidence and, boom! Brave-ah-na, a feeling more rewarding than the Zen afterglow following a spa treatment at a five-star hotel. Yep, seriously, THAT good.

I'd be remiss to not warn you that the journey to Brave-ah-na can be scary at times. You'll have butterflies in your stomach. Not to worry, though, because with the right support in place, it'll be the best road trip you've ever taken. So hop in, roll down the windows, jam the tunes, and get ready to Speak Up, Sister!

Lastly, if you want to dig deeper and get even more out of this book, visit **www.jamieempowers.com**, where you'll find additional resources. Or contact me directly at **www.jamieempowers.com/contact**. I'd love to hear from you!

Part 1

Chapter 1
Hit It to Me!

My family loves baseball. Growing up in Ohio we claimed not one, but two major league teams: the Cleveland Indians and the Cincinnati Reds. With just an hour's drive we could be sitting in a third MLB stadium, that of the Detroit Tigers; our house was less than 10 miles from the Michigan border. My grandpa on my mom's side cheered for the Yankees from the time he was a little boy. My own Dad coincidentally did as well. So, that's four teams right off the *bat* (Ha ha, get it? I love a good pun), all frequent topics of conversation while we sat at the picnic table over the summer.

Come fall, it was time for playoffs and the World Series would, of course, cap off every season. We lived in an average Midwest neighborhood with a shared interest in baseball, so the World Series was a big event. Each year, as the leaves turned colors, several dads would gather at our house to initiate the setup for our watch party. They'd assemble and work as a team, carrying the Dandar family big-screen TV, and I do mean BIG, not flat and light like today's, out into the front yard. They'd set it on top of a tall dresser and run extension cords out from the house. A pretty classy setup, I must say.

We'd all pitch in to gather every lawn chair and diligently place them in neat rows, so they resembled a façade for bleachers. My sisters and I would make tickets from construction paper, and we'd serve beer to the adults and Cracker Jacks to the kids, just like in the big leagues. The parents and kids would gather on each night of the World Series to watch the game and pretend we were all right there in the stadium, having a wonderful time. One year we even made a Goodyear blimp out of cardboard and strung it from one tree to another, giving the illusion that it was flying overhead. That might have been the year that the

9

local TV channel came out to showcase our baseball fandom on the evening news.

So baseball has been a love of mine since very early in life. Later, shortly after college, I was in my apartment watching ESPN when I saw an interview that has forever stuck with me. The subject was Derek Jeter, captain of the New York Yankees and one of the best shortstops of all time. The journalist casually tossed questions at Jeter and the conversation progressed nicely. It was similar to a casual game of catch, back and forth, back and forth…until one particular question disrupted the flow.

The journalist set it up.

"Okay, Jeter, it's a high-pressure situation. Bottom of the 9th, go-ahead run on third, the Yankees need this win to clinch the playoffs. You're standing at shortstop and the opposing team's star hitter steps up to the plate." He paused, looked Jeter dead in the eyes, and slowly and dramatically asked: "What's going through your head?"

Jeter didn't miss a beat. Without hesitation, with barely half a second passing after the journalist's last word, Jeter quickly yet calmly said, "Hit it to me."

He said it so fast and with such certainty, the journalist (and I) were both thrown off guard, captivated by what the captain himself had just said. I leaned into the TV, thinking, "What did he say?" mirroring the journalist's reactions. Taken aback, and with a shot of whimsy, the journalist smiled and asked Jeter to repeat himself.

"What did you say?"

Jeter, this time more slowly and intentionally, asserted, "Hit (pause) it (pause) to (pause) me (pause). Hit it to me," he said and looked the journalist right in the eye. "I want that ball. Especially when there's THAT much riding on that pitch, I want it. I know how to catch it. I know how to field it. I know how to get the out. Win the game. Hit it to me."

The journalist sat back and smiled. I too sat back and smiled, thoroughly impressed. It was both *impressive* and made a huge *impression* on me. Jeter's words and his demeanor were so impactful. He was neither arrogant nor cocky in what he said. He wasn't boastful or showing off. He was simply being authentic and demonstrating *unequivocal confidence* in his abilities. He had an unmistakable belief that his teammates, the fans in Yankee stadium, heck, probably the entire population of the Bronx, could rely on him in that moment. This was his job.

He knew how to do it better than anyone else, and he wasn't afraid to say it. He owned it with the self-assurance of someone who would go on to win FOUR World Series championships.

To achieve that level of confidence was certainly an anomaly. Jeter: a rare find, a diamond in the rough, a unicorn. Few others, if anyone, I thought, could match that degree of certainty with the performance to back it up. He was one of a small, select circle.

Or was he?

A few weeks later, I was having dinner with my girlfriend Robin. Robin was in her mid-30s and the CEO of a landscape architecture company, a significant achievement at any age, let alone this early and as a woman. As we ate, I relayed the dialogue from the Jeter interview. I was still thinking about it and excited to share it. I got to the end of the story, at which point I figured she'd mirror my excitement and awe in the rarity of his confidence. I imagined that Robin would react as I had and agree that such confidence was unattainable to average people like us.

Instead, she responded to the contrary.

"I have that, too," she boldly yet humbly stated. My eyes widened with intrigue. "You have what, too?" I asked.

With utmost poise and class, Robin replied, "I have that 'Hit it to me' feeling."

I was astounded. Bright-eyed, brimming with delight, I implored further. "You do? When?"

Matter-of-factly, very confidently, Robin said: "On Thursday nights. In my club volleyball league."

I laughed in supportive amazement. I mean, I already thought Robin was unbelievably cool and accomplished, all things that I too aspired to be. Yet *now* -- now she shot up even higher on my admiration scale, having articulated that while she was maybe not quite performing at the level of a professional baseball player, she too had attained unequivocal confidence in a league of her own! Confidence in something as mainstream and every day as a club volleyball league, for Pete's sake!

Huh. I was again blown away, but in a totally different way this time. This woman with Jeter-style 'Hit-It-to-Me' confidence was sitting right here across from me. Her confidence struck me as achievable, pragmatic, and practically palpable. I could barely contain my exhilaration at this new revelation.

Jeter was one thing. And honestly? While I've set some high goals in my life, becoming a shortstop for the New York Yankees has never been one of them. Robin, however, was something and someone entirely different. She provoked completely innovative thoughts in my mind. Some utterly transformative thinking.

If Jeter had a 'Hit it to me' skill and Robin had a 'Hit it to me' skill, then what was my 'Hit it to me' skill?

And what if I looked beyond athletic abilities? What about my professional life? Did I have 'Hit it to me' skills at work? The ones I and my team members both recognized? Activities or categories in which they continuously came to me for expertise and advice? What about my personal life? Maybe even in the context of a relationship; what were my hit-it-to-me traits? Was I one of the best listeners, or could I claim patience as one of my strongest virtues? (Answer: No, I most definitely cannot claim patience as one of my strongest virtues.)

Which hit-it-to-me skills did I aspire to develop so thoroughly and intentionally, I too could claim Jeter's level of confidence? Skills that, whether on a calm workday or amid a crisis, my team would know they can count on me to deliver? I'm the one who can securely catch the issue, work on the issue, and deliver an on-time, accurate solution. Heck, maybe I already had hit-it-to-me skills -- I'd just never dedicated time to think about them, let alone evaluate or improve upon them.

Whoa! This was a HUGE grand slam of a discovery in my life. Almost as exciting as a World Series win!

And so began the effort and energy to think about not only my hit-it-to-me skills, but those of the people around me, too. What skill sets did they excel in? The ones I knew I could rely on?

Allow me to digress at this point and play journalist with you. Let me ask you; what are YOUR hit-it-to-me skills? Where do you stand out from the crowd? Let's give it an acronym for ease in remembering: *HITM* (pronounced HIT-EM). Everyone has *HITM* skills. Some are well-known, some are in development, and several might simply be awaiting discovery.

HITMs are the tasks and accountabilities that you perform with excellence. Where you excel faster than your peers and you're known for reliability as it relates to a particular category. That's your _HITM_.

On a flight, I sat next to a woman and asked about her *HITMs*. Her initial response was, "Hmmm, I don't have any," she shrugged sadly. I refused to believe her and dug a little deeper.

"Really? You're a super smart computer programmer. You're fluent in technical languages that other people can't even name, let alone, use. Surely there's something that your teammates continuously bring to you because they know just how good you are at doing it."

She thought further. "Well, actually, you know every time a certain hiccup comes up with the Artex program, they ask for my opinion and for my help. Yeah," she looked back at me and nodded, "I know that program better than anyone else and I like working on it, too."

"Awesome! I have no clue what Artex is. Tell me more about that!" We both smiled as she shared more about the program itself AND how she felt in those moments when her team knew they could rely on her. Just watching and listening to her, I could hear the enthusiasm in her voice and see her posture stir with empowerment. She transitioned from speaking meekly to exuding success, self-reliance, and confidence, and all from briefly pondering her HITM -- a term as new to her as Artex was to me!

As child psychologist Roxanne Thompson says about kids and self-esteem, "Recognize the child's strengths and encourage them to use those strengths when they are up against a challenge." This builds resilience and helps kids stay on track. The same is true for adults!

Optimizing Strengths and Weaknesses

Another way to describe *HITMs* is as areas where you're above average and you take pride in it. We all have 'em, as we do our weaknesses. The beauty of this dichotomy is that no one person can do it all. There's an elegance and a flow that comes from working on teams who embrace strengths and adjust for weaknesses. Differences can be celebrated and optimized by intentionally pairing the right combination of strengths and weaknesses.

Take baseball, for example. I'm sure Jeter could hold his own to a certain extent at any position on the field. But when it comes to optimizing performance, there are other players who are the best at pitching, outfielding, and infielding. Putting Jeter in a slot someone else could play better doesn't make sense for optimizing team performance; nor would it help his confidence, assuming his performance is subpar compared to where he shines, at shortstop. Focusing on tasks for which we have both standout ability and high interest is a surefire way to build and boost confidence.

Identifying and being aware of both strengths *and* weaknesses is important. It helps you dedicate appropriate time and effort to both. Having an honest conversation with yourself, and even with someone else who'll offer you frank feedback, is important so we don't find ourselves in over our heads with no way out. This conversation will also help us know when to take on challenges and enlist resources for help. We'll talk about this more in the chapter on mistakes.

Nature and nurture both play roles in development of our strengths and weaknesses. Did you know that by the age of 7, most of our motor skills are developed? At that age I knew I wasn't going to be great at basketball, for example. It just didn't come naturally to me. I enjoyed a rousing game of H-O-R-S-E on the half court in our backyard, yet was never the best in the neighborhood, or even a valid competitor. I could perform at a baseline level, but it was defeating and self-deflating to play and never win. I didn't like what it did to my self-esteem. It hurt my confidence to keep playing a game where I was incredibly unexceptional. I was not motivated to keep at it. The other neighborhood kids got better, and I just did not. As for my grade school basketball team, it's completely fair to say they knew better than to throw-it-to-me. I showed up to play because I'd made a commitment; but, honestly, I didn't want to be there.

My sister, on the other hand, was a natural at basketball. I got way more satisfaction out of watching her growth and performance on the court and cheering her on than struggling with my relative ineptitude. I'm glad I gave basketball a shot, though, because I wouldn't have known otherwise. I checked it off my list and moved along to discover something else that would be my *HITM*.

Thankfully, shooting hoops is not something I've had to do in my adult life for a work event or team building exercise. That would be horrifying. But there are work-related tasks that I, and likely you, have had to attempt where no matter how hard we work, we fall short of our peers. It's certainly important to know our weaknesses, so we can plan accordingly or request additional training. That's just how work goes sometimes. Over the long term, though, your career satisfaction will be enhanced as you navigate through different roles and responsibilities. You'll find your niche, especially when you prioritize awareness of your *HITM* skills. Even the most poised, professional, successful people, male and female alike, have weaknesses and strengths. The successful ones know to acknowledge both – and build teams of people with complementary skill sets.

I worked for an oil and gas services company where our management team was very small, less than eight people. Each of us had a specialty, and each relied on other team members' expertise to lead the company. The price of oil had crashed, and some companies experienced massive layoffs. Our CEO took a different approach. We each played such specialized roles that letting any of us go would have hurt the whole company. It would have been like playing a game without a key position (like when a hockey player goes in the penalty box), exposing a major vulnerability or weakness. Instead, he retained all of us and reduced our individual compensation by 10%.

While nobody likes a 10% cut, it's far superior to a 100% cut resulting in a job loss. More importantly we were able to maintain the strength of our team by preserving our well-balanced mix of HITMs. An optimal combination of HITMs will maximize success and minimize failure.

Years later, I went through a strengths-building exercise with a team I managed. The technique I used was inspired by a foundational confidence-boosting exercise my parents did for my sisters and me when we were young. They allowed us, or rather pressed us, to each have a unique hobby. They asked each of us to choose an activity that we wanted to explore individually and enrolled us in lessons. For me, it was dance. Art for my middle sister, horseback riding for the youngest. Each was our hobby and ours alone.

I wonder now how integral that was in forming our self-esteem. We each got to do something that we liked and dedicated time and effort to becoming the family expert. Did we want to choreograph our own dance show when we played together? Yes, well, I was the natural leader on that. Was there some super creative project that involved painting? Well, Colleen would be the one to drive it, managing contributions from Sally and me. Did we want to set up a horse race and run them down our urban street block? In the absence of real horses, we used stuffed animals, but, boy, what an event it was, rivaling Churchill Downs in our imaginations. While her fellow jockeys, otherwise known as her sisters, played along, Sally orchestrated the whole thing. When it came to conversations about horses and family day trips to visit farms (something you can readily do in Ohio), it was Sally who was most at ease and familiar with the turf. It was her time to shine.

Later in my career, as the VP of sales and marketing at a financial technology start-up, I did something similar with my team of millennials. Upon getting their buy-in, each was designated as the resident expert in one of our four target areas. Now, instead of four generalists, we had four experts, one for product, for troubleshooting and problem solving, for systems, and for customer service. These were their designated *HITM* skills. Each still had accountability to meet a baseline performance level in each category, and when an opportunity or issue surfaced, the team expert was called in to save the day.

When opportunities came for external training, instead of sending the whole team, I sent the expert as it related to the topic. When he returned, I asked him to teach his teammates what he learned. I absolutely LOVED watching a teammate's confidence soar when his *HITM* skill set was enlisted to help a fellow team member. Not only was it a confidence booster for the employee to perform his *HITM*, it was a development opportunity for the team, it was helpful to the customer, and it grew the company's bottom line. A winning combination, all around!

Let's circle back to you and YOUR strengths. Taking time to identify and evaluate them will make for a more fulfilling, less frustrating, more rewarding work experience. It's a fun, exciting self-esteem boost when you're doing something that comes naturally to you – and you continue to improve the more you work at it.

Malcolm Gladwell and some other experts say it takes 10,000 hours to master a skill. Assuming one dedicates 40 hours per week to mastering one singular thing, that means 4.8 years. Almost five entire years spent on ONE thing. That's a long time, right? But *HITMs* aren't necessarily about mastery – rather about excellence as measured against your peers. Very few of us have responsibility for just one singular task at work. Most jobs include a variety of accountabilities. Put some intention behind the things that you both LIKE to do and are good at doing. See how it impacts your confidence!

Motivational public speaker and self-development author Brian Tracy declares you need only five to seven skill sets to set yourself up for success. So why not build that short list by considering what you enjoy doing and where you naturally stand apart?

Giving thought to your areas of excellence and/or to those that you're working toward is an essential tool for building confidence. You might reflect on categories or tasks where you tend to outperform others and are considered expert by your peers and colleagues. I've surveyed groups and had many conversations where I re-tell the Jeter interview story, culminating in my favorite question:

What is your Hit it to Me?

I love watching people light up when they answer, just like the woman on the plane. Their posture becomes stronger, their voice more animated. They smile, they lean in, they exude brilliance, and, dare I say, an aura, that is so positive and full of light and energy. Their confidence becomes practically palpable. It absolutely makes my day to watch it happen right before my eyes. And you know what? It makes their day, too!

The contagious nature of what ensues is quite special. As I listen to someone talk about her go-to skill set(s), I can hear her confidence rise in that very moment. And, get this: I notice my very OWN confidence rising as well. It's incredibly contagious. We experience privilege by proximity, as I like to call it. In a later chapter, we'll take a closer look at the neurochemistry of what's happening in our brains as we hold conversations like this. In the meantime, the important thing to know is that it is very easy to flip the switch on your confidence and that anyone can do it. Anyone can instantly channel confidence. By simply thinking and talking about your *HITMs*, you may feel a kick start.

People with authentic confidence light up a room, project a charismatic persona, and achieve desirable outcomes. They're respected, admired, and valued. They focus on what they do well and have an honest understanding of their weaknesses, too. They communicate with accuracy and humility. They're not necessarily the smartest person in the room, yet they know and optimize their strengths to get things done, a critical factor in achieving and exceeding workplace goals. They're fulfilled both professionally and personally.

Are they perfect? Nope. Do they have off days? Absolutely. And they know how to CTRL+ALT+DEL their personal hard drives and do a reboot when needed.

No matter how introverted (or extroverted) you are, no matter how you'd rank your self-esteem, no matter how little belief you have in yourself is at this moment, it is unequivocally possible to change and grow. You have the power and you'll learn how to do it here. It doesn't take Herculean effort; rather tiny steps will get you started. You may be surprised by how quickly a small shift in momentum can change your entire course. The shift can fill your sails and make you feel like an America's Cup catamaran swiftly cruising to victory.

Know Thyself: Identifying Your *Hit It to Me*

If you're committed to learning more about confidence and how to get yours rockin', getting started is quite easy.

First, now that we've talked about them it's time to identify them: what are your Hit It to *Mes*? If you've got yours ready to go, skip ahead and write them down now in the space provided. If you're still thinking and need some ideas, continue reading. I'll get you there!

If you're thinking that you don't have any *HITMs*, here's some tough love. I'm going to be very honest with you. I don't believe you. You have them. Some may be yet undiscovered, and I swear on the best bottle of wine in my fridge that you have them. In fact, I sincerely request that you ask close family members, friends, or co-workers to help you. If you're struggling to think of any on your own, ask people you respect, "What do you think I'm good at doing?"

Then decide if you also enjoy doing those things. Seriously, and I care about you. I didn't write this book for me; I wrote it for you. I believe in you. Putting a little effort toward identifying your *HITMs* helps you believe in you too and that is the best feeling of all!

HITMs can be both present and future tense. Something you aspire to do can qualify. Have you ever observed someone else in action and thought, "Hmm, that could be me. I could do that"? Great. Write that down. It's fantastic to have ideas not only of HITMs you currently possess, but also some that help elevate your career if you were to develop them.

Here are some possible *HITMs* for you:

- **Professional tasks** – Attention to detail, formulas in Excel, strategic thinking, ideation, conflict resolution, creative lesson plans or meeting agendas, patient care, charting, customer service, team manager, etc.
- **Personal tasks** – Remembering birthdays, listening well, being a great hug-giver (it's a real thing!), sharing a meal with a friend in need, calling your Mom on a regular basis and asking how she is, being the friend who'll always cheer someone up, etc.
- **Athletic abilities** – Weightlifting, cardio, distance running, volleyball, soccer, yoga, martial arts, meditation, hockey, roller blading, dog walking, crawling on the floor with kids, etc.

Have you thought of a few? I hope so! Did simply thinking about them boost your spirits? I bet it did!

Here are more thought-provokers. Very sincerely ask yourself the following questions:

- What do I LIKE doing?
- Do I notice patterns in what others ask me to do?
- To what types of meetings am I invited? Is there a pattern?
- Am I more of a people person, or a data person?
- What do others say I do well? What compliments am I consistently given?
- If I were to give myself a workplace performance review, how would I rate me and in what categories?

There's a variety of online resources offering formal assessments to help identify your strengths. In the context of this chapter, focusing on what you already know is all you need. If you'd like to take free assessments to help find your strengths, head to www.jamieempowers.com for a list of resources.

So back to you. Time for you to pause and think about your *HITM* traits. I invite you to put the book down, and consider things you both enjoy and already know that you're good, great, even EXCELLENT at doing. When you're ready, write them in below. Here are a couple of entries to get you started.

HITM Skills	**Have**	**Want**
1. Building PowerPoint Presentations	X	
2. Knowing my way around a P&L Statement		X
3. _____		
4. _____		
5. _____		

Here's another way to think about it. Fill in the lines below:

Tasks That I Do Well	Tasks That I Like Doing
_____	_____
_____	_____
_____	_____
_____	_____

Is there any overlap between the two? Did any of the tasks that appeared in the left column also show up in the right? If so, those are your *HITMs*!

For any Venn diagram fans out there, here is how *HITMs* look in that context:

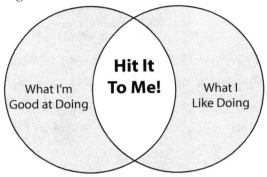

Working with all these suggestions on how to identify your HITMs, you're hopefully finding value in this exercise. To aid in your success, it's really important to think through what occurs within you when you hit the sweet spot – something you do well and love doing. You're rewarded for a job well done with internal satisfaction and external praise! It's invigorating and a self-esteem booster to work on things you like, so why not be intentional about naming these things?

That was task number one. For the second task, pay close attention to your HITMs. I'll let you in on the secret as to why. It's a tiny yet very important distinction. Most people think that confidence is built based on an ending, on outcomes. Winners are confident because they won, they believe, and losers lack confidence because they failed.

While positive outcomes can reinforce and further grow your confidence, they are not where confidence begins.

**It's actually when you take that very first step that
confidence sprouts.**

When you build confidence in one area, it transfers to another. Confidence built in your personal life will transfer to confidence in your professional life, and vice versa. Newton's First Law of Motion states that an object will remain at rest unless acted upon by an external force. Even a tiny movement created by some external force, also known as effort, leads to acceleration. It's a scientific principle that one small step leads to another, leads to another, and another, building confidence each time!

Taking any initiative, no matter how small, sets you in motion, and that's all you need to get started. You don't have to get all the way to the last PowerPoint slide of your boardroom presentation in order to check the confidence box. You simply have to speak your introduction to experience a little kick and get your momentum going.

Psychological studies show that it's actually NOT the outcome, but rather taking the first step, that begins building your confidence.

Let that sink in for a second. To build confidence, you don't have to win. You don't even have to have a favorable outcome. We love it when we do, but the simple act of TRYING will increase your confidence.

Isn't that liberating?! You don't have to *perfect* something to boost your self-esteem. If you focus on trying, on that initial step, on the initiation of a task -- that small move, by itself, will boost your confidence and create momentum to project you forward. Will you then be catapulted toward a successful outcome? Maybe, maybe not. Either way, you've done something you hadn't done before. You can evaluate the outcome, whatever it was, and refine and improve your approach for next time. Was it a success the first time? Cool! Was it a failure or a mistake? Never fear! We'll spend an entire chapter on how to handle that.

Prioritizing tasks you're good at helps you reinforce your confidence and cement your foundation. Recognize even tiny wins and savor the satisfaction of a job well done. Reserving time in your calendar for *HITMs* as an essential means of generating momentum to keep you moving forward..

The Virtuous Cycle of Job Performance and Confidence

Have you ever been in a spin class or on a Peloton bike? The flywheel is quite heavy when you first clip your foot into the pedal. It takes a decent push to get started. (Have you ever let out an audible "Uuuurgh" to get that sucker going? I sure have.) Yet once the momentum is there, the wheel spins with ease and it's exhilarating and rewarding to push ahead. One push of your foot boosts your energy and that energy then fuels your next push. The virtuous cycle of job performance and confidence looks kind of like that, with attention paid to one, in turn fueling the other!

There's a symbiotic relationship between job performance and confidence. It goes around and around, elevating you all the while. With confidence comes improved job performance, and as your performance is improving, your confidence rises in your ability to perform. Pretty soon your colleagues and managers are noticing, and praiseful comments are showing up on your performance reviews.

Increased confidence fuels your job performance, and successful job performance fuels confidence.

You are creating a virtuous cycle that leads to fulfillment and satisfaction at work. As others rely on you and look to you for expertise in your *HITM* area, they see you as a leader. Leaders get promoted and promotions can mean higher compensation. What might start as something small can quickly gain momentum.

What a gift it is to be in the invigorating vortex of a virtuous cycle!

I'll close out this chapter with a real-world *HITM* success story.

Krista was a manager at an energy company. Every Monday morning, it was Krista's responsibility to assemble and distribute a report for her boss and her team. Was she good at doing it? Yes, she had impeccable attention to detail and compiled that report with more accuracy than anyone on her team. Did she enjoy the task? Meh, not really, thus disqualifying it as a true *HITM*.

Another one of Krista's skills was her financial savvy. She had a great eye for putting together slide decks for investors. When it came time to pitch, everyone knew Krista was the person to build the presentation! Was she good at doing it? Oh, absolutely. Did she enjoy doing it? Yes, that, too! For Krista, this was a *Hit*

It to Me. Her performance as well as her confidence soared as she worked on her project. She derived satisfaction from producing, and from the kudos she received from the team. It was another huge pat on her back when her audience of investors signed the deal. Go Krista!

As you go through your day, try to compartmentalize your tasks, considering which ones light your fire. If you find several, that's awesome! In that case I would surmise that you are both successful and satisfied at work. If you're struggling, maybe it's time to ask for a special project, or take on something else new and exciting to you. If you're still having trouble after that, you may want to consider if there's a different role entirely that would speak to your gifts and strengths. To create a virtuous cycle, which is such a productive and satisfying place to be in your career, it's imperative to find tasks you enjoy and allow you to excel.

You don't want to be stuck on the basketball court if you dread basketball. It's not fair to your teammates and it's not fair to your confidence either. It's much more fun to thrive than to merely survive!

Staying mindful and protective of your confidence level at work is so important, because it props you up in every other area of your life. The bottom line is, YOU ARE AN AMAZING HUMAN BEING. You have many talents, some of which you know and some you've yet to discover. Be grateful and joyous for all that you are, and all that life's journey presents to you. Stand proud knowing that your HITM traits are unique and were given to you for a purpose. Be generous with them and grateful for them. I promise that, when you do, the rewards are limitless.

And those rewards are what we will explore in the next chapter. We'll also look at what's at risk when confidence is not prioritized or demonstrated. The stakes are high! From there, we'll check out how confidence sounds and how it looks. And then we'll take a full tour of the Confidence Tool Shed, where you'll have access to over 30 tools for building and boosting your confidence.

In Part II of the book, we'll take a close look at real-world scenarios frequently encountered in the workplace. Navigating them with confidence will help both professionally and personally. Job performance is one critical factor that drives your success. Confidence is the key to accelerating that success while helping you feel more empowered along the way!

What's at Stake?

Missing out on opportunities for you to shine, feel fulfilled, and get promoted! Homing in on your strengths enables you to stand apart from the crowd and make your irreplaceable contributions.

Key Points

- EVERYONE has a *HITM*, if not several.
- Awareness and development of your *HITM*, i.e., exceptional strengths, lead to satisfaction and increased performance.
- You create a virtuous cycle of increased confidence and improved job performance when you prioritize *HITMs*.
- A high functioning team optimizes each other's strengths and compensates for each other's weaknesses.

Confidence Challenge Checklist

- ❏ Name your *Hit-It-to-Me's*!
- ❏ Pick one *HITM* this week and prioritize spending time on it. Tell someone else what you're up to.
- ❏ Have a team building meeting to identify and maximize each person's unique *HITM* to increase overall team performance.
- ❏ Find three friends or colleagues and explain the *HITM* skill concept to them. Ask them, "What is your *HITM*?" Key in on how their energy changes!

To stretch and condition my confidence, one action I commit to is:

_____

_____

_____

Chapter 2
What is Confidence and What's in It for Me?

A dozen young men all planned to propose marriage to a young woman.
Eleven came with a rose. The 12th showed up with a ring.
Now, that's **confidence!**

What is a key that you can't carry on a keyring, but with it,
you'll never be locked out? **Confidence!**

My 6-year-old niece asked me, "What's the difference between confidence and
confidential?" I thought about it carefully and replied, "I am your aunt,
and you are my niece whom I love; of that I am **confident**.
I fed you ice cream before dinner. That is *confidential!*"

Confidence is a universal trait. It does not discriminate against anyone! It's
incredibly inclusive and available to all. Confidence isn't concerned about your
age, gender, race, culture, sexual orientation, socioeconomic class, education, or
profession.

It doesn't mind if you're a vegetarian, a proletarian, or a libertarian. Asian, Cajun,
or Malaysian? Doesn't matter. Career experience, new at your role? No problem.
Extrovert? Sure! Introvert? Yes, you, too! Jock, geek, hipster, band member. All
are invited to join the party. It truly is a one-size-fits-all and is attainable for
absolutely everyone!

In fact, if you're hosting a diversity-and-inclusion event and looking to highlight
a special guest, consider inviting Ms. Confidence! She doesn't discriminate
and embraces all. There's not a single genre of person who can be excluded.

Confidence doesn't even care what kind of roof you have over your head – or whether you have one at all.

There's a very inspiring and impactful non-profit organization called Back on My Feet. Through organized running programs, they help homeless people find a new place to live – and a job to earn the income they need to keep the house. Their mission is to help people "get back on their feet." It's an incredibly successful program. Of the foundational characteristics they require for individuals to succeed in their program, guess what's number one? Here's the answer as taken directly from the Back on My Feet website: "Our unique model demonstrates that if you first restore confidence, strength and self-esteem, individuals are better equipped to tackle the road ahead." Running helps the program participants believe in themselves. Anyone must believe in themselves before others will follow.

Have you ever noticed what quality all those webinars, seminars, and training classes teaching businesses skills consistently mention as a success requirement? Yep, again, it's confidence. The next time you watch a video or webinar to learn a side hustle, improve your well-being, market your product using social media, enhance your leadership skills, or accelerate your professional development, notice how they all include at least a small bit about mindset and believing in yourself. They each have a unique spin on why their program is best. Many do have a few nuggets of information and tips worth implementing. What they ALL have in common, though, is a confidence shout-out. It's been included in EVERY SINGLE webinar I've ever seen promoting a product or service to help improve your life. And I think it's fantastic. The common denominator for enriching and enhancing your life is having confidence.

The bottom line is that confidence is the bottom line.

It is your foundation. Your infrastructure for believing enough in yourself to be able to achieve what you want.

Picture a skyscraper, or heck, a two-story townhome will do. When the builders start building it, what do they start with? The foundation and infrastructure, of course. I'm no architect or construction engineer, but I do know that if they get this part wrong, they risk a disaster later, and a lawsuit! A flawed foundation may look OK for awhile, yet it's not sustainable. Trying to build atop something that's shaky at best will only wind up in frustration, patchwork, or implosion.

A proper foundation, however, leads to a strong, sturdy, reliable structure.

Confidence gives you the same supportive foundation you need to prop up your courage to try something new, to speak up in a meeting, to address an issue with someone who intimidates you, or to maintain poise in the midst of confusing changes at work. Confidence can also be a very magnetic force that attracts others to you. It garners respect, credibility, and likeability. It helps you solidify the platform you need to tackle whatever it is you want to achieve or build, whether it be a project, a business, your next job, or a relationship.

Whether you're starting a business, starting a class, going to work, setting small goals, setting high goals, playing in a club sport, or presenting in front of your team at work, confidence is a fundamental and foundational element for ALL success stories, no matter how big or small. Confidence helps women get the credit they deserve, the visibility they need, and the career they desire. The power is ours for the taking!

It's not that you won't have days of doubt and fear. You will. I will. We all do. Yet knowing that you hold the blueprint, the plan to reset your confidence and prioritize it, automatically sets you apart and ahead. It helps you ditch self-doubt and move with much greater velocity toward your goal.

You've got an achievable level of confidence inside of you at all times. Having that foundational belief cemented inside is my very sincere wish, hope, and dream for you. It's the mission and the reason why I wrote this book. There's too much at stake when you lack confidence, and so much to gain for having a firm grip on it, locked tightly inside your head and your heart.

What's at Risk Without Confidence?

Before we get into the gifts and advantages confidence brings, let's get clear on what's at stake and what traps your confident self will avoid.

Here are the three big drags on a life lived with too little confidence.

First, *envy* – one of the Seven Deadly Sins. Also called FOMO – Fear of Missing Out -- or ROMO, which is even worse: the Reality of Missing Out. Ugh, not pretty! Confidence gives you the power to shun the envy and the jealousy. You won't watch your professional life go by as other people advance. You won't say to yourself, "That was MY idea!" when you hear credit for an accomplishment go to another. You won't regret not trying things, nor will you be frustrated that, despite your intelligence and ability to outperform your peers, some are outpacing you. You won't be jealous of others' triumphs, because you'll have your own. You'll likely also be able to collaborate and learn from the people who are winning, because your self-esteem and confidence are in a healthy enough place to do so.

As Teddy Roosevelt said, "Envy is the thief of joy." When two similarly qualified candidates are up against each other for a job and one has more confidence than the other, guess who typically receives the offer? With confidence, the joy and the job are all yours! And best of all, you can say NOMO (No more!) to both FOMO and ROMO!

The second big cost of lack of confidence: *cocoon confinement*. Ugh, can you even imagine? Being confined in a cocoon for a long time? It's boring, it's lonely. It's dark, it's damp, it's crowded, the view isn't great, and good luck moving through your morning yoga flow. The tight boundaries of the cocoon impair your ability to do things, see things, and embark on special journeys. You can't see out and it can be rather lonely, too. Having confidence helps you break free of the cocoon's tight boundaries and spread your beautiful, majestic wings. You wouldn't want to hide those wings now, would you? It'd be like hiding your favorite outfit away in a dry-cleaning bag in your closet. What a disservice to you and your outfit! Bust it out, put it on, and let the whole world see. You have too much potential to be confined in a boring, dingy, stagnant space.

Third, too little confidence is *selfish*. The people need you. Withholding your innovative thoughts and ideas deprives those who need to hear them.

Be like Susan, an advocate for kids in special education. After mustering the confidence to stand up to someone who was denying evaluations these kids needed, she decided to take action. She felt she had to do it not just for herself, but for six-year-old Thomas, too young to speak up for himself. It worked. The kids received the evaluations they need because once-timid Susan knew what was at stake and that these kids needed her.

Research shows that women are more successful at negotiating for others than for themselves. Speak up, loud and proud. Others are counting on you. If you can't do it for yourself, be brave enough to do it for them.

As I was writing this section, I had the most jarring thought. It hit me so hard that I dropped my hands from the keyboard and raised one hand to my chest, over my heart. I took a deep breath and gazed at the field outside my office window. My thought was,

Suppose all the women in history too afraid to voice their ideas had actually done so. What would the world be like today?

Not being dramatic, but this thought brought tears to my eyes. What if every time a woman talked herself out of voicing an idea, she had actually said it out loud? Shared it with someone and took steps to develop it even further? How different and better off might we be had all the ideas pushed down and out of sight by the weight of fear, intimidation, or insecurity ... actually surfaced?

Think about how often that happens just in the present day, and multiply it by the number of women throughout history. It's a staggering and unfortunate amount! I find it very unsettling and something that needs to come to an end.

Let's not let this happen anymore, ladies. Let's change the course of history right now by acting in the present and impacting the future. Will every idea expressed be a game changer? Nope. Yet the sooner we get in the habit of regularly expressing our ideas, the sooner the game is changed, and the closer we get to achieving life-changing impacts. Please join me in having the courage and confidence to speak up and share your bright and brilliant visions.

The stakes are simply too high for anything otherwise. The confidence journey is upon us. Hop along for this fun and exciting ride!

What is Confidence?

There are many textbook definitions, synonyms and substitutes for confidence. Courage, boldness, self-assurance, nerve, guts, and chutzpah, to name a few. Here are three definitions of confidence, each having its own unique twist.

First, "a feeling or consciousness of one's powers, or of reliance on one's circumstances. 'She had confidence in her ability to succeed.'" This might be my favorite. It comes from the old-school Merriam-Webster Dictionary, first published in 1806, so it way predates superheroes with superpowers and Halloween costumes to emulate them. "One's powers" are very real, and while my abilities to teleport or leap tall buildings (or even modest-height buildings) are admittedly questionable, I do know my ability to channel my own confidence superpowers is every bit as strong as Thor's biceps. Confidence is a very real and capable superpower all of us mere mortals have and it's right at our fingertips.

Google's calls confidence "a feeling of self-assurance and certainty arising from one's appreciation of one's own abilities or qualities." ("She's brimming with *confidence*.") The key word is "appreciation." The vital ingredient of self-love is required for true confidence. Sure, it wavers on certain days, yet even an ounce of appreciation and love for oneself is a seed necessary for having and growing confidence.

A third (and admittedly left-field!) authority, the National Center for Biotechnology Information, defines confidence as "a faith or belief that one will act in a right, proper, or effective way." ("I have confidence in her as a leader.") I believe there is a moral component to confidence. Authentic confidence comes from knowing the difference between right and wrong and acting accordingly. The moral compass of a truly confident person points true north. Altruistic leadership doesn't necessarily mean you're the most popular, but it does mean that you do what's right and in doing so you set a strong, inspiring example for all.

Those are three fine definitions of confidence – and now I'll add my own take. Confidence is a constant quality, yet not a static state of mind. It's not an organ within your body that operates consistently without conscious directions from you. Nor is it an inanimate object, a sapphire ring for example, that you either own or you don't, with no in-between. Confidence has an amazing ability to be dynamic. It's like a light switch with a dimmer on it. The electricity is always there and it's up to you to control how brightly it shines. Over time, its dynamic nature trends toward a static state. Like anything you practice, you get so good at doing it, you can't imagine not knowing how.

Once you control your special gift of flipping on your confidence switch, you'll never be able to lose it. Unlike your favorite pair of heels after a long day, you cannot easily kick confidence away. Like your shadow on a sunny day, it will never leave you. As you're practicing your skills, it is natural to feel 'kinda' confident. When you're working your way up, though, 'kinda' confident is a degree of magnitude more confident than you were yesterday. You're trending in the right direction and moving along the right path. Get your steps in by continuing the journey!

The ebb and flow of confidence works like many other personal characteristics. How happy, sad, excited, disgusted, etc. you are varies thanks to a variety of influencing factors. Even the most confident of people experience days, hours, moments, when their confidence is rattled, when their self-esteem takes a dive. This is normal, however, and great news, actually! Science tells us what goes down must come up (or maybe it's the reverse). Either way, your confidence can easily rebound after a plunge. Putting even the tiniest bit of effort behind it will make it rise in an instant. It wants to pop back up, like a beach ball held beneath the water's surface.

"But some people are just born confident!" you might say. They come out of the womb standing straight up in their power pose and ready to conquer the world. Well, yes, there is some science that says confidence is a personality trait embedded in our DNA. But that's only one influencing factor. Your family, your friends, your surroundings, and your own mentality have a lot to do with nurturing and shaping confidence as well.

Let's look at a less desirable characteristic, stubbornness. My dad's side of the family is known for being pretty darn stubborn, or, said more nicely, determined and tenacious. My Hungarian genes gave me not only an innate ability to make a delicious chicken paprikash, but a propensity for being stubborn. Yet stubbornness is something I can turn up or down based on my awareness of it and willingness to do so.

I've learned to temper it, no question. I've worked at being a better listener, and more approachable and docile when circumstances call for it. By concentrating, I've succeeded at decreasing a seemingly undesirable trait like stubbornness – and a desirable trait like confidence can be increased the same way. At any time, in any situation. No matter what traits you display thanks to heritage, culture, family, and gender, you have the ability to change for the better.

If you have any doubt of your ability to build confidence, please just go with it for now. Just assume for the time being that this will work for you – because I know from the bottom of my heart that it will, and after all, arguing with a stubborn Hungarian might not be as easy as you think!

The Currency of Confidence

Most important, confidence can be summed up in three words. CONFIDENCE. IS. YOURS.

It is yours and yours alone. No one can take it away from you without your permission. I often think of confidence as currency you have in the bank. That's your bank account; you decide how its funds are disbursed. You wouldn't Venmo someone money for something they haven't earned, right? Or stand in the street throwing $100 bills into the air? Of course not, that's ridiculous! Think of confidence the same way: You alone make the decisions about how you "spend" it. It is no one else's for the taking.

The investment you make in confidence is something you'll be able to cash in on, over and over again. Protect it just as you would your bank account.

And the really cool thing? It compounds. Confidence compounds, meaning that when you grow confidence in one area, that confidence will help boost you in other areas too. When you crush a personal goal, for example, it has a compounding effect in that will likely elevate your performance in some aspect of your professional life and vice versa.

The Most Important Skill to Have

Tony Robbins, Zig Ziglar, and Suze Orman are excellent motivational speakers known for working crowds of people into a frenzy. They get audiences so hyped, they'll walk across hot coals while feeling no pain. Their motivational speeches are invigorating, energizing, and action-oriented. They help you set big, audacious goals and leave you feeling ready to conquer the world. They provide transformative experiences.

And I think it's absolutely awesome. Incredible achievements come from people who attend motivational speeches. I'm a huge proponent. Yet sometimes people depart the event, go back to work, and the hype and the excitement fizzles. The huge life goal they set in the arena winds up just being something that they wrote on a piece of paper. It never achieves liftoff.

I've been asked if I consider myself a motivational speaker. My typical response is to smile and shake my head, "No." I quickly dismiss my ability to motivate like the major stars do. What I do consider myself, however, is a champion of women.

My strategy is also motivating, yet it takes on a softer approach. It focuses more on mindset and *honoring where you are right now.* We all come with different starting points, which vary widely based on a whole host of factors.

I think the main factor is what season of life you're in. So what season are you in?

If it's your summer, your starting point is likely: Fired up and ready to go! But is it winter for you? You may need to wrap up in a blanket and sip hot toddies, talking and working through the darkness until you see flowers budding in the spring. Some people are ready for blue skies and high clouds, and others aren't quite there yet.

Tony, Zig, and Suze will exhort you to reach for the stars, which I think is awesome. I like to first offer support, though, by achieving something within a realistic grasp. If the stars are in a galaxy far, far away, then let's just start with reaching for the clouds instead. And not even the super high-up ones. What are those called again? I think they're cirrus. I like to start with the attainable clouds, like the stratus clouds that grace our sky at a lower altitude. They can be reasonable motivators and encouragement on any given day. Or, as one woman I was coaching asked me with a laugh, "How about the ceiling? Could I just start with reaching for the ceiling?" You bet! Where you start is not important. What matters is that you just start somewhere.

Once you have a firm and consistent belief that you can grab those low-hanging clouds, then you'll have the solid foundation needed for more. With just one confident day, you grow more capable of having another, and another and another. Once you've established a baseline and seen the difference that having confidence makes, and learned how to channel it, THEN you are able to reach higher and higher, all the way up to those world-changing goals and achievements that kick-a$$ women accomplish.

First, though, you must develop measures that become as habitual as getting out of bed in the morning. Add on rituals for pumping yourself up and giving yourself a bump every time your self-esteem needs a boost. Then use the resulting momentum to face whatever unfamiliar or intimidating situations lie ahead. If you're ready to ride the Harley, then ride the Harley! But if you stall and give up, that's not doing anybody any good. If you need to take the tricycle or two-wheeler out for a spin first, then by all means, get moving!

Again, it doesn't matter where you start, only that you START.

The Gifts of Confidence

The gifts of confidence are the best ones to unwrap! Here, I'll share my Top Five Favorites. I'm hoping that as 'confidence' stays in the forefront of your mind, you too will be able to name and claim them, as well as build your own list.

Fuel for Forward Motion

Have you ever felt stuck in a decision? Rather than being able to make a tough call, you find yourself in a mental tennis match. You watch your thoughts lobbed back and forth across the net. *Well, I could decide this way* (ball served), *but thennn, what if I don't like that way and I want to do this way instead* (ball returned)? *But the first way will allow me to accomplish this* (ball hit back again with a wicked backhand), *but then I'll compromise that* (ball slammed back with a solid mid-court bounce) and so on and so on. It makes my neck tired just thinking about it!

We all get stuck in decisions and part of the problem is that none of us have a functioning crystal ball. We don't get to know the outcome before we must make a choice to move forward. Getting stuck in a decision can be a very frustrating place that drains your energy. It's certainly no vacation. It can steal away time and effort that could be better spent on more important things.

Thankfully, there are practical ways to approach tough decisions. Ask for someone else's advice, list pros and cons, draw out a decision matrix. If you really want to get fancy, draw out a weighted decision matrix, like a friend did recently when she was trying to decide between two job offers. Doing all of those things will certainly help organize your thoughts. Getting them on paper helps you filter out less relevant information, essentially de-cluttering your thoughts so you can have a higher resolution view of what's most important. (Marie Kondo would be so proud.) Yet in the end, you will have to decide without knowing what will happen next. You will have to take a leap of faith, and confidence is what will provide the push.

Confidence will allow your inner monologue to go something like this: "Okay, so I don't know what the future will bring. I can't control all of the variables that affect my decision. I've spent time evaluating. I am a strong, intelligent person who is making the best decision that I know how to make. It will go the best it can go, and I know I can navigate whatever outcome results. Game on. Let's do this!" And you commit to a decision.

Confidence is the fuel that catapults you forward, knowing that while it's impossible to predict the future, staying stuck prevents you from ever getting there. It's like sitting on the tarmac for hours while waiting for your flight to take off – *ugh* – except this time, you're the pilot! And it's your responsibility and privilege to push that throttle forward and get that sucker in the air!

Side note: The word 'decide' comes from ancient Latin, where 'cide' which means to cut or kill. De plus cide: cut off. When you choose to decide, you're literally making a decision to kill off the other options, freeing your mind from the energy it takes to think about them, and allowing one choice to rise above the rest.

Gives You a Voice

My friend Maria is a diversity and inclusion strategist. Maria moved to Chicago from Mexico as a small child. Today she advises organizations how to leverage diversity's advantages. I heard her speak on a panel at a Women's Energy Network event in Denver. Afterwards I asked Maria what she witnesses as the biggest struggle for women in a working environment.

"They don't have a voice," she responded matter-of-factly. "They can be the smartest ones in the room, yet when it comes to speaking up, they can't do it."

Have you ever struggled with the same thing? You have something incredibly brilliant or even just additive to say, you can hear it loud and clear in your head – but making it travel from your head to your mouth is a big challenge, if not a dead end. Have you ever heard that little voice inside, felt your heart pound at the prospect of externalizing it, but succumbed to the fear of not saying it out loud? Do you regret it later on, driving home, saying it out loud within the safety of your car?

I've done that. I'll tell you what: regret it every time.

Thankfully, you can channel past regret into motivation for next time. Remember how Ursula, the Sea Witch, commandeered the Little Mermaid's voice? Can you imagine what kind of predicament you'd need to be in without owning your very own voice?! How tragic would that be? Oh my gosh, you'd miss it so, and others would, too! Don't be your own Ursula! Don't give others the opportunity to take your voice. With confidence, you won't let that happen. It helps you speak up and sing out with the exhilaration of Ariel when her beautiful voice was rightfully returned.

The gift of confidence will help you vocalize, so you are heard and seen. The reward could be even more thrilling than finding your Prince Eric. It could land you your next promotion!

Challenge = Opportunity

Imagine two different women driving to work on a Monday morning. The first pulls out of her garage, coffee tumbler secured in the cup holder, leather bag on her front seat, GPS monitoring traffic. She's navigating her way along the highway and sighs. Her brow is furrowed and her thoughts go something like this.

"Hmmm, I wonder what kind of week this is going to be. I wonder what problems and issues are going to hit me. Friday seems like a looong way away. I hope I can survive this week. Woe is me."

A second woman pulls out of her garage, coffee tumbler also secured in the cup holder, leather bag on her own front seat, GPS on. She's navigating to her office and she smiles. Her eyes are bright, her thoughts are optimistic. She's thinking:

"Wow, I wonder what kind of week this is going to be. I wonder what issues or challenges are going to come up that I'll get the chance to tackle. I wonder what I'll learn and what successes I'll have. It will certainly be fun to celebrate at happy hour on Friday! Hmmm," she muses, *"Prosecco or rosé?"* And she laughs, envisioning toasting with her friends.

Same Monday morning situations, but two very different mindsets. The first is an example of the Eeyore Complex. The Woe-is-me, I'm slow and sad, everything is a downer mode of thinking that the Winnie the Pooh donkey embodies. The second mindset is what I like to call the Tigger Complex. It's upbeat and positive, bouncing with anticipation of good things to come. It's happy and optimistic regarding whatever reality lies ahead.

Now picture the posture of these two women as they walk into work. Our Eeyore Complex friend looks a little sluggish, shoulders low, eyes pointed downward, probably causing others to wonder if she needs a hug. Once in the office, imagine how she starts her day. I see her tossing her bag to the side of her desk, slumping into her chair, and begrudgingly turning on her computer. How will others react to her? Will she be greeted with enthusiasm? Will it be presumed that she's a good contributor? A team player interested in contributing her fair share? Will she be invited to meetings because people want her opinions and enjoy the energy she brings to the conversation? I'll let you decide.

As our Tigger Complex woman enters the office, she greets the janitor putting fresh liners in the trash cans. She smiles at the receptionist and asks how her son's soccer game went over the weekend. She hangs her bag on the hook of her door and sits at her desk, back straight, and eyes focused on her calendar. She's ready for the day, giving off vibes of *confidence*. Consider the same questions. How will others react to her? Will her enthusiasm be reciprocated? Will it be presumed that she's a good contributor, ready to help the company and improve the lives of others? Will she be invited to meetings because people want her opinions and enjoy the energy she brings to the conversation? Again, I invite you to decide.

Confidence gives you the ability to program your mindset so you can treat the most mundane or even challenging circumstances as opportunities. By definition the word *opportunity* is a set of circumstances that makes it *possible* to do something. (Notice: *possible*, not its opposite, *impossible*.) Confidence gives you the superpower to shift your thoughts so challenges look like opportunities.

Test the Fence

I have to admit this is my favorite of my Top 5 Gifts of Confidence. If you like dinosaur movies, you'll especially like this one too.

Remember *Jurassic Park*? The first film in the franchise became the highest-grossing movie ever when released in 1993. Well, whether you saw the first one or any that followed, the scene I'm about to describe pretty much happened in each one. To properly do it justice, I'd like to ask you to join the cast of the movie. Congratulations! You have been awarded the prestigious role of the Brontosaurus. I can see the Oscar nomination now…

So there you are in the jungle, ambling along and socializing with the other dinosaurs. Everything seems to be going fine until you reach a barrier. It's a fence, actually. You stop and look back at the large area behind you, where you've been roaming around all this time. Suddenly it looks smaller, and it feels, well, limiting.

You look back at the fence, and see the vast park on the other side, with people milling around. You realize that while things are comfortable and familiar on this side of the fence, it doesn't compare to what looks like the infinite landscape over there. You're sure curious to find out more. You, the Brontosaurus, start to evaluate your position here on this side of the fence. Sure, you have food and shelter, and an okay job at the elementary school cafeteria preparing lizard-turtle-and-egg lunches for the kid dinosaurs. But now you begin to wonder, "Is this it?" Is this all I'm destined to do for the rest of my career, limited to this small space with only a handful of options?

You're interrupted from your reverie as you focus on the humans across the fence. You reflect further: *Wait a second.*
I'm smart and strong and brave. Why am I confined over here, to a certain job pool, with mediocre benefits, while on that side they're free to explore and go after whatever they want? Why do I have to stay on this side of the fence? I'm probably as capable as they are of achieving great things — maybe more so.

This makes no sense, you think. Is that fence really so strong? or is its strength an illusion I've simply never questioned, because that's what I was told?

Now let me go off script and acknowledge what an excellent point, you, Brontosaurus, have made. It's the stuff of prehistoric diversity & inclusion conversation!

In the movie, the dinosaurs begin to realize the unfairness and ridiculousness of these imposed limitations. As their realizations sink in, these women, er, dinosaurs, start to assert their rights and *test the fence.*

Gently at first, poking dino fingers at the barrier. And they're kicking it soon enough. They scratch their claws more and more forcefully, testing the limitations of that fence until their momentum and their courage rise so high, they put the full weight of prehistoric quadrupeds into the assault and, lo and behold, break right through! They penetrate and find themselves standing face-to-face with the people on the other side – who are now scared witless, realizing the unjustness of confining these beautiful, strong creatures.

Perhaps at first both dinosaurs and people doubted whether the dinosaurs had the courage, the cunning, the strength and the tenacity to make it. But now that the fence is rubble, both know there is no turning back.

Some may watch *Jurassic Park* cheering for the humans and fearing the dinosaurs. I cheer for the dinos. When they break through and get to look into the eyes of their captors, captors with no idea of the magnitude of their true potential, I applaud with delight. Incidentally, an average brontosaurus weighed a whopping 36,000 to 49,000 pounds, or approximately the equivalent of 222 high school football players. (I looked it up for you.) Imagine what we as women can accomplish with collective confidence, armed with more than enough weight and determination to break barriers that have held us back for so long.

Thankfully, you need not struggle into a brontosaurus suit to test the fence. Confidence gives you the ability to not just think about testing it, but to be bold and fierce about it. To be courageous and start pushing on the boundaries that hold back women in the workplace.

Another term you might associate with this challenge is the "glass ceiling," an imaginary, transparent blockade holding women back from executive roles. A good friend and coach of mine said, "I often find myself thudding my head against that ceiling, and one of these days I'm going to crack it!" Recent research from McKinsey and Company reported the glass ceiling problem is actually improving. Unfortunately, the study identified another, bigger issue called the "Broken Rung." They name the rung as the true obstacle preventing women from climbing from entry level to a management position, even as a precursor for an executive role. We have to start testing the fence to get to the other side.

So when someone talks over you in a meeting, or you're continuously passed over for a promotion, or excluded from a project that fits your skill sets, confidence gives you the ability to test the fence – by speaking up, speaking out, scheduling a meeting with your manager to discuss your career path, and by putting together a plan of how you'll get to the other side. It might be green and lush and comfortable on the old familiar side of the fence. However, at some point, you might just get bored and feel unfulfilled or underappreciated. You may realize you have way more to offer than your current, limited job requires. You may just want to reach for the other side where your skills, passions, and aspirations can be fully realized.

Confidence is a wonderful gift to help test and break the fence to get you to the better side.

Contagious

Ever caught yourself yawning as you watched someone else who started a few seconds ago? Overheard a baby giggling and, without even realizing it, joined in laughing yourself? And have you ever smiled at a stranger on the street and had them return it as they walked by? The contagious nature of human interaction is pretty darn neat.

Just about everything is contagious! Sadness and happiness, discouragement and enthusiasm, laziness and vitality – we're all exposed to their contagious nature. As people with souls, capable of empathy and energetic connections, it's human nature for us to "mirror" what another is doing, good or bad. In a study published in 2008, Marco Iacoboni talked about the science behind mirroring, and what is happening from a neurological standpoint. He identified mirror neurons in our brains that activate as we observe others. They cause us to subconsciously imitate what someone else is doing. They are responsible for our impulse to demonstrate empathy by responding in a compassionate and appropriate way.

Old clichés that attest to the contagious nature of human interaction. "You're only as good as the company you keep." "Birds of a feather, flock together." "Show me your friends, and I'll show you your future." And there's a modern contribution credited to motivational speaker Jim Rohn: "We are the average of the five people who most closely surround us." If you're hearing that for the first time, let it sink in. Who is closest to you at this moment, either in physical proximity or connected via social media? Do you find yourself acting differently depending on the cast of characters in proximity – playing one role around co-workers, another with close friends, still another with distant acquaintances? Do you like these people? Do you want to be like these people? Pay close attention, because the longer you're around them and the more you interact with them, the more likely you are to resemble them, for better or for worse.

Yet another cool thing about confidence is that it, too, is extremely contagious – in not one but two ways.

First, you can catch confidence simply by being close to someone else who has it. Think about a mentor, a teacher, or a coach who's inspired you. Do you feel uplifted and encouraged after having spent time with this person? Are you at a 2 when you greet them and a 10 when you part? Are there people at work, friends you have, or even fictional characters in movies that leave you noticeably more confident? That's confidence contagion! One of the best ways to build your confidence is to surround yourself with confirmed sources.

Second, when you radiate confidence by delivering encouraging, positive, motivational, and affirming words to others, you likely boost your own mood and confidence in the bargain. It's a boomerang effect: what you toss out, comes back to you. Simple physics, you might say! Simply by carrying yourself with confidence, others observing you may very well wind up mirroring you. The simple act of changing your posture and even thinking yourself more confident can change your mindset and that of people nearby. You can catch confidence from your own self by enlisting the help of the body-mind connection and adjusting either mentally or physically.

We'll go much deeper into this in the next chapter. In the meantime, here is an example.

Lydia is confident but Madison is not feeling it. Lydia says encouraging words to Madison. She offers reassuring advice and cites a past success of Madison's. During this exchange not one, but two magical events occur. First, Madison's confidence is boosted as Lydia, a trusted friend, shares her sincere and inspiring feedback. Second, Lydia's confidence is boosted too – because she encouraged Madison with sincere and enthusiastic words. She did something nice and, sees the difference it made for Madison, and feels it herself too.

How about that? The more you give, the more you get. Confidence truly is the gift that keeps on giving. Put it on your Christmas list. Put it on your birthday list. Yet don't wait for somebody to buy it for you. Simply dish it out, and you'll discover not only that you'll receive it in return, but also that you've had it all along.

There's a lot of reciprocity when it comes to confidence. It's an infinite resource, the best renewable energy source out there. And neurologically speaking, it's not just those mirror neurons that get to party. Oxytocin is a hormone activated by friendly, encouraging interpersonal connections, sometimes called the 'Love and Connection' hormone. Something simple like a smile can even get it moving. So pop the Champagne bottle and crack open the White Claw. When you speak positive words to someone else, you're creating an open invitation to a confidence party. And what a fun time it is

Remember this riddle from when we were kids? "The more you take of me, the more you leave behind. What am I?" Answer: Footsteps! Ha ha! Think of confidence the same way. The more confidence you give out, the more you get! No riddle or mystery there. Just a known fact!

Rehearse Until It's Verse

As we've discussed, it's a common misperception that confidence grows only from outcomes and endings. The notion could propel a whole episode of MythBusters: *It's only once you cross the finish line that confidence is built.* Nope, myth busted! Or: *It's only when you close the deal or nail the presentation that your confidence increases.* Again, false! If you build your confidence only once you've mastered something, what would give you the courage to even start? Fortunately, in the moment you begin a new challenge or step outside your comfort zone, the confident light is switched on, lighting the path ahead. Confidence certainly is reinforced by your successes, achievements and wins, yet those milestones are not where confidence starts. It starts in the exact moment when you simply *try*.

Think about this the next time you're around a tiny human who's learning how to walk. Observe their motions and imagine their thoughts. They have such determination and they appear to think really hard about taking that first step, letting go of the ottoman and going for it. And once they start, they usually make it at least a few steps, if not the span of the entire room. And then what do they do? They fall. They land on their bottom or their top, or somewhere in between. And then they laugh and some larger human cheers them on, both immensely proud. The outcome is not a perfected walk, immediately mastered and flawlessly executed, but rather a messy, bumbly, tumbly walk. It's perfectly imperfect, yet that little attempt is all the toddler needs to boost her confidence to keep going, and try again.

So many things in life are like this. Cognitive tasks are like this. It can be incredibly intimidating to try something new, yet we tend to forget that starting is usually the hardest part. After we start, we're usually fine. And the best part is knowing that the start, not the finish, bumps your confidence right then and there. Think of a top female executive. (I really hope you know at least one!) Her confidence is apparent, her manner exuberant, and her performance excellent. But even she didn't start like that. She practiced from an early age and worked her way up. She dedicated time to maximize her performance. Or what about that guy at work? The one who nails his presentations every time. He didn't come straight out of the gates like that. He's practiced many times and knows it's his thing, probably his *HITM*, thus further propping up his confidence and job performance every time he presents.

So whether you're a master or a novice – whether you're excited to dive deep into a new task or are more comfortable wading around the shallow end – all you have to do is remind yourself that no one knows how to do something perfectly the first time they do anything. Or the second, or the third or maybe even the 273rd time. You may be thinking to yourself, "Cool, I just have to try and fake it 'til it I make it! Right?" Well, actually, there's a better way!

We all know the phrase, "Fake it 'til you make it." It means that if you bluster your way through as best you can and pretend you know what you're doing, that'll be good. I've actually heard this recommended during a formal confidence training class and it made me cringe!

Wellll, I have a slightly different take on it. A way to rise above merely "faking it," because I think you're capable of more – and you are worthy of more.

By 'faking it,' you are selling yourself short. To me, "Fake it 'til you make it" implies something fraudulent. I mean, you're faking it. You're telling yourself that this is pretend. You're not instilling a strong belief that you can actually do it. There's an element of doubt. Are you actually faking the task you're trying to do? Well, no, of course, not. You ARE doing something. While doing something for the first time, you may not know exactly how or what to do, yet you are, unequivocally, doing something, and you're doing the best you can.

There's danger and risk in telling yourself that you can just fake it because of how predictive and powerful thoughts are. They direct your performance.

Think about it. If you're just faking it, then how can your efforts actually be legitimate? How can you actually be working toward an achievable goal that, like many things, may take a few iterations to get there? Picture the wobbly toddler again. Is she confident that she'll get there? Absolutely. Are her onlookers confident? You bet. Does she have her strut perfected? Absolutely not, but there's nothing fake or fraudulent about what she's doing. She's trying, and she believes in what she can achieve. She's simply practicing and rehearsing until she reaches the point where her walking skills are automatic and she doesn't even have to think about them.

Faking it suggests that you don't necessarily believe you're going to reach your end goal. Rehearsing implies that you can see the end goal and are taking the appropriate steps to get there.

At this point I'd like to invite you to serve yourself better and ditch the language of, "Fake it 'til you make it." Replace it with:

Rehearse until it's verse.

Rehearse until it's verse. When you're trying something new and you're unsure of the outcome, you don't have to pretend to fake it until you make it. All you have to do is tell yourself that you're rehearsing, simply rehearsing, and you're in a safe zone for mistakes or blunders as long as you work through them and keep going. This isn't the night of the big show, or the day of the final deadline. This is merely the dress rehearsal. You're preparing, and practicing, and working on your performance. Perhaps you practiced the guitar, the piano, or the oh-so-sophisticated recorder, and reached a point where you no longer had to look at the notes. You knew the melody by heart! The refrain and the verses were committed to memory and became instinctive. You rehearsed until it was a memorized verse, and you grew comfortable and confident.

You did it then, and you can do it now. Most of the time, in a situation where your performance will be measured or judged, you'll have the opportunity to rehearse first. And in some cases, that's just called "experience." Unforeseen circumstances will arise, yet when you encounter them, you succeed by recalling past experiences and many, many previous opportunities where you had the chance to rehearse.

Switching your mindset from "faking it" to "rehearsing it" alleviates the pressure of feeling you're more likely to fail than to succeed. If you do succeed the first time, awesome! If you don't, though, what's better than failing while seizing an opportunity to learn? That can be even better than succeeding right out of the gate.

When you no longer feel like a fraud, but rather like a normal human rehearsing her path to excellence, it reduces a lot of stress. It's so liberating! It's so relaxing! As "firsts" and new challenges naturally come up in a workplace environment, adopt the mindset that everyone starts somewhere, and you too will begin by rehearsing right now.

Your mission, should you choose to accept it – and you're reading this book for a reason, so I know you will! – is to elevate your self-talk from "I'm going to fake it" to: Rehearse until it's verse. If you don't get a task right the first time, congratulations! You just boosted your confidence in spite of the outcome, purely by trying. Giddy-up, girlfriend! You stepped up to the plate. Maybe you even took a swing. Either way, be very proud!

And since you are rehearsing, you're probably wondering how to sound and look the part. We'll focus on that in the next chapter.

What's at Stake?

Living with jealousy, loneliness, and selfishness instead of *thriving* with empowerment, enhancing the lives of others by sharing your gifts, and continuously testing barriers that are incredibly invigorating to cross.

Key Points

- Confidence comes from within and is a choice you make.
- The contagious nature of confidence creates energy that is easy to catch, easy to give, and won't stop growing once initiated.
- You're not faking anything! Life is about practicing and doing your best.
- It's in that first step, no matter how tiny, that confidence starts to gain momentum.

Confidence Challenge Checklist

- ❏ Dish out encouragement to someone and see what boost it provides for you.
- ❏ Find a confident person to intentionally spend some time with. Grab lunch, have a drink, go for a hike. Be particularly open to receiving her energy, and see what it does for your own.
- ❏ Identify a "fence" that's holding you back and start planning your attack.
- ❏ Ask a confident mentor, friend, or colleague what confidence does for them.
- ❏ Share what confidence does for you with someone in a more junior role than you.

To stretch and condition my confidence, one action I commit to is:

_____

_____

_____

Chapter 3
Does This Outfit Make My Confidence Look Big?

The Look of Confidence in Action

The board of directors at an energy company hired leadership coaches for each member of the executive team. Linda, the only woman on the team selected a man as her coach. She wanted to know how her male counterparts perceived her and asked for his feedback. In a very frank conversation, the coach told her hair was distracting because it was so long, like Rapunzel long. Her attire needed an upgrade, both from a fashion sense and to reflect her position on the company organizational chart. And, the coach advised, her office looked as if she were still working in her previous, junior role.

"Ditch the maps," he told her, referring to her wall decor.

Linda transformed his feedback into action. She went to her stylist and got a fresh cut, leaving her locks shorter yet still at a length she chose, below her shoulders, giving off a more professional vibe. Not blessed with much fashion sense, she reached out to another woman whose wardrobe she admired and asked her to take her shopping. She took down the maps, replacing them with matted, framed photos and leadership quotes.

Two months later, the CEO called her into his office.

"Linda!" he exclaimed. "I have to tell you, out of everyone who's been a part of the executive coaching program, you are light years ahead of the others. Your performance is noticeably improved. I'm very pleased with the changes in your work output." Linda smiled at him and thanked him for his feedback. The bigger smile she shared, however, was with herself. She shook her head in disbelief as she thought, "I didn't change a damn thing about my performance." Not a single person had mentioned her new haircut, outfits, or office decorations, yet now her performance was being noticed like never before. Way to go, Linda! The power of perception is an incredibly potent force!

Fair? Maybe, maybe not. Yet basing our judgments on presentational factors is human nature and something we all do. Key to note, is that Linda was excited about making these changes. She was comfortable with the suggestions. She stayed true to herself. Had the coach suggested changes that went against Linda's values, she would not have complied.

Separately, I do have to wonder if Linda's performance actually did improve, though perhaps not drastically. Perhaps her perceptions of herself changed while she strutted her stuff in her new suit, with her new haircut, reading the inspirational leadership quotes hanging in her office – and it had a positive effect on her work.

The Sound and Look of Confidence

Confidence makes a great first impression, and a second, and a third. It comes across in a variety of ways. Sometimes it is heard. The volume, intonation and timing of spoken words have definite capacity to transmit confidence. The way someone stands, walks, and enters a room instantly conveys confidence to friends and strangers alike. The manner in which someone is dressed, and body language – does she plant herself proudly or fidget? – can transmit confidence as well.

Certain behaviors and attitudes embody confidence. Personality traits such as authenticity, humility, and honesty communicate confidence as well, subtly or not. The opposite also is true. For every confident trait, action, and behavior, there's an opposite quality that can signal a lack of belief in oneself and plant doubts in observers. Minor shifts can instantly change the impressions one is giving off.

In this chapter we'll talk about the wide variety of ways confidence comes across externally. In the following chapter, we'll review, step by step, the playbook for creating and maintaining confidence. But first, a word from the Ethics Committee.

Using Your Powers for Good, Not Evil

When I was in grad school, one of my favorite classes was Sophisticated Statistics, aka data analysis. I learned all kinds of cool ways to calculate numbers in order to solve problems, forecast revenue, and describe trends. Unlike previous math classes I'd taken, there was usually more than one answer, or rather more than one way to get to an answer, and myriad ways to interpret the numbers. There was a literary component to it as well: the task of presenting and analyzing the numbers left a lot of room for interpretation. Even when reaching the exact same mathematical solution, different teams would present different cases as to why it was what it was. It was objective and subjective at the same time.

Outside the class, I started paying closer attention to numbers, specifically the way numbers were reported in news stories. I remember a report about a major oil spill in the Gulf of Mexico. Journalists continuously updated the quantity of oil spilled versus the quantity of oil recovered. They were trying to convey the severity of the situation by citing the amount remaining in the Gulf. Having spent part of my career in energy, I had some professional context around this type of data, so I listened very closely.

I noticed something interesting. When news accounts mentioned the amount of oil spilled, it was done in terms of gallons spilled, the key word being gallons. When they reported the other side, the amount of oil recovered, they talked in terms of barrels. Barrels. Think about that for a moment. Gallons versus barrels. Gallons are a much smaller volume than barrels: kind of like comparing inches and feet. Twelve inches equals one foot, but based on the numbers alone, the inches sound a lot bigger. While we all know that 12 inches equal 1 foot, most people are not familiar with how many gallons are contained in a barrel, or really even think about it.

Here's the math. One barrel holds 45 gallons of liquid. When news reports said 45,000 gallons had spilled, but ONLY 900 barrels had been recovered, the numbers make things sound terrible, right? But a closer look at this data tells us 900 barrels equals 40,500 gallons, so the incident featured a 90% recovery rate. Bad, but not as bad as it sounded.

If you merely compared the numbers without considering the metric being used, you'd walk away from that news story thinking only a small percentage had been recovered. Highly inaccurate! Was the media intentionally misleading the general public to turn them against the company responsible for the spill? I can't say for sure. But the message communicated to the untrained ear was rather manipulative. It would have been just as easy to report numbers that could be fairly compared.

Now, I'm not here to start a debate about the oil and gas industry or the news coverage it gets. I use this as an example of how people in power, in leadership positions, people who come across as confident, can use their persuasive powers for good or for evil.

Back to Sophisticated Statistics. On the final evening of the semester, our professor, Debra Smith, (Gosh, I loved her!) had a very serious conversation with us. She emphasized the importance of applying our new-found statistical savvy with a high level of integrity and ethics. Throughout the semester, we had acquired skills which could be used magnificently or malevolently, for right or wrong, with good intentions or bad. Nothing in her final message would appear on the final exam. The woman who had imparted her wisdom and knowledge, along with a great sense of humor and an obvious love for teaching, wanted to instill an essential lesson within us all: When it comes to data analysis and life in general, there is a lot of gray area. We'll often be faced with choices that can go either way on the morality scale.

"Honor your true value by *making good decisions*," she said to us. To close out the conversation, she made her final profound point, by looking each of us in the eyes, and slowly and deliberately saying, "It's up to you." [Long pause.] "It's up to you." It gives me goosebumps to this day, more than ten years later.

I share Professor Smith's words with you to make the point that confidence and strong leadership work the same way.

You have the power to ignite positive change that lifts others up and catalyzes improvements for the greater good. You also have power to make selfish decisions, usually in pursuit of a short-term gain of some kind, that may (or may not) come back to bite you later. We know of leaders like Hitler or Osama Bin Laden who demonstrated strong leadership qualities and, I'm sure, projected confidence. Their energy, like all energy, was contagious. How compelling it must have been to provoke the terrible things it did. Now, I'm assuming that you, my reader, have only good intentions – that you want to make the world, your employer, your family, or yourself better. We're all faced at some time or another with situations that will challenge us, that will put us in places where compromising our integrity could serve an immediate purpose. It may be tempting, but deep down you know it's not the morally right thing to do.

I love the phrase, "The right decisions aren't always the easy ones." Another one I love:

The softest pillow is a clear conscience.

Authentic confidence and strong leadership come with high integrity and broad visions of things that can be done for the betterment of humanity, big or small. I've noticed that the leaders I know and respect the most, the ones with the kind of confidence worth striving for, whose words and actions make the world a better place, all have consistent behaviors. Without comparing notes they all embody certain consistent qualities. Their recipes for success share several common ingredients.

I want to share those ingredients with you here. If you already exude them, awesome! Keep prioritizing them. If you're working on them and aware of them, that's a step in the right direction. And if these are foreign to you, you've never cooked them up before, I want to highly encourage you to add them to your grocery shopping list. I promise the meal you wind up preparing and serving will be far more enriching and satisfying than a quick-fix, microwaveable alternative.

Before we begin, I want to ask for your participation. This is so important, let's go deeper.

When you think of someone with confidence and strong leadership characteristics, who comes to mind?

These can be people you know or don't: leaders of organizations, athletes, political figures, co-workers, or friends. They give you a consistent impression of their confidence and self-belief. Not cocky or arrogant, but simply confident. They've done good things, they lift others up, they've achieved goals which benefit the greater good; maybe they've even impacted your own life, using their gifts and talents to help you in some minor or major way.

Pause for a minute and give it some thought. When you're ready, write down their names here. There's no timer on this book (unless you're reading the e-book and the digital library deadline is looming!), so stop and think. Who are those people? We'll come back to this again in later chapters, so jot down a few names now. Feel free to write down a few adjectives you'd use to describe them as well.

1._____

2._____

3._____

All righty! Great job! I'm thrilled that you spent some valuable time thinking of these individuals. You may even want to send them a note letting them know you chose them. I bet they'd appreciate hearing from you.

There are some unwritten characteristics that coincide with confidence. We're about to pull back the curtain on these lesser known qualities. Let's get excited about having first-row seats for the big reveal!

I've Got Sunshine on a Cloudy Day

Someone with genuine confidence is consistently positive and encouraging. This doesn't mean she never has an off day or bad moments, but her general outlook and attitude toward life is hopeful and optimistic. She likes to think about why something will happen or work out, rather than why it won't or can't. She focuses on what is possible, not what isn't, and on how brightly a vision can burn rather than quickly extinguishing it. When you ask how her day is going, you'll frequently hear, *"Wonderful, Excellent!" "Couldn't be better!"* And she means it! She means it because she sees problems and issues as opportunities. (Remember the Third Gift of Confidence, from Chapter 2. See Challenges as Opportunities!) By framing things in a positive way, she tends to draw others toward her.

Sometimes described as charismatic, she holds her head high – and, in doing so, creates the energy that attracts good things and good people. She's happy to offer an encouraging word or remind you how awesome you are. She may even deliver helpful feedback, or point out an area in which you could improve, something you hadn't yet noticed yourself. You'll appreciate her feedback because it's delivered mindfully, in a way you'll be able to digest it easily, gratefully, and without hurt feelings.

Vow of Gossip Silence

In a sales environment, there's an unwritten rule: Never talk down your competition. If you resort to saying negative things about them rather than positive things about your own product or service, it's a big red flag that your offering is inferior.

Sh*t-talking about your competition, be it a company or a person, doesn't tell anyone why they'd want to work with you, or give them confidence in your ability to meet their needs. If, on the other hand, you tout the numerous benefits of your own proposition, it gives the customer plenty to think about and consider. It's a far more successful and sustainable sales strategy.

Let's look at an example using the help of our good friend, Wine.

In this first scenario, Red Wine is talking down its competition, White Wine. Listen in.

"I mean, did you notice how see-through White Wine was? Gaf! Who would want that kind of promiscuity? Her structure?" [Scoff!] "It's not full-bodied at all, more like scrawny. And I heard that her grapes..." [Pauses, leans in and whispers for dramatic effect...] "...were harvested by a machine. A machine! Can you even believe it? Rather than by hand? How classless!

"And did you hear what happened when White Wine and Seltzer got together in the cooler? Well, let's just say that cooler got awful hot! Know what I'm sayin'?" (Wink, wink!) "Oh, and the flavor? She will leave your taste buds at a complete loss..."

Aaaand, Scene! Notice Red Wine cannot come up with one good thing to say about herself. She's only slamming White Wine in order to score points. This is a clear indication that she lacks selling points of her own. Red Wine has very low self-regard, and may doubt her ability to serve a purpose, help solve an issue or fill a gap for the customer. If Red Wine does not believe in herself, then why should her customer or anyone else, for that matter?

Now let's look at a second scenario. This time, Red Wine's pitch takes on a different focus. She has plenty of characteristics that are worthy and valuable, so the conversation goes another way, as she describes her attributes. Let's listen in again. See if you notice the difference.

"2012 was a particularly good year. That was my year. My grapes were harvested from vines grown in organic soil, over the finest rock minerals, and delicately picked by hand. I was fermented in an oak barrel and stored in a cave where a consistent temperature was maintained. I was then tested by one of the most renowned wine connoisseurs in the entire valley and given kudos for a job well done. People smile and relax when they have me. They ask for more and take me to meet their friends. It's a pleasurable experience for all that will leave you already asking when we can meet again."

Aaaand, Scene! Wow, a little different, right? Red Wine, confident in her own features, advantages, and benefits, can describe herself in accurate terms. She can tout legitimate reasons why she should be uncorked at table. She never even bothers to mention her competition, White Wine. She doesn't have to put down White Wine or gossip about her to make herself look better. She's prepared, well-spoken, and poised.

Well, I don't know about you, but that's the kind of person I'd sure like to have on my team. Let's toast *this* glass of Red Wine, shall we, ladies? Oh, and White Wine? Who's that? Her name is familiar, but I can't remember anything about her.

Again, as sales (and life) philosophy will tell you, if you are truly confident in your own offering, there's no need to speak ill of your competition. You set yourself apart not by putting down others, but by demonstrating your strengths, communicating your abilities, and backing them up with actionable results. Feeling the need to talk down others suggests something missing in the person doing the talking. While throwing shade or spreading gossip may feel satisfying and attention-grabbing in the moment, it will do absolutely no good in the long run, and you'll be the one left in the dark.

"Catty makes me batty," is a phrase you'll often hear me say at the start of empowerment workshops. Workshop attendees agree to create a safe place by ensuring that the comments we're sharing are positive and encouraging only. So at this juncture, I'd like to invite you to take a vow with me. It's a vow I took very early in my career. And I'll renew my vow right here with you right now. Let us gather here today to take the Vow of Gossip Silence.

Having graduated from an all-girls high school and participated in sorority life in college, I'll tell you that I've experienced quite a bit of gossip. Despite my Catholic upbringing, I was no saint. I participated too. You know what, though? Never once, not a single time, in the enormous sample set of gossip that I heard and sometimes even spread myself, did I ever once see a single good result. Gossip hurts feelings. It can damage reputations and ruin friendships. And it almost always comes back around at you in some way, with timing that inevitably sneaks up on you. It's hurtful. It's immature. It's completely unnecessary. It can be spread verbally and digitally as cowardly attempts at boosting one's own self-esteem. I assure you, gossip will never once have a long-term positive effect. Have you heard the expression, "Every time you point a finger at someone else, there are three fingers pointing back at you?" Gossip is toxic and spreads faster than the common cold. It's contagious. It's not worth risking your own reputation by attempting to trash someone else's.

When I first entered working life I did not expect gossip, especially in a male-dominated workplace. But while it might have been less catty, it was still plentiful. And it was admittedly tempting to participate. I had the option to sink to that level, risk my own reputation, and hurt someone else's – but I turned my back on that path when I took my Vow of Gossip Silence. I've carried myself with more confidence and self-respect, ever since. I've never once regretted it, and on the rare occasion when I slip and say something that falls into the gossip category, I call myself out. I identify it and say aloud, "You know what? That's not the direction I want to take this conversation. Leadership doesn't speak that way."

Think back to your list of confident people. Do *they* gossip? Share salacious information? I bet not. And if they do, you may want to re-evaluate their presence on your list.

So again, I invite you to commit to the Vow of Gossip Silence. Invite your friends and co-workers to commit as well, for that matter. Unfortunately, the Vow will not insulate you from gossip in the workplace. Especially if you're a manager, you may have to intervene. And you'll know to go directly to the source to solve the problem, rather than talk to third parties about the gossiper, which only wastes time. A behavior cannot be corrected if the offender is not told of her crime.

Avoiding gossip saves time, energy, and effort and, dare I suggest it, increases work productivity when employees are spending time and conversing appropriately. If you don't believe me, ask my co-worker, Lisa. You know Lisa. She's the one who wears expensive clothes yet still manages to look cheap. She sure spends way too much time in the breakroom. Once I even saw her coming out of the supply closet, looking a little flushed. Come to think of it, I saw Tom emerge with a little afterglow himself! Hmm, I wonder if...

Just kidding! I wouldn't share a story like that, because that would be gossip, my friends. So repeat the Vow of Gossip Silence with me:

I, (State your name) , do solemnly swear to not spread gossip.
I'm worth way too much to risk my own reputation, credibility, and
respect by tastelessly talking about others. So help me, God!

Amen, sister, amen!

Not All Confidence Starts that Way

Sometimes we simply have to choose to persevere in circumstances when we aren't feeling it. Any honest leader will admit to moments when they weren't feeling confident yet had to move forward anyway, overruling the voice in their head telling them not to. And guess what? They made it. And we can all make it too.

Sure, you will get rattled. You will have that morning where bad news strikes, or you spill coffee on yourself and it's too late to turn around and change. Or you lose a big deal at work, or don't get to use the curriculum you think best for the kids you teach. Those unexpected moments can shake your confidence, but they don't have to shut you down.

Think once more about your list of confident people. Clearly, they project confidence. That's why you chose them. Do you think perhaps they've experienced moments in which they, too, were rattled, or not really feeling it on the inside, but chose to project it on the outside? I promise you that they have. They bounce back and so can you. The author and motivational speaker Josh Shipp has a great definition of perseverance:

Perseverance is stubbornness with a purpose.

Nelson Mandela has another excellent line about perseverance:

It always seems impossible until it's done.

Jokey-Jokerson

Last, but not least: while I've yet to find scientific proof, I hypothesize that genuinely confident people consistently have a sense of humor. Or, at a minimum, don't take themselves too seriously. While I'm sure there some very confident people are entirely serious-minded, I'd like to suggest that true confidence often comes with a sense of humor.

Whether you're someone who is quick-witted and on point with workplace-appropriate jokes, or simply someone who can laugh at herself and recognize that perfection need not be the goal every time, it's really helpful to have a sense of humor. Life's too short to not be able to laugh at yourself – and at others, for that matter, as long as they know you're laughing with them, not at them. I recently heard a keynote speaker flub a line, then follow with: "My bad. When I brushed my teeth this morning, I forgot to remove my foot from my mouth!" And she kept right on rolling. The crowd smiled and everyone carried on, no confidence or respect lost.

You don't have to be the life of the party or the comedian of the group, yet a light-hearted attitude and sense of fun are good habits to practice. And, psst, guess what? Humor helps keep you from taking things too personally and over-thinking, too. It's like a bonus gift, or a BOGO deal on Black Friday! More on that later…

In summary, the four over-arching personality traits of confidence are:

1. Positive and Encouraging
2. No Gossip Zone
3. Perseverance
4. Sense of Humor

The Sound of Confidence

There are two primary voice characteristics you can instantly leverage to project confidence. The first is volume and the second is pitch. To explain volume, I'll lean on a lesson taught to me by my favorite marketing professor in college, Dr. Roger Blackwell. One day in class, he shared some advice about what to say on a professional voicemail greeting – and, more importantly, *how* to say it.

"Think about it," said Professor Blackwell. "When job recruiters start calling you, they'll already have a sense of who you are per your resume. When they call and hear your voice for the first time, either live or via your voicemail message, they'll instantly be making judgments about whether you're a fit for their company. In a split second, hearing how you pronounce your name, keying in on volume as it correlates to confidence, they could decide whether they want to schedule you for an interview, or hang up and move along to the next candidate. Why? Simply because of how you sound. Is that fair? Maybe, maybe not. Does it happen? Yes. Can you do anything about it? Well, yes, pronounce your name with authoritative volume and confidence and you won't have to worry about a thing until interview-prep time!"

Dr. Blackwell then demonstrated as he projected his voice with confidence and proclaimed a sample voicemail greeting.

I remember looking at him and smiling. He was so cool. He said his name with elegance, with this cello-like tone. Had I called Professor Blackwell and reached his voicemail, I sure would've wanted to continue a conversation with him. Whether recording your voicemail greeting or introducing yourself in person, make it a priority to say your name clearly and with authority. No need to shout or overwhelm the listener, but practice saying your first and last name like you believe it – or, better yet, like you believe in you so they can believe in you.

When I'm giving live presentations, I like to play "Opposite Day" to dramatize this point. I first ask audience members to introduce themselves to a neighbor using a quiet, soft-spoken, wimpy voice, the opposite of how they should do it. I watch their body language and hear them inevitably giggle as they complete the task. Then we flip it right side up.

"Okay, now do it with authority, like you mean it."

The second time around, I see the body language is much different. Shy giggles turn into "Hell, yeah!" head nods and robust "Ha"s(!). You see and feel the energy shift in the room. Just reading this, can you envision the scene and feel the difference? The first-time voice is unsure and meek. The second one is proud and strong. The former voice isn't very engaging, nor inviting to the listener to stick around. The latter draws the listener in and starts a conversation on a strong foundation. Quick note for introverts: you need not be the loudest voice in the room. Just articulate your words and maintain an appropriate volume level. *That* projects confidence.

Proof of why volume is so critical comes from my adorable 2-year-old niece (what 2-year-old niece isn't adorable, right?) practicing her ABCs. What began as a very boisterous, "A, B, C, D, E, F, Geeeee!" softened to a quiet whisper when she hit the traditionally difficult part of the song, "L-M-N-O-P." Ever since kids started singing the ABC Song in 1835, they've been unsure of and confused by the L-M-N-O-P part. The letters lack distinction because the tune forces them to blend together. Fun fact: nearly 200 years later, there's now an updated version of the song accessible via a Google search near you. It changes up the tempo to force kids to articulate the letters. Today's version comes out sounding more like "ellemenopy," which is a full word, rather than individual letters and one which some clever(?) parents have actually named their child. (I can think of three letters to describe that! #WTH.)

Anyhoo, when my niece got to L-M-N-O-P, where uncertainty and skepticism lies, I noticed that I had to lean in closer in order to hear her sweet little voice. She involuntarily dialed it down to a whisper at this part, only to regain full volume at "Q-R-S," and a resounding finish of "W-X-Y-and-Zeeee!" Naturally, the crowd went wild. Think about this, though: she whispered the part that confused her, the part she was unsure of, the part she subconsciously did not have the confidence to say properly. She lowered her voice as a means of protection from admitting her own uncertainty. "I'm saying it quietly because I don't know this part well," her mind was telling her. The second she arrived at the letter Q, however, she grabbed back her confidence with the force of sticky hands heading toward a cookie, as demonstrated by the return in her voice's volume and enunciation.

As adults we do this, too. My good buddy, Ned, is the CEO of a large customer service company. He told me of a conversation he had with his board of directors going into 2020. 2019 had been a rough year and he knew he would be asked, "Ned, how will performance look this year?" When the question came he responded, firmly and confidently, with no dip in the volume of his voice: "We're going to have better performance this year and meet or exceed projections."

Period. End of story. The board nodded. Imagine if Ned had responded, "Well, um, (scratches his head, gets quiet), I *think* we'll meet or exceed projections..." How would the board have reacted? They probably would have started looking for a new CEO. Now, did Ned have a crystal ball? Could he predict the future? Of course not. But having confidence in himself and his plan convinced the board that he had a good handle on the company's future. The board believed in him because he believed in himself, and demonstrated it with his voice.

When thoughts you're unsure of are put into words, they tend to come out more quietly. Think about the volume of your voice when you're first pondering an idea, brainstorming, or thinking out loud tentatively. Compare it to your volume when you express familiar thoughts in which you have confidence. Me, I'm definitely quieter as I'm considering or evaluating something, yet more vocal, and I enunciate better, once I've gone through my thought process and reached a conclusion. The bottom line: convey confidence by speaking with appropriate, even authoritative volume, and beware of soft talk in situations where your performance is being observed and measured.

The pitch of your voice is another component to consider. Toastmasters International is an organization that teaches public speaking and leadership skills. Their take on pitch: "A thin, high-pitched tone lacks authority and appeal." Sometimes a speaker indicates uncertainty by raising her voice to a higher pitch at the end of a sentence, making what is meant as a declarative statement sound more like a question. This speech pattern is also called upspeak, uptalk, or rising inflection. It can be meant as an attempt to frame a point in a more welcoming, less aggressive manner. But listeners may interpret upspeak differently – wondering whether the speaker even believes what she's saying in the first place.

Let's look at an example.

Mandy, an entry-level employee, is sitting in a team meeting. Her boss asks, "Mandy, where do you think we should hold the next company retreat?"

"I think the next retreat should be held in... Palm Springs?" As Mandy responds, the inflection in her voice is steady until she gets to Palm Springs. Then it rises – upspeak in action – implying that she's unsure of her very own response. Imagine what facial expression accompanies Mandy's higher-pitched conclusions. (Body-mind connection at work here. We'll talk about it more in the next chapter!) She scrunches her nose and looks at her manager for approval rather than agreement. He returns her gaze, a bit frustrated and confused because when he asked Mandy a direct question, he expected a direct answer – not something that sounded more like another question in response.

But let's try this again and give Mandy a second shot.

"Mandy, where do you think we should hold the next company retreat?" asks the boss.

"The next retreat should be held in Palm Springs," responds Mandy evenly. Period, end of story. No upspeak, and notice she also dropped 'I think' as a prelude to her sentence. Smar move, Mandy. These two little words are superfluous. Of course it's what she thinks since she's the one saying it!

Her boss returns her gaze and says, "Great. Palm Springs it is. Let's get to planning that."

Cool, eh? By displaying confidence with a direct response to a question, and leaving out the upspeak at the end of her sentence, Mandy gets to go to Palm Springs! Sounds like a nice reward to me! Not all incentives for ditching upspeak will be as glamorous as Palm Springs, but doing so will get you to higher places, including on the company organizational chart.

When you have something to say and want to be heard, then be heard. Speak up with pride, Sister!

Appropriate volume and pitch are the two key variables. Speed and added filler words come into play as well. There's a lot of conflicting evidence, though, on whether speed and filler words help or hurt you. While the jury remains out on that, aim to focus simply on volume and pitch, and you'll be ahead of the game. Don't sell yourself short by sharing those brilliant thoughts and ideas in a tiny mouse voice. Contribute courageously, in a calm and collected way, like the beautiful, brave lioness you are.

The Look of Confidence
Self-confidence is the best outfit. Rock it. Own it!

Have you ever sat in a public place and people-watched? A shopping center, college campus, corporate headquarters, or airport? I have. Next time you're suffering through a flight delay and what feels like an infinite period sitting at Gate B7 in the East Concourse, do a confidence observation exercise.

Look around. Observe people. Watch them walk. Watch what they do when they sit, talk on the phone, or chat up a fellow traveler (if anyone still does that). Watch how they work on their laptops, snap selfies, or interact with family. What assumptions do you make about the people you see? What messages are sent by their clothes, accessories, postures, and mannerisms? Can you create a story about someone simply by watching their interactions or observing their body language?

Sure you can. We all do it, often without even thinking about it. Right or wrong, we all make judgements based on what we see. It's human nature, and a survival mechanism, to be aware of the behaviors around us. We base beliefs and theories about who's a friend and who's a foe on those field observations.

It's survival of the fittest out there and the corporate jungle is no exception. It's a huge judgment zone where we can use confidence, and confidence-based job performance, as shields and secret weapons for surviving and thriving.

In this section, we'll see how confidence looks. I'd like to invite you to play a fun game with me called "Confident or Not?" You'll look at pictures of people and based on what you see, decide whether the subjects are confident... or not.

Ready? Time to bust out your inner game show contestant. Here we go!

Confident or Not?

For Round 1, we'll start with this cutie... Is he confident, or not?

What do you first notice about him? What are some of the first things that come to mind? His gaze, his smile, or his stance? If you had to vote either confident or not right now, what would you say?

Did you say *confident*? Ding, ding, ding! Excellent work. You are correct. Let's discuss why.

This young man is making direct eye contact in a warm and focused way. This is a still picture, but we assume he's holding his gaze, a sign of confidence and belief in himself. His smile is subtle, yet sincere. He looks authentically happy, yet not giddy or crazed. Lastly, his stance. His arms are casually crossed, and he's leaning slightly against the stone wall. If someone were to try to push him over, his stance is such that he'd withstand it or bounce back quickly. Round 1 is a tick in the Confident box.

For Round 2, take a look at this woman:

What do you notice about her? Outfit, hair, stance? Confident or not?

Again, the correct response is *confident*!

Why? She's well put together, a sign of self-care and belief in her own self-worth. Her clothes are well tailored. We assume she recently picked them up from the dry cleaners. She's well groomed. Her hair, nails, and makeup are appropriate for a professional environment. She looks feminine, sophisticated, and smart. Similar to the young man in Round 1, she's also crossing her arms, signaling sturdiness but not closing off others. It's almost like her arms are the rungs connecting two legs of a ladder. They are there for support and to assist in reaching higher levels.

Again, well done, contestant! Let's move on.

For Round 3, consider this gentleman:

What do you notice about his body position, his hands and his eyes? Confident or not?

Not confident? Correct! You are really good at this

Why? Despite his well-groomed appearance, he's in a sitting position, hunched forward. His hands are touching his face, a classic sign of doubt and disbelief in oneself. Body language expert Traci Brown, a close friend of mine, will tell you that hands near the mouth are an indication of lying. Our bodies speak louder than our words. When we put our hands near our mouth, it's a subconscious signal that we're trying to cover up or hide our words. It's hard for our bodies to lie when our minds know the truth. Hands elsewhere on our face can indicate insecurity. We may not be intentionally lying, but if we're internally uncertain, it's human nature to put hands on our faces.

Think back to the story of Mandy responding to her boss about Palm Springs. In the first scenario, when she responded with what sounded like a question of her own, where do you picture her placing her hands? Did she scratch her forehead, or rest her chin or cheek on the palm of her hand? I bet she did. It goes right along with the insecurity heard in her voice. But in the second scenario, when Mandy responded with authority, it's hard to imagine her hands anywhere near her face. I bet they were on the table in front of her or even resting on her hips.

This poor gentleman's eyes are cast downward, and the vibe he's sending is certainly one of disappointment and even defeat.

There are plenty of times when it's appropriate to be thinking through something. Just as the famous sculptor, Auguste Rodin, who created the famous statue *The Thinker*. Know, however, that when you're presenting your final thoughts or wanting to persuade someone, you must be convinced first before convincing others. Hands near your face subconsciously communicate that you're not quite there. It's a great test you can use on yourself as you're preparing an important project. You'll know you're ready when, as you rehearse your delivery, you can do it with your hands casually hanging at your sides or relaxed in your lap. If you find yourself rubbing your forehead or putting them anywhere near your mouth, your preparation is incomplete.

(Sidebar: Hand-watching can be a great lie detector in personal and professional settings. Have some fun the next time you're on a date, at a family dinner, or collaborating at work. See if you can detect dishonesty! Whether you call out the offender or not, well, that's up to you!)

For Round 3, the correct answer is: *not confident*!

In Round 4 we see a woman shaking hands with the man across from her:

What's her story? What assumptions are we making about her? How would you rate her handshake?

Survey says… *confident*!

Similar to the woman in Round 2, she's well-tailored and well-groomed. Her hand is locked into a firm handshake and she's making eye contact. Speaking of handshakes, if you recognized hers as top notch, you just earned extra points here on the "Confident or Not?" show. Mastery of this very important gesture is a prize in and of itself! And no matter what your gender, a proper handshake is an essential element of a confident greeting. Here's a story of a handshake lesson as given to one of my male colleagues.

The morning of a trade show where our company was exhibiting, the CEO, Sam, greeted James, an operations manager. As Sam and James shook hands, Sam said, "Hey, man, do that again. Shake my hand again." James gave Sam a confused look but complied by again extending his hand.

"Now," Sam said, as his firm grip met James's, "Don't break eye contact with me while you're shaking my hand. I notice that you don't maintain eye contact. When you do that, it conveys the wrong message to our customers. Our customers only believe in you if you believe in yourself. When you look away, it tells me that you don't believe in yourself. Keep that eye contact with me and with them, too, okay?"

I stood within earshot, pretending I wasn't listening. I didn't want James to feel further embarrassment, yet I was fascinated by this conversation. James responded very humbly. He could have turned defensive or aggressive, and called on ego to protect his pride. Instead he modestly and sincerely replied to Sam, "Yep, I know I do that. Thanks for pointing it out. I'll work on it."

I busied myself rearranging brochures, but I was so impressed with James. And I was impressed that Sam offered that important feedback in such a matter-of-fact, quick, moving-right-along kind of way. Fairly or not, women, more often than men tend to be associated with wimpy, dead-fish handshakes, but this is not a gender-specific issue. Moral of the story: nobody likes a dead fish. So, briefly, here are the four steps to a winning handshake:

1. **Firm grip.** Shake the other person's hand with the authority of an inspector in the grocery store fresh fruit section. Squeeze that pear too hard and you'll have a juicy, sticky mess. Don't squeeze hard enough and you'll have "bitter face" at home later on, when you bite into the unripe fruit.

2. **Smile.** Be friendly, not flirty, genuinely happy to be adding someone new to your network.

3. **Make and hold eye contact.** While they are saying their name and you're saying yours. Be sure to maintain eye contact.

4. **Introduce yourself** by saying your name with confidence, as described earlier in this chapter.

Nailing your handshake is absolutely crucial to conveying confidence. Since it's the first contact you have with someone and it typically happens within seconds of meeting, it sets the tone then and there. A limp handshake signals: that you can be pushed around, have no backbone, and are unlikely to bring much to the table. Is that true or not? The other party doesn't know and doesn't care. Immediate assumptions will be made, and a first impression is hard to revise. A firm handshake, combined with eye contact and confident pronunciation of your name will establish instant credibility, convey your true value, and help you get down to business faster.

The Round 4 final answer: *confident!*

Now for the fifth and final round of "Confident or Not?" Take a look at the following picture:

There's a lot going on in this picture! Since it's our last round, we'll break it down by category!

- **Apparel:** All eight people in this photo are dressed the part. What do you think – confident? Yes! *Confident!*

- **Eye contact:** On the left side, the two gentlemen in the middle appear engaged in the conversation, as do the two women at right who are farthest away. All four are leaning in, making eye contact, and have one or both of their hands visible and on the table. For this category, the correct answer is *confident!*

- **Body signals:** At left, the woman closest to us and the man farthest away are both looking at their phones. What are they checking? Important information relevant to the conversation? An email from a key client? Are they gossip-texting each other? (Violating the Vow of Gossip Silence right in our faces?) Are they playing Angry Birds, or swiping left on a dating app? We have no idea. The impression they're giving, however, is that they couldn't give a rip about the meeting and have better things to do. If you were their manager or even their teammate, how would you rate their level of engagement? Would you consider them reliable, valuable, and indispensable? They're not projecting interest in the team discussion, nor conviction that they want to contribute. They may well be confident people, yet their disinterest here works against them. Does disinterest mean lack of confidence, though? Maybe! Life in the workplace isn't always black and white. Habitual disinterest, regardless of confidence, is not a desirable trait. What say you, Game Show Participant? Confident or not? Without further information, this one is too tough to call.

- **Facial expressions:** The two employees at right, closest to us are, well, um, they could easily be accused of RBF, otherwise known as Resting Bitch Face, a gender-neutral term in my opinion. Does RBF send a positive and encouraging signal, or at least neutral? Nada. Is it possible to be angry and confident at the same table? Yes, it is. But since this game, just like real life, turns only on what we can see, not on a thorough understanding of everything happening in these people's lives, we have to base a quick call on the evidence at hand. Confident or Not? *Not!*

Finally, a bonus category. Look at the positioning around the table. Sometimes I refer to this tactic as "Survival in the Woods." Remember taking wilderness survival class as a kid? (If you never did, this might be one to add to your Physical Confidence Booster List, coming up in the next chapter!) What did they teach you to do if you encountered a bear in the woods? Obviously, you want to get out alive, so you're taught to make yourself as big as you can. Stand and face the bear directly. Don't turn sideways. Wave your arms above your head. Take off your jacket and swing it around. Establish your presence and give the perception that you're bigger than you are. Doing so will make the bear question the wisdom of fighting something his size or bigger. He may well back down and walk away.

This same survival skill applies in a workplace environment. Make yourself BIG. If I were coaching the woman on the right, I would have her push in and raise her chair. The chairs in this photo aren't the adjustable kind, yet when you encounter ones that are, make sure to raise yourself up so you're at least at eye level with your peers. Don't ever let them look down on you physically, lest they do so mentally as well. I'd also tell the woman at right to make herself big by claiming some tabletop "real estate." Spread out with a laptop, a notebook, something that allows you to claim more surface area. It's a good idea to take notes in a meeting regardless and having a tablet to do so helps in literally establishing your place at the table. Bring in a water bottle or coffee tumbler, too. Establish your turf to show them that you belong and that you plan on staying awhile. Make your presence big and known to stave off bears in the woods and the boardroom too!

Okay, players, what's your final answer for the two people sitting closest to us

on the right side? Not confident! But suppose they easily tweaked a few things —
like engaging, pushing in their chairs, and bringing a notebook, what would you
say then? Confident!

Congratulations, you astute contestant you, you have won the game of
"Confident or not?"!

What We Perceive is What We Believe

You played very well, and caught on with relative ease to perceptions of what
is confident and what is not. Simply by looking at people in photos, you were
able to assess if they'd be reliable, sure of themselves, and valuable contributors
in your place of work. But let me ask you an important question: What do
we actually know about any of them? Do we know what degrees they have,
or their IQ scores? What about what kind of morning they had, professional
accolades they've achieved, or personal issues that might be weighing on them?
The answer, of course, is no, we don't know. We don't know anything, but we
made assumptions and because they are all that we had to rely on, that's what we
believed and what we acted on.

So if we make our own tweaks, is it really just this easy to sound and look the
part? Yep, it sure is. Nothing overly complicated here.

It really is just that easy to sound, look, and project confidence.

What we perceive is what we believe. What our voice and body convey is what
observers believe, without asking us for clarification. In the "Confident or Not?"
exercise you likely made further assumptions about whether you'd want to work
with them or seek advice, or whether you could count on them to carry their
weight and contribute appropriately to advance the collective goals of your
organization. There are many conclusions we, as humans, draw about others
simply because of the messages they're projecting and how we interpret them.
Whether our conclusions are true or false, we may never know, but perception is
reality.

**What you are projecting is what people perceive. And what people
perceive is what they believe, regardless of the true reality.**

What adjustments might you consider to project your own confidence? Test out
something different next time you're walking into work, sitting in a meeting, or
speaking with colleagues. See how you can elevate your own confidence simply
by playing the part.

Confidence is *your choice*. Anytime, anywhere, no matter how you're feeling, you can choose confidence. It's your superpower, your secret weapon for instantly feeling better or feeling "badder" (because you're a bad a$$, of course!), and busting out your "A game." You can use confidence to protect yourself, soothe yourself, and promote yourself. You've got an endless supply, so *use it to your advantage*. Test it out early. Test it out often. And *slay* along the way!

Now that you're an expert in projecting confidence to an external audience, we'll shift focus – to getting centered in confidence for the most important audience of all: *you!*

There will always be times when you're afraid or intimidated. Confidence helps you mitigate the fear so you can work through it and perform regardless. Things may not be perfect the first time. That's okay. Just that first ounce of confidence fuel will often be all you need for your first step forward. You might be trembling on the inside, but when you look confident on the outside, no one will ever know. You're able to protect yourself by remaining calm and not allowing a "crazy town" state to overtake you. Have you ever been highly emotional and made a super good decision in that moment? Logic and emotion activate in two separate locations in your brain. Some neurologists say the two cannot function simultaneously. Channeling calm and confidence helps keep you in a place of logic and professionalism. It can simultaneously prevent a slip to the Dark Side. Unless Darth Vader is your boss, the Dark Side is certainly not where you want to be while at work!

A question I sometimes get is, "But isn't it dishonest to project confidence when I'm not really feeling it? Am I being disingenuous by faking it?" First, remember that you're *not* faking it. You're *rehearsing*. You have a goal and you're just practicing to attain it. Second, didn't your organization hire you, choose you over other candidates, for your strengths, experience, and attitude? They hired you to get sh*t done because that's who you are: a well-qualified candidate and an incredible asset. Does that mean you'll be free of failure, fear, and family or friend drama creeping into your professional life? Absolutely not. Yet knowing how to manage and work through it helps you maintain sanity and keeps you on an upward trajectory.

Company cultures vary regarding tolerance of – and forgiveness for – personal life issues affecting your performance. I've worked for the full spectrum. One boss texted me relentlessly during my grandma's funeral, but another let me work from home while I went through a painful boyfriend break-up. I was given that privilege because he knew I wouldn't abuse it. It was a rare lowlight in my life. Yet because I'd proven my value through prior job performance, my understanding boss gave me the breathing room I needed in order to come back strong and do what the company paid me to do.

Not all companies or bosses would do that. He was my all-time favorite boss, and did a particularly excellent job of developing and managing me as an employee as well as caring about me as a person. He embodied the Goldilocks approach… Not too much, not too little, but rather just right. That company culture was a good fit for me. You'll have to decide what spot on the tolerance spectrum looks like the best fit for you.

At the end of the day, all organizations have a mission, and they hire you to do a job. Confident You is the one who'll be able to crush it over and over again, allowing you to survive and thrive in any environment at any time.

Decide who you need to be at work to be successful – frame your own, personal definition of success – and project accordingly. Remember: because of the power of the body-mind connection, what you're outwardly projecting is catalyzing your thoughts and vice-versa. It's almost like your "Inner-Siri." Tell her, "Hey, Inner-Siri! It's time for me to strut my stuff!" And now that you have the steps to get you there, simply follow the path and re-calculate whenever necessary!

What's at Stake?

Letting self-doubt call the shots shows up in your voice and your posture. People respond accordingly. Project your own confidence to send a message to them, and yourself, that you are a power player.

Key Points

- Tiny changes in voice and posture instantly project confidence both inwardly (to your most important audience, you!) and outwardly to your peers and colleagues.

- Staying positive, encouraging others, and making ethical decisions demonstrates great confidence and excellent leadership characteristics.

- What people perceive is what they believe. Put your best foot forward by establishing yourself confidently in both verbal and non-verbal ways.

Confidence Challenge Checklist

- ❏ Identify three people who embody the characteristics of positive, non-gossiping, ethical players. What else about them do you admire?

- ❏ Notice your voice in the next meeting when you're challenged. Do a volume and pitch check!

- ❏ Establish your place at the table like a boss the next time you go into a meeting. See if it changes how the meeting goes for you.

- ❏ Share one of the techniques you learned to improve the appearance of confidence, and challenge others to uphold it in their work, too. Compare notes on the results.

To stretch and condition my confidence, one action I commit to is:

_____

_____

_____

Chapter 4
Channeling Confidence:
Unleashing Your Superpowers

Anyone else have Underoos as a kid? They were sold as the "Underwear that's fun to wear." I loved mine.

Underoos came in a variety of designs. The matching top and bottom featured cartoon characters, movie characters, and most memorably, comic book superheroes. They had Underoos for boys and Underoos for girls. I happened to be the proud owner of none other than Wonder Woman Underoos. My set spent way more time as my outermost layer than underneath my regular clothes.

I vividly remember bossing around, er, demonstrating good leadership skills, to my two younger sisters, who wore Incredible Hulk (For a girl? Why not?) and My Little Pony Underoos as we conjured up all sorts of beat-the-bad-guy, save-the-day, stop-the-crisis, avenge-the-nemesis scenarios. My parents played along, sometimes moonlighting as the bad guys or helping us make a highly secure 'jail' out of a cardboard box to securely hold the villains.

I look back on my four-year-self brimming with courage and confidence, her superpowers tangible, with undaunted power to execute on story lines and goals. Can you recall your own childhood, when your imagination trumped reality, and you saved the world as readily as you might post a picture of dinner today? As kids, our imaginations knew no limits. We believed we could leap tall buildings in a single bound. We were excited, pumped up, and free of doubt. What a magical time!

But then, like a car slamming on the brakes, SCREEEEEECH! – how quickly it comes to a halt. Hashtag Adulting starts to happen real fast. Fantasy, fairy dust, and fun are overpowered by responsibilities, reports, and reconciliations.

Our imaginations dwindle as we grow out of our Underoos and toss aside the superpowers they gave us. Our brains retire the superhero plot lines and transition to fretting about mounting responsibilities. Before, we used blankets to make forts in the living room. Now they smother creativity, imagination, and the limitless possibilities we explored as kids.

But is it all gloom and doom? Is this a permanent situation? Are our superpowers forever banished to planets unknown? Holy hell, Batman, of course not!

I'm thrilled to say our superpowers are just as present in this moment as when we were kids. All we have to do is prioritize them more intentionally.

So while I continue to wait for Victoria's Secret to release a mature and sophisticated version of Underoos, something I could wear to work on a Tuesday for an important meeting (unbeknownst to anyone but me, of course), we have other tools and techniques to revive our superpowers.

We can choose from a battery of options depending on the "villain" we're facing. Some days may be low self-esteem days, for example, when we're struggling just to get moving. Other days may mean important meetings, or high stakes situations in which you interact with someone who intimidates the heck out of you. Never fear! No matter how you're feeling or what situation you face, there's a confidence tool for that. Do you have days, or even seasons of life, when you feel more or less confident? Yep, me too. Based on my starting point, I'll use different confidence-building techniques. Some, when done regularly, become as routine as brushing your teeth.

To dive into techniques to channel confidence and unleash our superpowers, we'll start with learning how to leverage the body-mind connection. This connection is an amazing phenomenon that accelerates confidence growth via the direct link between our mental and physical abilities.

Let's look at a scientific experiment as proof of not only how powerful our thoughts are, but also how much change we can effect by carefully and intentionally selecting thoughts that serve the highest and best version of ourselves!

Warning: The following information may very well have you #mindblown!

In 2007, Time Magazine[1] wrote about a study conducted at Harvard Medical School. Neuroscientist Dr. Alvaro Pascual-Leone measured the brain activity of people in motion, *physically* performing a task against the brain activity of people sitting still, simply *thinking* about the same task.

Here's what went down. Dr. Pascual-Leone set up two groups of volunteer musicians, Group A and Group B. Each member of Group A was led to a room that contained a piano and was given instructions to play the piano for two hours per day for five days in a row. The volunteers each sat at a piano and their fingers moved over the keys. They could feel the ivory, hear the notes, and smell the piano frame's mahogany wood. Their brain activity was scanned and measured using something called a Transcranial Magnetic Stimulation (TMS) test.

Each member of Group B was led to an individual room and given the same instructions with one key exception. There was no piano in the room. They were directed to simply sit and *think* about playing. No ivory keys to touch, notes to hear, or mahogany to smell. Using their imaginations only, they "played piano" for the same time frame, two hours per day for five days in a row. Their brain activity was scanned using the same TMS test.

What do you think the brain scans showed? Likely wildly different because surely physical activity produces a much different result than just pretending, right? The results may very well astound you!

When scientists looked at Group A's brain scans they saw that, as expected, the motor cortex of Group A, the ones physically practicing piano over five days, expanded. When they compared this to the scans of Group B's, the ones playing pretend piano, they observed that, get this, the images were nearly identical. Their motor cortexes had expanded as well! It did not matter whether a volunteer had actually played the piano or not. The brain responded very similarly. Real-life and imagination registered the same way.

They concluded that:

The mind does not distinguish between
reality and imagination.
Merely thinking about something produced practically
the same result as actually doing it.

Wow! Isn't that super intriguing? Whether someone was physically playing

---

1 Sharon Begley, "The Brain: How The Brain Rewires Itself," Time, January 19, 2007, http://content.time.com/time/magazine/article/0,9171,1580438-1,00.html

the piano or just imagining it, it rendered nearly similar changes in the cortical pathways. Check out the chart that compares the scans of Group A and Group B:

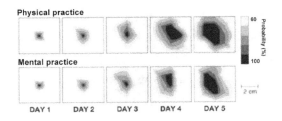

They are incredibly similar. *So,* you may be asking, *does this mean that if I imagine doing sit-ups, it will have the same result as actually doing sit-ups?! Well, hot diggity, let's flop on the couch and imagine those crunches right now!* Ha, I wish! It doesn't exactly work that way, although there are studies that suggest that there is an element of truth to that. For now, though, let's reflect upon your 4-year-old-mind. When it was pretending, imagining, and acting out Disney movie scenes, the brain was lighting up in the same way as if what you were imaging was actually happening. That's why it seemed so invincibly real.

Upon further reserach, Dr. Pascual-Leone further explored a characteristic of the brain called brain plasticity, or neuroplasticity, a name first used in 1948 by Polish neuroscientist Jerzy Konorski. Simply put, neuroplasticity is the brain's capability to change and adapt in response to experience. It happens gradually, just as it takes not one, but several trips to the gym to earn you some ripped abs. We each exercise, you build upon your previous effort, rather than continusouly start at square one. Over time, your arms are beautifully toned, and eventually you can't wait for tank top season. Neuroplasticity works the same way. The more you practice visualizing something, the more of a reality it *becomes*.

When I first learned about how the brain changes in respo nse to thoughts, my mind was truly blown and I was deeply intrigued. It made me consider how one could take advantage of this and capitalize on the results

I recalled a story I'd heard when I was in high school. I was on the diving team, and long before we perfected any dives, we did what all novices do: we practiced in the natatorium by repeatedly jumping off the one-meter board and awkwardly landing in the water. The water surface was incredibly unforgiving. We actually wore heavy wet sweatshirts to defend against the harsh slap of contact. Over and over, we smacked into the surface, as with each attempt edging closer to a smoother, less punishing entry.

I heard that in China, however, they had a different technique for novice divers. Before a first-timer was ever allowed to catapult herself from the diving board, she and her teammates met for an entire year, never getting wet. They sat in a room and visualized their dives: inwards, reverses, twists, the whole portfolio of options. They simply visualized the motions, step by step, and performed perfect dives in their heads, including sting-free entry. When they finally stepped out onto the board a year later, they were far more prepared. They felt the smack of the water much less often than I had the pleasure of experiencing.

Dr. Pascual-Leone's experiment supported the Chinese technique. While I was using my body to practice the dive, the Chinese divers were using their minds. After a certain period of time, we both had similar results, although I had more bruises! It truly blows my mind.

So if harnessing brain plasticity works for piano and it works for diving, where else can it apply? Let's look at another everyday activity demonstrating just how powerful our thoughts are in controlling our brains. This time I'll enlist the help of Netflix.

Recall, if you will, the last time you watched a scary or suspenseful movie or show? The one that makes you shiver just thinking about it. Any *Ozark* watchers out there? Good god. Or *Get Out*? Eek, I can barely think about it without recoiling in fear. There's the classics, *Silence of the Lambs*, *The Blair Witch Project* and *Cape Fear* – all terrifying. Do you have one in your head?

Think about what happened to your body as you watched that movie.

You're sitting on your comfortable couch, in your perfectly safe house, doors locked, windows closed. You're casually tossing popcorn into your mouth, when, all of a sudden, something jumps on the screen. The popcorn goes flying as you clutch the person sitting next to you, the dog, or a pillow. Your heart pounds, your stomach has butterflies, and you are laser-focused on the screen. You're actually experiencing an increase in your heart rate, possibly your blood pressure too, and certainly a widening of your eyes. Why are you experiencing these things? Are you physically in danger? Are you truly suspicious that someone lurks inside your house, so much so that you've tapped "9" and "1" on your phone, hovering your finger over that second "1"? Are you doing physical exercise that would cause your heart rate to increase? Of course not. You're merely watching and *thinking* about what you're seeing. Your mind's imagination is hard at work. All that is happening is doing so not in the middle of a dark forest with serial killers on the loose but rather in your motor cortex, in your very own safe living room on your comfortable couch, offering further proof of the power of your thoughts! The power of your mind! And it's solely responsible for the physical changes you're feeling. Whoa!

Late one night, after my Mom had gone to bed, my Dad was watching *Bird Box*, the Netflix thriller starring Sandra Bullock (love her!). Suddenly the household printer, located in an adjacent room, spit out a page for no known reason. My Dad heard the whirring sound and freaked—so startled, he said, he just about rocked himself out of his La-Z-Boy. I laugh thinking about it now, and so did Dad once he regained his composure and checked his blood pressure. Had he been watching, say, SportsCenter, or a comedy, an unexpected printer noise would not have elicited nearly the response it did when his brain was being exposed to scary things and conditioned to respond in 'fight or flight' fashion.

Scary movie side note: scientific studies show watching *The Shining*, featuring a madman played by Jack Nicholson, burns 189 calories. Yep, 189 calories! Shocking that it hasn't shown up yet as a weight loss ad in your Insta feed, eh?

The power of our thoughts is immense! What we expose ourselves to, and the things we think about, truly chart our course. They help determine our direction of travel, as we also have the power to consciously choose where and how we want to go. This is wonderful and amazing news! Just as we have the ability to think ourselves scared, we also have the ability to think ourselves safe, or strong, or assured or whatever we want to be.

It's the same superpower that convinced us kids in our Underoos that the cardboard box we made into a rocket ship had actually taken us into space. This ability still exists in our minds, and now we can use it more strategically, to guide our very own reality. Do you want to be happier? Think happy thoughts. Do you want to be calmer? Think calming thoughts. It sounds so simple, almost trite, but when you visualize what you want to be, your brain responds – and helps.

It works for emotions, negative or positive, too. If you're having one of those days and just want to be mad and angry, a few thoughts can get you there. If you'd rather be happy or optimistic, start envisioning it now and by the time you reach the end of this paragraph, your mindset will already have begun to shift.

Here are two more quick examples to convince you of the superpowers of your thoughts!

The first example works better in person, but you'll get the idea. It's fun to use with live audiences because it works every time. "Listen closely and simply imagine if you will, nails on a chalkboard," I'll say as I simultaneously make the motion of scratching my nails on a chalkboard. Inevitably, audience members will wince and recoil. Even if you've experienced only smooth, silent white board and not green chalkboards, the mental association is so strong between the phrase, "nails on a chalkboard," and the imagined sound, it's as if the sound had actually pierced the room!

The second example is the lemon experiment. A speaker describes a lemon to you, at length and in detail: its color, skin, pulp, and seeds. Then you're asked to make the physical motion of squeezing an imaginary lemon into an imaginary glass of water and, finally, to take a big sip. What do you think happens? Yep, you guessed it. The drinker of the imaginary lemon water puckers. You may even be puckering right now, just reading this and mentally processing it. Heck, I'll confess that I'm puckering as I'm typing – and I already knew the story! Our minds are certainly powerful, aren't they?!

Let's start reviving and re-conditioning our mental abilities to be as strong and convincing as when we were kids. And while it's fun to imagine ourselves as princesses in castles or astronauts in space, let's also use these abilities to channel and direct our well-being, our belief in ourselves, and our confidence. We can use this superpower to think ourselves confident. Just as easily as we can pull up a Netflix movie, we can train ourselves into a confident state of mind. Simply by imagining it, by picturing ourselves as confident, we actually shift our brains into a state of confidence. We are confident. And thanks to neuroplasticity, the brain doesn't go back to the beginning. It retains confidence, so next time, you naturally start from a stronger position.

As a closing thought I am passing along the precautionary warning that Dr. Pascual-Leone himself, passed along to me in a recent email exchange. He requested that I share this with you.

> *"One better be careful with whatever one thinks because the induced changes in the brain may not be advantageous. In other words, it is important to think and do mental rehearsal but it is critical to be aware of the power of such thoughts."*

Choose wisely, my friends!

The Mind-Body Connection

The mind-body connection has quite a following in the scientific world. There are dedicated blogs, research studies, courses, books, and entire conferences held in its name. It's a fascinating and compelling topic.

Simply described, our thoughts have the power to direct our body, and our body's posture and position can influence our thoughts. Our mind and body talk to each other in a biochemical language.

Your thoughts can direct your body and
your body can direct your thoughts.

An article published by the University of Minnesota's Center for Spirituality and Healing described it this way:

"Our thoughts, feelings, beliefs, and attitudes can positively or negatively affect our biological functioning. In other words, our minds can affect how healthy our bodies are!...

"On the other hand, what we do with our physical body (what we eat, how much we exercise, even our posture) can impact our mental state (again positively or negatively). This results in a complex interrelationship between our minds and bodies." [2]

Have you noticed how your body reacts when you have stressful thoughts? Do you get that nervous or uncomfortable feeling in your gut? It might be TMI, but I've had major GI issues while under extreme stress. Have you ever felt yourself approaching a point of emotional explosion, yet were able to talk yourself back from the cliff edge by taking a few deep breaths, or by standing or sitting up straight? That's your body-mind connection at work. You know why we ask kids on the verge of a meltdown to pause and count to 10? Because concentrating on counting urges the mind to shift focus, as the body follows, it achieves a calmer state, offering further support to less frantic thoughts, and ideally preventing a tantrum.

How about the last time you were excited? Like when you learned the release date for the next season of *Big Little Lies*, did you slouch and cross your arms and glower? Of course not! You, like me, probably pumped your fists, nodded your head, or maybe even jumped up and down. Emotions come with fairly standard physical responses and as body language experts say, our bodies tend to be much

---

2 Patricia Hart, MD, "What Is the Mind-Body Connection?", University of Minnesota, https://www.takingcharge.csh.umn.edu/what-is-the-mind-body-connection

more honest than our words.

You can lie to yourself, yet your body can't lie to you.

Here's an experiment. Clear your mind and concentrate on saying the following words to yourself, either in your head or out loud:

"I'm so *sad*."

Say it like Eeyore. Slow, depressed, whiny. Notice what your head and body do. Did your body slump and your head fall?

Now say:

"I'm so *happy*!"

Say it like Tigger. Energetic, excited, spirited! Notice what your head and body do. Did you sit up straight? Wiggle your shoulders? Did your face smile?

If you answered yes in both cases, your body-mind connection is firing away. If you didn't notice a physical response, then it may not have been a spontaneous enough exercise to allow your body to respond involuntarily. The next time you naturally experience an emotion do a quick body-check and observe what's happening.

For now, let's celebrate the natural wonder of the mind-body connection and test-drive it on a road trip to Confidence Country! (Wow. Super corny, I know.)

Physically Channeling Confidence

Remember the Bible story of David and Goliath? David was the good guy; Goliath, the bad guy. David was the little guy; Goliath, the big guy, said to tower over nine feet tall. The two were primed for a fight, the betting odds were highly in favor of Goliath. In the absence of pay-per-view, a crowd gathered to watch the contest live, assuming they wouldn't be there long. David had no chance against Goliath.

Well, they were right about one thing. It was indeed a quick fight, yet the guy left standing was not the one of superior size and stature. By placing just one rock in his slingshot and launching it, David hit Goliath square in the forehead, forcing him to the ground. The crowd, along with the Biblical equivalent of Las Vegas bookies, went wild! David, with God in his corner, overcame someone twice his size and ten times as strong.

When I visualized this scene I wondered what stance David struck as he sized up Goliath. I pictured Goliath, too: smirking, cocky, poster giant for arrogance, barely glancing at David, having no idea of the power behind David's faith – no idea of David's confidence. I envisioned David standing up straight, chest out, eyes focused, with thoughts of determination emanating from his brow.

And then it hit me, as if an LED lightbulb went off over my head. *Oh my gosh! Was it David, the pipsqueak from 1063 BC, who struck the original power pose?* David who stood tall and puffed out his chest as he sized up his target? Hallelujah, who knew?!

Maybe the original power pose came not from a TED Talk stage, but the Valley of Elah. Is Amy Cuddy aware of this?

Dr. Amy Cuddy is the brilliant Harvard social psychologist, who, with Dana Carney and Andy Yap, published a research paper in 2010 in which they coined the term "Power Pose." Amy presented it at a TED Talk. I highly recommend watching it. I have to wonder, though, if David with the slingshot struck the pose millennia before Amy named it and long before Madonna sang about it. I look forward to asking Amy when I someday meet her. I bet we'll have a good laugh over it.

What exactly is a power pose? It's defined as standing in a posture which people mentally associate with being powerful. Assuming a power pose is believed to trigger feelings of assertiveness. It's the pose superheroes get into before calling on their powers to fight the bad guy or save the world. It's also a tool you can use each and every time your best, brightest, baddest self has an important job to do.

A power pose delivers almost immediate gratification. It can positively and powerfully affect you as fast as Wonder Woman spun into her star-spangled tights, ready to ensnare the bad guy with her lasso.

Here's a success story.

Molly was a candidate for a promotion, the youngest, first-ever female to be considered for the role. I had the pleasure of eating lunch with Molly after she found out who'd been chosen. Over salads and scallops, Molly excitedly recapped the minutes leading up to the meeting that would decide her fate. "I was excited, but nervous. About to leave my office for the meeting. All of a sudden, I hesitated. 'Wait! Not yet!' a voice shouted from inside me. I shut my office door.

"I struck my power pose, I said my mantras, took deep breaths, and, wouldn't you know it, I got *hyped!* I felt confident. Ready! I grabbed my notepad, I opened my office door, I walked to the meeting, and we began to talk.

Molly's eyes shone at the memory of her moment of truth. "Our conversation went *so* well! Jamie, I crushed it! And they awarded me the promotion right there, on the spot!

"I got it!"

Both of us clapped and screamed with delight, drawing glances from our fellow diners, and not caring one bit. I was beyond thrilled for Molly! She'd followed the simple physical and mental steps impeccably, and gosh, did she perform well in that meeting. Leading with confidence, she demonstrated her intelligence, her qualifications, and her vision. She believed in herself – and the selection committee did, too. Incidentally, Molly's new title came with a 20% bump in compensation, and a bonus. Not a bad return on a 2-minute confidence boosting exercise, eh?

So, raise your hand if you too would like to earn a promotion! Great! Let's get your power pose A-game going.

The first time you do what's coming up next, you'll probably want to be in the privacy of your home, bedroom, or office. Maybe grab a trusted friend and try it together. Whatever you do, choose a place where you won't feel any judgement. Also, remember two things already working in your favor. First, you are neurologically conditioned to be the master of your thoughts, and your thoughts rule your body. Second, you're in practice mode, simply rehearsing. No pressure. You're not "faking it 'til you make it." You're simply 'rehearsing 'til it's verse,' as if you're reading through a script for the first time, long before you're expected to be stage-ready on opening night.

Here we go!

Strike Your Pose

1. Stand up straight with your feet placed slightly more than shoulder width apart.

2. Point your chest forward and upward, and keep your lower back straight. Too far, and you'll feel like you're on your way to a backbend. Angle your shoulders slightly back.

3. Ball your hands into loose fists and place them on your hips, with your elbows bent. Think about the way superheroes pose on movie posters and comic book covers.

4. Lift your chin slightly, and gaze upward.

5. Hold your pose for two minutes, breathing deeply. Inhale positive, confident, strong thoughts. Exhale negativity, doubt, and fear.

Wowee! CONGRATULATIONS! How do you feel? Awesome? Silly? Doubtful? Somewhere in between? If this is your first time trying a power pose, my guess is that you felt some, however slight, improvement in your mood and confidence. A seasoned power poser, feels a bigger high; if you're a veteran, I'm sure you're psyched to repeat.

You know how a yoga instructor can offer several variations for positions? The power pose works the same way. So here are some alternative ideas for hand placement. You may like one more than the others. The goal is to find the one that works best for you – or maybe a rotation is your jam. All good, Sister! Whatever works!

- Keep your elbows straight and put your hands down by your sides, a few inches from your hips.
- Push your hands straight out to the side as if the room walls are closing in and it's your job to hold them open. Now, PUSH! Bonus: This serves as an excellent toning exercise for those triceps! (And it's my personal favorite!)
- Throw your hands straight up in a V formation. I like to do this one with my palms open, envisioning confidence, positivity, intelligence, and creativity flowing right into my hands like a glittery jet stream and circulating throughout my body.

The power pose is a journey. Over time, as you become more comfortable, you'll be able to incorporate intention. You'll get bold. You'll channel your inner superhero and unleash your superpowers, stat. To accelerate your learning curve, focus. Eliminate distractions. Practice anytime – for high-stakes situations, low stakes, or when you get out of bed each morning. It's a great meditation for starting your day. And we haven't even come to the mental part yet!

Mentally Channel Confidence – Add in Affirmations for Double the Effect!

Remember how Molly added her mantras to her power pose? Mantras, also called affirmations, are words you say to yourself to create and cement positive messages in your mind. You can literally change your own neuropathic highways by prioritizing and repeating affirmations on a regular basis. I set an alarm in my phone to remind me!

So now that you've got your physical pose down, let's add affirmations, the mental part, in order to really amplify your confidence game.

To start, think of three positive, powerful, upbeat words that describe you — either the way you feel in this very moment, or the way you want to feel. These are the three characteristics you want to embody to conquer a challenge or situation. They are your mantras or affirmations.

Recall the powerful impact of your thoughts. Your brainwaves begin creating your reality as you start envisioning what you want to be, what you want to project, and what you are.

Here are some examples of affirmations:

I am BRAVE. I am STRONG. I am SMART.
I am FEMININE. I am FIERCE. I am a WARRIOR.
I am COMPASSIONATE. I am CAPABLE. I am CHARISMATIC.
I am a BAD ASS. I am a ROCK STAR. I am a GODDESS.

Find your three. Feel free to borrow from this list, too:

- Resilient
- Unstoppable
- A Winner
- Determined
- Loyal
- Efficient
- Reliable
- A Problem Solver

- Awesome
- Witty
- Intuitive
- Creative
- Fearless
- Outgoing
- A Leader
- Fierce

- Courageous
- Consistent
- Tenacious
- A Warrior
- Powerful
- Deserving
- Tough
- A Team Player

When you have your three affirmations, write them in the blanks below:

I am _____

I am _____

I am _____

You know what happens next. Say your affirmations repeatedly. Over and over again, while you're in your power pose. (Note: You're not committing to these three forever. Change up as often as you like!) Declare your three affirmation statements at first in your head, then in a whisper, then out loud, then even louder, gaining speed and volume like a wave barreling toward the shore.

Feel the declarative nature of the words, 'I *am*.' It's not, I *want* to be, I *might* be, or Someday I *could*, but rather, I *am*. Right here. Right now! You can elevate to a shouting level and yell your affirmations until your decibel level rivals that of a Foo Fighters concert. *ARE YOU FEELING IT???* Is your confidence palpable yet? Do you notice a shift in your energy?

I swear I can feel it from here! Get it, girlfriend! You are most certainly ready to *crush* it!

Standing in your power pose, repeating your three affirmations, visualize your confidence. Imagine yourself excelling at your upcoming meeting, presentation, or event. Watch yourself in action like you're watching a movie starring you. You are impressive. Conversing like a boss. Owning it. Wrapping things up with all the success you deserve, maybe more.

You can use this powerful confidence-boosting tool anywhere. Standing is best for your power pose, yet sitting in your car works, too. You can sit, raise your chest, place your hands in various positions (keep at least one on the wheel if driving!), and you can absolutely recite your affirmations at whatever volume you please. If you're in an Uber, invite the driver to join in! Heck, blast some Beyoncé and feel your power rise from within. I've done this in parking lots, elevators, and public restrooms. Find your spot and make it happen. You will thank yourself for it, I promise!

When to Channel Confidence?

Anytime, of course! Beyond meetings and presentations, additional proactive opportunities to channel confidence include the moments prior to a critical conversation; a networking event, dinner party or any occasion when you'll meet new people; the first day of a new job; and, by all means, before a job interview.

Athletes use confidence-boosting techniques before games and events. Students use them before tests or prior to working on an important assignment. They even work for dating! A blind date, first date, seventh date, or maybe before you meet your SO's parents. Strike that pose, say those affirmations, and bring your most confident self to the party.

When Does Confidence Get Rattled?

Confidence-rattlers fall into two primary categories: unfamiliar situations and high-stakes moments.

The unfamiliar can occur in a variety of ways. A meeting agenda is changed at the last minute. A task at work takes a new direction and you find out late. You find yourself in a situation where you're the only (fill in the blank) person of your gender, age or race.. You attend an event you've never attended before, meet new people, or have to make a presentation before a new group, in a new room, using A/V equipment you've never seen before. All can rattle confidence.

Tips to familiarize the unfamiliar are interspersed throughout this book. Most can be summed up with two words, preparation and curiosity. A little preparation and introspection regarding what your day will hold, will go a long way. Shifting your mindset in unfamiliar situations from one perhaps of intimidation or feeling like an outsider to instead one of curiosity and 'what can I learn here?' is powerful in helping you maintain confidence.

As for high-stakes scenarios, where you have a lot to gain or lose depending on the outcome: When interviewing, will you get the job? When you take the Series 7 exam, will you pass and be certified to trade securities? In a performance review with your manager, will you receive praise or admonishment? When you're running a charity event, will you hit your fundraising goal? All prime opportunities for rattling confidence and all very normal ways to feel. You have a choice, though. You can *choose* to see the pessimistic side or you can choose to see the optimistic side. And since thoughts become things, it's critical to select words and thoughts that will direct you to a place of success.

It's okay to feel scared, nervous, or anxious. And it's not that you can necessarily reduce how high the stakes are, but when you make the choice to choose thoughts that help, rather than hurt, a shift will happen. Think, what do I have to gain from this situation, rather than what am I losing? Or as you'll often here motivational speakers say,

Instead of why is this happending to me,
why is this happening FOR me?

Small shift in words, big shift on impact.

Focus on positive self-talk. Don't listen to that tiny inner voice saying negative things about you! If all you can hear is, "I can't believe I did that. I screw up everything. I'm never going to get this right;" pause, breathe. Tell the negative thoughts to get-to-steppin' and replace them with positive language. "Okay, that didn't go how I thought it would, so what will I do about it now? There is always *something* you can do. Your value is not determined by the outcome of any single event, but rather by your choices in the aftermath. There's always a way out and a way up. You are better than the situation you are in, and the only true mistake you can make when you're knocked down is to choose to stay down.

You are a warrior.

In tough times or difficult seasons of life,
prioritizing confidence is a must.

Charlie Batch was an NFL quarterback who spent most of his career with the Pittsburgh Steelers in the early 2000s. He has a fantastic solution that helps both familiarize the unfamiliar and manage high stakes situations.

Proper preparation prevents poor performance.

I love both the alliteration and the message of Batch's sentence, especially because his self-preservation depended on it. Over and over again, NFL Sunday after NFL Sunday, Charlie practiced in preparation for three or four 320-pound defensive linemen to come barreling toward him. In the business world, we often have opportunities to properly prepare and prevent poor performance. When we seize those opportunities, we reduce the unfamiliar and increase our protection from people and situations that can rattle us. The stakes will remain high, but the more we can prepare, the more confidence we'll have that a favorable outcome awaits us. Can we prepare for everything and never be blindsided by a lineman? Absolutely not! But cultivating the habit of intentional preparation elevates us to where we're less vulnerable and more immune to getting rattled. Preparation fosters familiarity, and familiarity frees your mind from worry.

Proactive or reactive scenarios, in your professional or personal life, there's no limit to where these techniques apply. Tap into them before the next Parent-Teacher Association meeting, when you need to have a stern conversation with your kid's coach, in negotiations with a car salesman, or when you have to get on the phone with an airline to untangle a reservation snafu.

As Wonder Woman, the superhero my Underoos transformed me into said,

"Sometimes you just have to throw on a tiara
and show them how it's done!"

What's at Stake?

Your confidence muscles want to be flexed and you have the strength. If they remain dormant, you'll risk never experiencing your true strength. Start flexing now and see how quickly your strength builds.

Key Points

- You have 100% autonomy to control your thoughts and choose those that serve you.
- The thoughts you have are shaping your brain in the same way lifting weights shapes muscle.
- Your body is a powerful tool for shaping thoughts and you can use this to your advantage.
- Strike your power pose before any "A" game situation and enjoy enhanced results!

Confidence Challenge Checklist

- ❑ Create awareness around your thoughts. Ask yourself if you'd talk to someone else that way. No? Be just as nice, encouraging and supportive to yourself as you are to others.
- ❑ Name the thoughts that are holding you back and reverse them, i.e. 'I can't do,' that becomes 'I can do that.' 'That will never work out for me,' becomes, 'That will work out for me.' Give it a try!
- ❑ Be a poser! A power poser, that is. Practice your power pose along with your affirmations for two minutes every day, for seven days.
- ❑ The next time a situation is coming up where you feel nervous, see what you can do to familiarize the unfamiliar and prepare for the high stakes event.

To stretch and condition my confidence, one action I commit to is:

_____

_____

_____

30 Ways to Boost Your Confidence

Chapter 5

Congratulations! You *slayed* the basics of mentally and physically channeling confidence. I'm *stoked* for you! This chapter offers over 30 additional techniques to channel and boost your confidence. Have fun playing around with them and finding what works best for you. Invite a friend to try some out and compare results. Different techniques may work at different times, so enjoy the journey while experimenting.

I divided the confidence boosting tips into three categories: Mental, Physical, and Situational.

Ten Mental Confidence Boosters

These mental boosters may be practiced anytime, anywhere. Since they all happen inside your mind, you can use them while you're by yourself or in the company of others at work, home, or school. They take no preparation and very little effort. Use them as secret weapons and share with anyone else who may benefit as well.

1. **Breathe**
   When you feel rattled or threatened, one of the best and easiest things you can do in the moment is simply to, BREATHE. Shifting the focus to your breath and away from whatever is irritating will calm you and keep your thoughts in a logical, rather than emotionally upsetting place.

2. **Create space and be calm**
   Step away if you can. Create distance between yourself and the source of stress. Using your breath for assistance, aim to remain calm, controlling your thoughts and allowing your body to follow along. Remember, you control your thoughts. They don't control you.

3. **Use your lucky charm**

   Pick a specific tangible, easily accessible object – a bracelet, medal, special stone, or photo – to play the role of your private power source. The object should serve as a reminder of your strongest, bravest, most confident self and be called upon when needed. I carry a small silver charm, a baseball mitt holding a baseball. In moments when I need to summon confidence, I discreetly squeeze that little charm in my hand.

4. **Channel your inner RBG**

   Supreme Court Justice Ruth Bader Ginsberg (RBG) was the ultimate Shero. I want to share a trick I use to channel RBG's superpowers. In times when I know I should speak up but am hesitating, this is my go-to method; it's among my favorite and most frequently used techniques. I think to myself: *What would the Honorable Justice Ruth Bader Ginsburg do in a situation such as this? What move would the 5'1" powerhouse of a woman make? Would she sit and say nothing, or would she voice her opinion? She would absolutely voice her opinion! And so should I! Speak up, Jamie!* And I'll tell you what: almost like magic, the mere thought of Justice Ginsburg instantly stimulates me into action. She would be SO disappointed in me if I didn't. And who am I to not follow cues from the Notorious RBG? Ready, aim, fire! If some other figure motivates you in this same manner, that's cool, too! Just make sure you designate someone (maybe it's one of the leaders you listed in Chapter 3!) whose example will serve as a kick in the pants for you when needed! And if you're able to, tell them thanks!

5. **What's the hardest thing you've ever done? Compare your current situation**

   Think about this for as long as you need. What's the hardest thing you've gone through physically, mentally, or emotionally? Was it running a marathon? Climbing a mountain? Overcoming a disease? Surviving a breakup? Pulling all-nighters to meet an academic or work deadline? Getting your kids fed, bathed, and to bed on time every night? Is the challenge you're facing right now at all comparable to that hardest thing you've endured? Maybe, maybe not. But if you survived the hardest thing, surely you'll get through this, too. Put things in perspective.

6. **Consider all possible outcomes, negative and positive**

   Are you familiar with the Biblical phrase, "Who of you by worrying can add a single hour to your life?" It appears in two Gospels, Matthew and Luke. Yet you need not be religious to see the message: Worrying won't accomplish a darn thing. It may actually set you back. In a frantic state of worry, confidence is further out of reach. To bring it back in to a high-stakes situation or otherwise, use this quick fix. Pause to consider *all possible outcomes*, worst case to best case and all points in between. We often gravitate toward, and dread, the worst case scenario even though the worst case rarely happens. Go ahead and acknowledge the worst case, but also the best case, and then consider what's most likely to realistically happen, which is usually something in between.

7. **Focus on what you can control**
This one comes up a lot in work environments where a lot of change occurs, especially when it's poorly managed and communicated. So much change can make you feel as if you're flying off the rails. It's a struggle to measure progress, because management keeps changing the plan. How can you keep score when you don't know the rules? Instead of focusing on factors you can't control, choose some you can and prioritize them. With this one, it's a good idea to run your chosen priorities by your manager to ensure the two of you are aligned in your thinking.

8. **Choose three words**
Danielle Hill is a woman I admire more every time I'm around her. Danielle is COO of The Riveter, a coworking space 'built by women for everyone.' She is one of my favorite introverts who shared her confidence-boosting technique with me. In high pressure situations when she feels herself getting emotionally worked up, she stays calm and maintains confidence by repeating this phrase in her head, "Red fish, blue fish, yellow fish. Red fish, blue fish, yellow fish." Sometimes she'll change the color or add a fourth fish to the mix. She forces her brain to focus on something pleasant, and it changes her mental state so she can continue running on logic instead of emotion.

On the hit NBC drama *This is Us*, Justin Hartley's character, a recovering alcoholic, used a similar technique. When he felt pressured to give in and have a drink, he repeated three words that soothed and reminded him to stay true to his goals. These words helped interrupt a threatening stimulus and shift focus to something better.

Apply this technique anytime something or someone rattles your confidence. What words soothe you? Maybe "Mountains, sunsets, manicures. Mountains, sunsets, manicures." Or "Puppies, push-ups, and pinot." Or maybe three names of people far more important to you than the jerk trying to intimidate you. This small clandestine trick can be your own little secret – distracting you from the negative and keeping you in a mental state where you maintain professionalism.

9. **Prepare with a mental walk-through**

    "Prepare" is coming up on the list of Ten Physical Boosters as well. But on the mental side: Before an event, schedule some quiet time to mentally walk through what's coming. Whether it's a presentation to colleagues, a fundraising event, or your sister's bridal shower, think it through in advance in as much detail as possible. Use all five senses. Visualize the room you'll be in. Notice where people are sitting, and what's on the tables. Smell the aroma of food or coffee. What does the food taste like? Hear the music that will be playing, the voices due to speak, or the mimosas as they fizz.. Does the room feel warm or cold? As mentioned earlier, every memory we form is learned through our senses. Envisioning your future event including sensory details is some of the best nerve-calming, confidence boosting preparation you can do!

10. **Invite negative thoughts to leave – with authority**

    Sometimes you just need to take charge and do it like you mean it. There may be times when you get thrown off kilter during one meeting and have to proceed right to another. Or you receive discouraging feedback from a customer right before you have to meet with your manager. You have to keep right on performing despite setbacks. In those moments, deliver yourself some mental tough love by saying, "Self, I'll deal with Situation A later. I'm not going to risk my job, professionalism, or reputation by letting Situation A interfere with Situation B. For now, Situation A will have to sit on the shelf. I'm not letting Situation A take away my power. It didn't ask, nor did I give it permission to do so." Visualize yourself locking those negative, interrupting thoughts in the supply closet and then walking away. Don't let them deplete your confidence currency!

*   **Bonus booster! Pray**

    This is a personal preference, of course, yet if you believe in a higher power, a confidence deficit is the perfect time for a conversation. I like the classic Serenity Prayer myself:

    > *God grant me the serenity to accept the things I cannot change,*
    > *The courage to change the things I can,*
    > *And the wisdom to know the difference.*

    Share what's happening with your higher source and ask for help. Who knows? Celestial confidence may come your way before you get to "Amen!"

Ten Physical Confidence Boosters

These physical boosting strategies take a little more planning and effort. You'll be rewarded for the time and energy you put into them, so think of them like an investment in yourself that produces a big return.

1. **Do something hard**

   Pick out a BHAG: A Big Hairy Audacious Goal, as Jim Collins instructed in *Good to Great.* Take a leap out of your comfort zone. Surround yourself with the right resources and make a plan to get promoted, run a marathon, or win an award. The more difficult it is, the greater the confidence boost you'll feel when you show that BHAG who's boss.

2. **Do something easy**

   If you're not quite ready to achieve something big, start small. Set what I like to call a SAG: Small Achievable Goal. Track and celebrate your victories and use SAGs to build momentum. Choose your difficulty level based on where your head is, yet don't sell yourself short by choosing something too easy. Remember, if reaching for the stars seems insurmountable, reach for the ceiling instead, or whatever altitude is just beyond your reach. Just be sure to reach.

3. **Try something new**

   What's a hobby you've always wanted to try? Sewing? Singing? Swimming? Pottery? Painting? Pickleball? Coding? Cooking? Calligraphy? Grab a friend and take a class or go alone. Download an app that'll teach you. I used the Simply Piano app to dust the cobwebs off lessons I'd taken about twenty years ago. It was a ton of fun, and knowing I could still play a few tunes definitely put some pep in my step. Try something you have absolutely no clue how to do. Walk in a novice and walk out educated, enlightened, or empowered in some way! Confidence compounds, so make an investment of yourself in one area and it will transfer to others as well.

4. **Exercise**.

   Yep, get your arse to the gym and lift something heavy. I mean really heavy. The heaviest thing you can lift without risking injury, even if for a small number of reps while maintaining form. You can also run, elliptical, or stair climb — and at a faster pace than you think. Try it, just for a minute. Pat yourself on the back afterwards, then do it again. You'll walk out feeling more energized than you did when you walked in. I promise! If you're on the fence with this one, use the buddy system. Grab a friend to hold you accountable. Group classes are a good fix, too. If the gym is absolutely not your thing, try yoga, go to the park, or ride your bike. Take a walk in nature. It's all good for body, mind, and soul!

5. **Train for something you never thought you could do**

   Is there a race or other physical event you want to try, but never pulled the trigger? Give yourself a gift. Commit to it right now. I recommend something where you'll cross an actual finish line or compete with others. A 10k run, or a half or full marathon, for example. And if those sound like too much, there are competitions for everything from swing dancing to poetry to cooking. Pick something!

   When you start to notice progress as you're training and working toward your goal, it will boost your confidence like nothing else. You are conditioning your body and your mind. The mental and physical discipline you acquire as you achieve your goal makes you tough – and will stay with you long after you've crossed that finish line. This one is so powerful! But be careful, you might get addicted!

6. **Dress for success**

   Coco Chanel said, "Dress shabbily and they remember the dress; dress impeccably and they remember the woman." Amen, sister. I'd love some help from Coco today, as I must confess that I'm a terrible shopper. I've never enjoyed it and have a horrible time picking out things for myself. When I had an important event coming up, dressing the part meant I had to go shopping. Rather than rely on my own dubious fashion sense, I enlisted a personal shopper. (Nordstrom and Macy's offer this service!) Anyhoo, oh my gosh – I highly recommend it! She asked me a few questions over the phone before my appointment, and I was blown away with the items she selected for me to try. She was my "clothing whisperer!" I walked out with several new outfits, all of which made me feel like a total rock star/warrior/ goddess. Confidence box checked!

   Make sure your closet has a power suit, power shoes, power purse, power underthings, or whatever clothing, accessory, or footwear makes you feel you can conquer the world. No one has to know it's your personal *confidence couture*, but they are sure to take note of your swagger. I feel obligated to advise that you work within your budget, as this can get out of hand. A few well-tailored pieces should last a long time and return your investment tenfold.

7. **Prepare with a physical walk-through**

Remember the mental walk-through on the previous list? A physical walk-through helps too. One of the best things you can do to prepare for any big situation, especially a high-pressure meeting or presentation, is to walk the room where it will occur. If you plan to use audio-visual equipment of any kind, do a test run using the very computer, microphone, and slide clicker you'll use on the day of the event.

Go through the agenda and anticipate disruptions that could occur. Find the exits, restrooms, and water cooler. Know how to get a hold of tech support if something crashes. Assess what lighting and temperature will be like during the exact time of your event. A room that's cool in the morning could feel like an oven in the afternoon, so dress appropriately.

8. **Practice**

Whether your upcoming big moment is a crucial conversation with your employer, a job or media interview, speaking in front of a group, treating a patient, teaching a lesson plan, or negotiating a deal, each can be practiced in advance – with a partner or even individually. I rehearse presentations in my car, on my bike, and on the elliptical machine. I prepare notes and deliver my planned talk out loud. Even when you have no audience, practicing allows you to polish and rock your confidence at the time of the event.

For both novices and professionals, continued practice makes the unfamiliar familiar, calms nerves, and improves performance. A confidence boost follows. Tom Brady played quarterback for the Patriots for 20 years. The guy won three league MVP awards and six Super Bowl rings. Brady's a phenom, GOAT (Greatest Of All Time) perhaps, but guess what he still does before every game? You'll see him physically throwing the ball and even 'shadow throwing' as his hands, arms, body, and mind go through the motions. Proper practice prevents poor performance!

9. **Write down bullet points**

Anytime you anticipate speaking up in a meeting (which I hope happens in every one of your meetings), it helps to collect your thoughts ahead of time and put them on paper. It's like sprinkling written words with confidence dust. Writing down complete sentences isn't necessary. Just phrases in bullet form will help you organize and prepare. The mental activity of reducing a big thought to a tight bullet

point helps you speak more articulately when the time comes. Up your
game even more by practicing them out loud. Bring your bullet points
to the table, impress your managers. You never hear a manager say, "I
was really disappointed in how well you prepared for that meeting."
Bullet points help you score points!!

10. Clench your fists

In a pinch, this confidence-booster works as fast as a light switch. If
you feel a threat looming and your confidence starts to waver, clench
and pump your fists. My buddy Wade says that he does this before
real estate negotiations, sometimes so intensely, his fingernails leave
impressions on his palms. What will clenching your firsts do for you?
You won't know until you try! This technique makes me reflect a
little deeper on the fist bump, and wonder if that's a little confidence
booster, too. Regardless, get those fists pumping, that blood flowing
and those endorphins rushing!

✳ Bonus booster! Look in the mirror

Look in a mirror – in the bathroom, in your compact, or even into
your phone in selfie mode – and repeat after me. "I AM WORTHY. I
AM WORTHY. I AM WORTHY." *Hell yes*, you are! Look deeply into
those beautiful eyes of yours and see the capable and confident woman
staring back at you!

Ten Situational Confidence Boosters

We talked about the contagious nature of confidence. Here are ten ways to
create a situation where you will catch it! These take a little bit of effort and are
well worth your efforts and investment.

1. Surround yourself with confident people

At work, school, church, in social groups, professional organizations,
or athletic endeavors, be intentional about joining groups. Surround
yourself with people who lift you up. Downers need not apply.
Connect with people who talk about visions, goals, projects, interests,
and future plans rather than bringing others down. Oprah Winfrey
says, "When you talk about other people, you are really just talking
about yourself, highlighting your own insecurities." You and I have
taken the Vow of Gossip Silence and declared, "We ain't got no time
for that!" Seek out groups of women with healthy self-esteem, groups
that do cool stuff, people that ask what you're up to and how they can
help. Find people who encourage, enlighten, and elevate you…and do
the same for them!

2. Observe and learn from others

Especially at work, pay close attention to colleagues whom you respect and admire. What traits in particular do they demonstrate that attract you? Emulate the positive behaviors and attitudes and be vigilant about ditching the negative. Use this as an opportunity to create or enhance good habits and break ones that serve you poorly.

3. Attend a conference or see an inspirational speaker

Are Michelle Obama, Rachel Hollis, or Oprah coming to an event near you? Invite a girlfriend, or just buy one ticket and go by yourself. Look at sites like Eventbrite.com or Facebook groups to find options. There are a lot of great speakers whose names you may not recognize but will appear at women-specific events. Their stories will not disappoint. While you're at these events, be sure to network with other attendees. The energy will flow and you'll walk out a more enriched woman!

4. Set a daily confidence alarm

For this one, there's a handout waiting for you at www.jamieempowers.com/resources. Click on 'Freebie' and scroll down. The abridged version of this booster is: Set an alarm in your phone that goes off around the time you start work. It's your reminder to send a text or email to someone else to boost her day. For example, "Good morning! Just wanted to wish you a wonderful day!" Or, "Hey, rock star! I have a feeling that today is going to be AMAZING for you! XO." You'll be surprised at what dishing out these little boosts will do for both the recipients – and for you!

5. Phone a friend

Who's that friend whose mere presence always perks you up? The one guaranteed to brighten your day and make you smile? I find this booster so important, I keep a list of people on my phone. When you're in need of a pick-me-up, give one of your Sheroes (She + Hero) a call. Ask how she is, if there's anything you can do for her, or just tell her that you wanted to hear her voice.

One of the best bridesmaid toasts I ever heard was at my friend Allyson's wedding. Brooke, the matron of honor, gave a beautiful speech. One line in particular really stuck out. Brooke said, "Whenever I forget how awesome I am, all I need to do is call Allyson and she reminds me every time." Awww, don't you love that? That's the friend you want to phone.

If you don't think you have these kinds of friends yet, try being one for others. Be contagious to someone else!

6. **Keep a highlight reel**

   Otherwise known as a digital scrapbook of compliments, highlights, and accolades that remind you how fantabulous you are. Keep a folder on your personal computer and save emails, text message screenshots, and excellent performance reviews from your managers. Browse through it when things just aren't going your way or even during a season of roughness. Just the other day, I accidentally came across an email a colleague sent to me after I'd moved on to another company. It was so nice and complimentary, and it totally made my day – several years after he wrote it. I had completely forgotten about it, and it sure did brighten my day to re-read it. I have since added it to my highlight reel folder and I sent him a thank you note to let him know how much it made my day, many, many days later. That small gesture on his part had such a big and lasting impact for me.

   Pro tip: Compiling your highlight reel is a lifelong activity – and a private one. Make sure to save yours in a personal file you can always access no matter what job you have. A copy of an excellent performance review could be something you showcase on a future job application or in an interview. God forbid you save it on your work computer, then unexpectedly lose access. As long as you're not violating company policy by keeping a personal copy, be sure to do so!

7. **Listen to podcasts**

   This is a very personal choice and really depends on where you are in your life journey. While I'll share some of my favorites here, I encourage you to search for others that speak to you. You know you've found the right ones when they make you feel invigorated, inspired, smarter, or funnier, and have improved your well-being in some way. Some faves of mine: TopThink, on YouTube; *The Wall Street Journal's Secrets of Wealthy Women* podcast, hosted weekly by Veronica Dagher and found on the wsj.com website; anything involving David Brooks, the *New York Times* columnist, The Michelle Obama Podcast, the *TED Radio Hour*, co-produced with NPR and hosted on npr.org; Judi Holler's *FearBoss* found on iTunes and Spotify, and *The Guilty Feminist*, a comedy podcast hosted by Deborah Frances-White and found at guiltyfeminist.com. These are a few like. You'll find inspiration in others, too, I know.

8. **Watch motivational videos**

   Videos of motivational speakers are found all over the internet and especially on YouTube. Again, choose who and what motivates *you*. Finding some that resonate with you might take some time. Not to worry. Enjoy the journey along the way and ask your friends and colleagues for recommendations. My suggestions include Rudy Francisco, Suze Orman, and Tony Robbins.

Graduation speeches can be good sources of inspiration and motivation, too. Coaches' pre-game locker room talks are sometimes recorded and accessible. Speaking of sports, if you're a college football fan, pull up your favorite team's highlight reel. If it has the same effect on you as watching Ohio State football highlights does for me, you will not be disappointed! All I have to do is watch a few minutes and I am *primed* to close a deal, run a marathon, or crush a sales pitch. Bring it on!

On days when my friend Anna knows she has to bring her A-game, her go-to video is a fashion show. The women strut the runway with attitude, ownership, and major moxie. "Gets me fired up every time!" says Anna.

So whether it's sports, speeches, shows, or whatever subject motivates you, watching the right videos will have your inner cheerleaders wildly wiggling their spirit fingers all over the place for you!

9. Watch movie scenes

There are an infinite number of motivating movie scenes. They're often the ones that lead into the climax of the story. Watching certain scenes from *The Hunger Games, Top Gun, Star Wars,* or the *Fast and Furious* series can get you *pumped up*. Again, this is a very personal choice, so make a note next time a scene gets your adrenaline flowing. It's pretty easy to find good clips on YouTube. Pull up the video and use that endorphin rush to up your workplace game!

10. Create a playlist

You know those songs you listen to while you're getting ready for a big night out? Before a hot date? Or during the last few miles of a distance race? Do you have them saved as your GET FIRED UP playlist?! If yes, then great! I hope you're rocking out on your way to work, before an interview, and prior to speaking in front of a group. Get those songs organized on Spotify right now. Crank it up anytime you need of a boost. The same songs you play before a big night out, the ones that make you feel attractive, engaging, and intriguing, can double as motivators for feeling analytical, entrepreneurial, and strategic. Listen to 'em and sing along loud and proud! And, pssst, if you head to the Feebies page on www.jamieempowers.com, there may be one waiting there for you!

* Bonus Booster! Use the buddy system

Invite a friend to test this out with you. Research shows that when
you are accountable to someone as you work, you have a 65% chance
of achieving a goal. If you and your accountability partner(s) commit
to ongoing meetings, your success chances increase to a whopping
95%. Find a partner, or several willing participants who share in your
dedication, and choose a strategy for practicing and boosting your
collective confidence. You'll have a confidence convention going in no
time!

Last but not least, if at any point during your exploration of these Top 30
Confidence Techniques you experience frustration or feel you're failing, there's
always one more thing you can do. Ask for help. If you're really trying and it's just
not coming together, find a friend, family member, counselor, or mentor to help
you. Share your struggle with someone you trust. I'm sure they'd be honored to
lend a hand. Your confidence is too important to take a back seat.

27 Floors to Confidence

To bring this chapter to a close, I'll share a case study of how one woman
"elevated" herself to confidence by calling on several confidence boosting
techniques. That woman is me, and the scenario started out as my own personal
disaster.

Here's what happened.

There was a time when I invested in a real estate project as a "side hustle." The
investment did not go as planned and I found myself working with a bank to
mitigate the damage. The details aren't relevant here, but believe me when I say
it was incredibly upsetting. I had a demanding day job and the bank wasn't open
on Saturdays, so I made a 7:30 am appointment one weekday, tucked in before a
scheduled 9:00 am meeting with a nearby customer.

I was nervous and anxious as I drove to the bank. I parked and fed the parking
meter for an hour, or so I thought. I went inside, saw my banker, and reviewed
the bad investment. It was all very stressful and troubling, and I was mentally
beating myself up the whole time. (Example of what NOT to do when it comes
to self-talk.)

The meeting ended and I walked back to my car, trembling and grumbling the
whole time. When I got there I saw a bright yellow envelope wedged into the
driver side door: a ticket.

I rubbed my hand on my forehead, yanked the ticket out and opened the door, tumbled behind the wheel grumbling some very un-classy words, threw my purse onto the passenger seat, pushed the start button, and proceeded to burst into tears.

Tears *streamed* down my face. All my anger, insecurity, disgust with my decisions, all the pressure I felt from a personal situation which had nothing to do with work – and it all exploded out of me like a volcanic eruption.

Vision blurred by tears, I drove the short distance to my customer's building. I parked again and shoved my credit card aggressively into the parking meter. "Jeez, lady, what'd I ever do to you?" I'm pretty sure I heard the meter say in protest. I turned and entered the building lobby, still tearful, now dabbing my face with the frantic fervor of someone trying to get red wine out of a bridal dress. I found the elevator bank and pressed the up button.

As I waited for the elevator, I now made a concentrated effort to focus on my breathing. *In through my nose, out through my mouth. In through my nose, out through my mouth.*

The elevator doors slid apart. I stepped in and pushed the button for the 27th floor. I began to climb upward. *Upward.* Not downward, not sideways, not in a loop-the-loop, but *upward.* Physically, emotionally, and mentally, I began to move in an upward direction. I had a job to do and it was growing closer, as the elevator rose floor by floor, whether I liked it or not.

With each floor, I wiped my tears, I dabbed my face. Somewhere around the fifth floor I struck my power pose and I clenched my fists. "Single Ladies" by Beyoncé popped into my head.

My hips started moving, my knee started doing that thing from the video, and my arms made the pumping motion – not even close to emulating Beyoncé's rhythm, but I couldn't have cared less. I was feeling it and I was going with it.

My head started telling me, "I can do this. I can do this. I can do this." And then, "I've got this. I've got this. I've got this." As my thoughts and body soared to a higher place, I felt the negativity, the stress and ugliness, fall away. I let them plummet down that elevator shaft. Calm, confidence, and invigoration came over me as I ascended.

My ears popped and the elevator dinged, awakening me from my trance-like state. I had arrived. Oh yes, I most certainly had. The rattled, weepy, insecure girl who had entered at the ground floor stepped out, transformed. I was the self-assured, professional, go-kick-some-a$$ businesswoman I knew myself to be.

The elevator doors parted and I was instantly greeted by my customer, Patrick. "Hi, Jamie! We're ready for you."

"Great!" I responded, "Let's get started." We smiled and shook hands. The meeting progressed as planned. I closed the deal we'd discussed for months.

An hour and a half later, I rode back down those 27 floors and exhaled. I reflected on everything that had occurred. There will always be things beyond your control – things that happen at the worst possible moment. Navigating around them in a work environment can be incredibly tricky. Your keys to surviving and thriving in spite of them are the tools offered here to channel and project confidence, both internally (you are your most important audience) and externally. Bad things happen, whether it's a parking ticket or spilled coffee or a meeting that doesn't go the way you wanted, you have the ability to make a choice. You can allow bad things to bring you down further and lash out inappropriately and immaturely – at an innocent parking meter, for example – or you can rise above bad things, making what happens next better for yourself and anyone around you.

So whether you're a superhero about to throw on your mask to go save the day or just you – wonderful, intelligent, innovative, you – the next time you push an elevator's up button, it's too good a metaphor to waste! Use your elevator ascent as an opportunity to reflect on all the ways you know how to channel and rock confidence. Maybe it's a day when you're about to go bat sh*t crazy, or maybe you're dressed for success and about to crush it. Whether you're going up 27 floors, or 82 floors, or just two, use your transit time to practice your techniques.

Above all, know, with unequivocal confidence, that you have the power to elevate yourself – at any time, on any day, anywhere. And you might just give the person monitoring the elevator cameras a smile and a boost to their day too!

What's at Stake?

It's like being an ostrich or a penguin. You have wings. Wings! But you can't fly. Avoid staying grounded by channeling confidence and giving yourself the mechanism you need to not only fly, but to soar!

Key Points

- You can channel confidence in a variety of ways: mentally, physically, and situationally.
- Prioritizing at least one confidence booster each day will condition and strengthen your confidence muscle.

Confidence Challenge Checklist

- ❏ Practice your power pose along with your affirmations for two minutes every day, for seven days.
- ❏ Create a habit by committing to one booster from each category – mental, physical and situational – and practice it 7 days in a row.
- ❏ Grab a friend and grow the list, adding new boosters to each category.

To stretch and condition my confidence, one action I commit to is:

_____

_____

_____

SPEAK UP, Sister!

Part 2

SPEAK UP, Sister!

Chapter 6

Personally, My Dear, YOU Don't Give a Damn!

I was in Mrs. Peterson's class, at my desk, rocking pigtails and my plaid jumper uniform, happily learning my ABC's and 1,2,3's.

All of us first graders were tasked with completing a worksheet. Even for first grade, it was relatively simple. There were eight shapes on the sheet. Within some shapes the number "1" was written, while others contained the number "2." Our instructions were to color all the "1" shapes yellow and all the "2" shapes blue. Pretty straightforward, right? I eagerly grabbed my Crayolas and set to work, biting my bottom lip (which I still do to this day), swinging my little knee-socked legs and the navy blue Docksiders adorning my tiny feet. I was incredibly fixated on completing this very important assignment.

Time passed. Eight fully colored-in shapes later, I reached the bottom of the page. I pushed back from my desk and inspected my work. It was at that moment, however, that the boy at the next desk glanced over to inspect my work. As his eyes met my paper, we simultaneously realized what I'd done. I was horrified and he was giddy with jest and vitriol.

"You colored them backwards!" the boy exclaimed. "You colored the 1's blue and the 2's yellow! Ha ha, you totally did it wrong!"

"You're going to get a –" and here the boy paused for first grade-level dramatic effect – "a frown face!" he cackled.

The frown face sticker, of course, being the equivalent of a very, very bad grade on Mrs. Peterson's scale. I had never, ever received a frown face. I was devastated at the very possibility. The boy at the next desk elbowed the kid on his far side, pointing again to my paper, making fun of me.

I felt *awful*. My feelings were hurt, my confidence was shattered. Most of all, I was overwhelmed by the idea that my error would disappoint my beloved Mrs. Peterson. What was a 6-year-old girl to do?

I decided to take matters into my own hands. With the memory of my father's words in my head – "Come to me with a solution, not a problem," he would say – I grabbed my crayons and executed a new plan. "I'll just re-do it and it will be fine," I surmised. In my inner monologue, I added, "Screw you, Jeremy (name *not* changed to out the guilty). I'll show you and your snotty comments."

I forged on and colored over the blue with the yellow, then over the yellow with the blue. And to my horror, a terrible truth we had not yet covered in art class was revealed before my inexperienced eyes. Yes, as art theory tells us, yellow and blue most certainly make green.

My worksheet was a complete mess. It looked like a lawn in dire need of a mower. The more I colored, the worse it got, and the more Jeremy delighted in it. I made it through all eight shapes a second time, bottom lip jutting out in fierce concentration and mounting shame, and it was at that moment that Mrs. Peterson walked up to my desk.

I was utterly embarrassed and colossally defeated, on the verge of puddle-sized tears.

Mrs. Peterson, whom I love to this day, looked at me, then Jeremy, and decoded the entire ordeal. She instantly knew what had happened. Gosh, she was smart. "You got the colors mixed up, but used your problem-solving skills to try to fix it. Is that right, Miss Jamie?" She asked.

"Yes," I whimpered softly from my Crayola-green vortex of self-defeat.

She smiled at me. I remember her reddish-pink lipstick as she did so, some of which always found a home on her teeth. "Do you want to start over? I have a clean sheet."

God bless her, that Mrs. Peterson. She was full of encouragement, understanding, and phenomenal detective skills. She got right inside my 6-year-old mind.

I started the worksheet over and did things right this time. Jeremy scowled and made a grumbling noise. I sneered back at him. We saved lessons in maturity for a later time. The bell rang and we all ran outside for recess. The ordeal was behind us, Mrs. Peterson's opinion of me was preserved, I earned a smiley face, and all seemed well in my little orbit. But, darn it, my feelings were still hurt by what Jeremy had said. I had taken it immensely personally, to the depth of my small soul. Why did I let his words affect me so much? How did I let Jeremy's opinion of me overpower my own? I imagine he forgot all about me the second he darted out onto the playground and dove onto the swings. But me? Not me. I carried it with me throughout recess and beyond. Maybe right up to today, as I share this story therapeutically and clear all this out!

Taking things personally is very easy to do and many of us are guilty. You might be surprised to know, however, that there are fairly common reasons why we do it. Even better, there are coping mechanisms and ways to get ahead of this compulsion!

A piece of wisdom to commit to memory right now comes from Eleanor Roosevelt. In one of her many profound statements, Mrs. Roosevelt said, "What other people think of me is none of my business." Let that sink in for a minute.

What other people think of me is none of my business.

Other peoples' opinions are theirs and theirs alone. It's true. You cannot control someone else's thoughts, so why bother being affected by them?

Think about this in reverse, too. Do you ever have thoughts about others? Thoughts that would mortify both of you if they could read your mind? Of course! We all do. And sometimes they even slip out. In taking Eleanor Roosevelt's advice, however, we should shake it off. Move along. Don't give others that power, especially when they, like Jeremy, have likely long moved on.

Another favorite quote of mine is from Albert Einstein: "Great spirits have always encountered violent opposition from mediocre minds." You're the great spirit. Don't let mediocre minds rain on your fabulous parade.

The Why

Imagine if a comprehensive list existed of every single conversation and digital interaction you've had over the past two years. If you could review those interactions and categorize them as good or bad, reassuring or upsetting, affirming or disturbing, uplifting or degrading, which would you take most personally? I think for most of us the good would grossly outweigh the bad and the overall list of what hurt us personally would be relatively small. But, *yowza!* A few might really sting!

While taking things personally is an ailment that plagues both men and women, women seem to struggle with it more. As it turns out, our DNA is partially to blame.

I've come across several research studies which conducted similar experiments.

In the standard scenario, toddler-aged girls and boys are led into a room filled with a variety of toys, from dolls and stuffed animals to balls and trucks. The children get no instructions (unlikely to impress toddlers anyhow!), nor adult supervision. The researchers simply place the kids in the room with all kinds of toys, stand back, and observe.

Invariably the little girls gravitate toward the dolls, tea party sets, and miniature kitchens – toys generally considered nurturing and inclusive. The girls aren't very aggressive (with the exception of the occasional "Mine!"), or competitive. They don't keep score. Anybody ever play a heated game of tea party? No? That's because nobody "wins" tea party. It's a shared activity in which everyone feels included, collaborative, and happy. And what grown woman still doesn't enjoy a girlfriend get-together over tea, petit fours, and fancy dishes?

The boys, on the other hand, gravitate to the trucks, drum sets, balls, and bats. They create noise, destruction, and competition. Who can bang the drum the loudest or kick the ball the farthest? They devise win-lose scenarios.

Without any cultural cues or parental pressure to be a "strong little man" or "good little girl," the boys' play is naturally more competitive, explosive, and physical while the girls are more social, inviting, and considerate.

Fast-forward to middle school, when many girls and boys join scouting organizations. I have great respect for the Girl Scouts organization and enjoyed my team earning badges, but there's something I recognized in my adult life that really sours my sweet tea. The Girl Scouts' pledge starts off, "On my honor, I will try to…" The Boy Scouts' begins, "On my honor, I will do my best to…" Did you catch the distinction? Girls Scouts pledge to merely *try* things, whereas Boy Scouts pledge to *do* things. The former view is obviously more passive. It bugs me! It makes me wonder what kind of subconscious imprinting takes place when girls in formative phases recite that pledge over and over, and what developmental advantage Boy Scouts might gain being conditioned to DO, not just try. That's where I'd rather *Tagalong*.

Organized sports are regular after-school activities. Coaching styles and individuals will certainly vary, but if you had to generalize, which of the two genders would you say is cattier? Holds more grudges? When I pose this question to groups I usually get amused head nods, followed by, "Yep, the girls." And personally, I must agree. When we ladies walk off the field after an aggressive game of soccer or field hockey, or leave the basketball court, the penalties, fouls, and dirty looks tend to come right along with us. We don't leave the drama on the court. With boys, however, the literal blocking and tackling and other physical encounters on the field of play tend to be left out there. Opposing team members can literally go from attacking each other during regulation time to walking across the sidelines afterwards, as if through a magical disarming warp zone, and ask each other, "Hey, man, want to go play X-Box?" "Want to grab a soda?" Boy athletes don't seem to bear nearly the weight of grudges or hurt feelings as girl athletes do. I have a friend who's a former National Hockey League player. He's told me stories about punching an opponent to the point where one or both were bleeding, then meeting up at a bar not long afterward to share a few beers and rehash the game. Wow, definitely not taking things personally!

As women in personal and professional settings, we generally work hard to promote "tea party mentality." We strive to avoid hurting others' feelings. We're nice. We make sure our coworkers and friends are included and satisfied. There's an underlying commitment to treating others the way we want to be treated: We're mindful of the Golden Rule. So when these norms are violated, when we are the recipient of something hurtful, negative, or unexpected, it doesn't immediately compute in our brains. We haven't been conditioned to just let it go. It doesn't sit well. We might feel symbiosis has been disturbed and internal fires are a' ragin'! "That's not how this game is played."

In a business environment, this conditioned reaction can be dangerous and disadvantageous for women. If we become trapped in taking things personally and ruminating (more on rumination in the next chapter) our unaffected male colleagues (and some women, too) are already moving along. They're focusing on key tasks and forging ahead. We risk being left behind.

A high-powered CFO had taken part in a particularly contentious meeting. He was on both the delivering and receiving ends of strong language and dissenting opinions. Shortly after the meeting, he commented to someone else who was still reeling from the harsh exchanges: "It's just business." He shrugged. In other words, his advice to his still-rattled colleague was, "Shake it off, Sarah. I did." We all have thresholds, of course, when it comes to what we can or should tolerate in a professional (or personal) environment. Yet this CFO didn't feel disrespected, hurt, or angry at his sparring partners in the meeting. He wasn't hyperventilating at the LaCroix fridge sputtering, "I CANNOT believe he said that!" He simply shook it off and moved on to his next cash flow statement, since it was his business to do just that.

Breaking Free

Okay, great! If it's just that easy, show me now! Teach me to forget about those personal stingers and get on with my life.

Absolutely. Here we go. To release yourself from the stranglehold of taking things personally, here are some strategies to try.

Do not make assumptions

When someone directs communication toward you that hurts your feelings or causes you to feel defensive, first take a hard look at what is fact and would could be fiction. What do you know to be true in the context of that moment? Did the other party spill coffee on himself during the morning commute, putting him in a foul mood? Perhaps she just learned a loved one is ill. Oftentimes the other person's circumstances have nothing to do with you, yet their behaviors surface as if they do. Are their own insecurities to blame? Perhaps they're wary of your success? I don't know. You likely don't either. If you must assume something, assume you're seeing their own insecurities on display. Acknowledge you cannot know all that's happening in someone else's life — what unseen factors might be causing them to do or say hurtful, unnecessary things...*none* of which have anything to do with you.

Try to interpret the circumstances at their most basic, spin-free level. Evaluate only the content of what was said. Resist the temptation to analyze the emotions and body language that came with it. While the delivery may have been irritating, annoying, and unprofessional, it's no one else's business. In my experience, the more energy I spend trying to interpret someone else's business, the less I can focus on my own business, or my own job for that matter.

And if you've ever falsely interpreted an email, a comment, or a message, only to later learn the author's intent was completely different from your take on it, know that you are not alone. My friend Kelly experienced this when a co-worker was going through a rough time at home. When she learned of his divorce, she realized his abnormally quiet demeanor, brief email responses, and diminished presence in meetings had nothing to do with her. She had taken his behavior very personally, but he was going through something very personal that had nothing to do with her.

Just the facts, ma'am

Focus on the facts you know to be true. I once worked for a company whose culture was very negative and condescending. I would read inbound emails and feel my blood pressure start to boil. I'd start to return fire with my own ammunition, allowing myself to sink to the level of my correspondent – a much lower energy vibration than I normally strive for.

And then I learned a better way. While working for this company, I managed to attend a two-week seminar in the Bahamas (I know, poor me) about leadership and living the life you want to live. It was at this seminar that I'm proud to say I evolved to rise above this whole fight-fire-with-fire-via-email thing. I learned to remove the feelings and emotions I was injecting into email. Fueling the fire only made it burn hotter. Instead, I'd add water (beautiful Caribbean blue water) with a newfound approach to unpleasantly contentious emails.

Here's what I did. I'd re-read heated inbound traffic as if I'd never met the person who composed it. I made zero assumptions, and, thus, did not allow myself to take the content personally. I no longer let myself hear the voice of the person behind the email or picture his face. I'd neutralize the sender in my mind, give him the benefit of the doubt and match that same energy in a reply that was factual, professional, and stripped of any negative tone or superfluous emotion. This immediately lessened my frustration and made my communication more effective. Sometimes I even composed a response, held it unsent in my Drafts folder until the next day, then re-read it. It's amazing how stepping away for a bit can heighten your ability to focus on facts, not feelings, and perhaps alter your response.

Use this technique in live settings as well. It's a little trickier when you know a person, you're looking him or her in the eye, and you're on the receiving end of comments and opinions that rub you the wrong way. Do yourself a kindness, however. Pause for a second and pretend there's no feeling or emotion in what they're saying. Seriously, consciously, intentionally wait just a few seconds. Take a sip from your eco-friendly water bottle. Consider the words, alone, of the person who's throwing attitude your way, and respond to those words only, not the accompanying emotion or implications. You'll be surprised how disarming and productive this can be. It can shift the energy of the entire conversation and free you from walking away hurt or angry. I'd even suggest you'll walk away empowered and confident. #winning!

Poison, anyone?

Realize that taking things personally is like refusing to forgive someone. It is like poisoning your own drink and expecting the other person to die. You're allowing the other person to win and causing yourself to lose when you take things personally. I'd sure feel like an idiot if I kicked the soccer ball into my own team's net. Don't give the opposing team the satisfaction.

Logical or emotional?

Recall the last time you were highly emotional about something. Once I cried when my computer suddenly shut down and rebooted, costing me 15 minutes of work time during a particularly high-pressure day. At that moment, I was basically taking it personally that my PC had rudely taken it upon *itself* to selfishly interrupt my day for IT updates only to run more efficiently in the long run, of course. I was being neither logical nor fair. ("Hello Pressure, I'm under a bit too much and should heed this as a warning sign!") I wasn't my best self, nor was I delivering my best work. It wasn't until I took a few deep breaths, considered the basic facts of the situation, and realized that my emotions were unnecessarily extreme that I found my rhythm and productivity again. I've been thankful for unannounced Microsoft updates and forced breaks ever since!

What's MY truth of the matter?

When you take something personally, step back and ask what is it inside of you that is causing you to feel exposed or to react so strongly?.

This can be a tough one. Sometimes you have to face things that are uncomfortable. Things you take personally may have some nugget of truth to them, or strike at a tiny vulnerability you might not even be aware of. If you do take time to honestly reflect on it, you may discover a self-improvement opportunity, or even feel gratitude or relief for having a blind spot exposed.

In the case of my first grade coloring debacle, if I were to be very honest, part of the reason I took Jeremy's comments so personally is because I was embarrassed – because I messed up. I was ashamed and didn't want to be wrong. I especially didn't want an audience observing and relishing my blunder, let alone such an immature kid. Gah! 6 year olds! Yet looking back, Jeremy was *right*. I had done the task wrong and he took it upon himself to articulate exactly how. In hindsight, the mature, not-taking-it-so-personally-me would have reacted more like this: "Gosh, Jeremy, you're right. Thank you for pointing that out. I made a mistake. I'm going to ask Mrs. Peterson if I can have a new worksheet and start over." And then I would have calmly stood and followed through with my perfectly articulated plan. I bet that would've shut Jeremy right down.

It was my own issue, not his. Jeremy certainly wasn't helping, but this was primarily about my own self-talk and disappointment, not his stinging words. If I could have separated the two in the moment and simply started over, the Crayola-green vortex of self-defeat would never have stuck with me all these years. I highly doubt I'd even remember it now.

Who's the common denominator?

Another opportunity for pause and reflection: ask whether the person pushing your buttons treats everyone this way, or just you. If it's just how they are, knowing that should help you take it less personally. You're not unique. The behavior is consistent no matter who's on the receiving end. That doesn't make it right, yet you can take it less personally when you know you're not the bullseye on someone's dartboard.

Whether or not you're one of many, though, I invite you to confront the offender. Have a side conversation and confidently and professionally ask why is it that this person seems to communicate negative energy around you. Perhaps their own awareness will improve as a result, and they'll stop. Perhaps not, in which case you'll need to make choices about setting boundaries in order to garner appropriate respect and treatment. (For more tips on managing confrontation, see Chapters 8 and 14!)

Lesson Learned

While I clearly did not fully dissect the Crayola Caper until much later in life, it was pretty darn early in my career, that I had a similar, but adult-sized experience. It was so extreme, so left field, that I could not possibly have taken it personally. And was thankful to learn a very valuable lesson early on.

I was assigned a sales territory in Colorado as an interim representative covering for Joe. I was brand new at the job, still in training, and was given Joe's territory as a practice ground.

One Tuesday morning I walked into a key customer's store to introduce myself. I entered the front door and walked alongside the counter, smiling and saying my hellos. I headed to the back where I was told the manager's office was located. He caught sight of me, before I caught sight of him and he jumped up, emerged, glared at me, and aggressively and loudly inquired, "Are you the new paint rep?"

Taken aback – I think I legitimately retreated a bit – I responded, "Yes, I'm filling in for Joe while he's on sick leave."

The manager hesitated not a second and launched into a complete tirade, proceeding to light me up about who knows what: All kinds of stuff that had happened before my time at the company. And I had literally transferred to his territory only four days before.

"Jim!" I interrupted him firmly. "Jim? That's your name, right?"

He paused his rant. "Yes," he said in a slightly quieter voice. Louder wasn't really possible at that point so any reduction was an improvement.

"Okay, Jim, I'm Jamie. I'm here to help you while Joe is not available. I'm committed to getting to the bottom of everything you're talking about. But I can't do that when you're yelling it at me. Could we go sit down in your office and talk about it? I'll listen to your every word and do my best to address the issues *if* we can have a calm conversation about this."

Jim's entire posture changed. He looked at me and motioned into his office. "Sure," he said, "Let's do that."

Sheesh. There are a few Conflict Resolution 101 lessons sprinkled in here, yet the main takeaway in that moment was not to take his rant personally. Rude? Yes. Unprofessional? Absolutely. Uncalled for? No doubt. There was absolutely no way, however, I was going to give this jerk the power to upset me nor would I take his immaturity personally. He knew exactly nothing about me, and I had exactly as much on him. Afterward, while I worked to resolve Jim's problems, I didn't carry the weight of his issues with me. I didn't take it personally and I didn't fret, or attach false assumptions or emotion to it.

Honestly, he was much nicer and calmer every time after that.

Summing It Up

Whether the challenge to your confidence is your first-grade nemesis, your boss, a co-worker, a close friend, or the demanding customer sitting across your desk, we all have good days and bad days, our insecurities and our securities. Not taking things personally can be a tricky skill to master. As with so many things, though, try to be grateful for the chances you get to practice it. With every occasion it will grow easier. Next time it happens, and then the time after that and the time after that, it will become more familiar and quickly managed. If you continue to struggle, talk it out with a trusted friend or advisor, and review the key concepts here to build confidence and empower yourself.

Keep in mind that whether the flashpoint is a heated face-to-face conversation or a spicy email exchange, sometimes the best way to change direction is to simply pause the game. Either reset your own take-it-personally-clock or ask those involved if everyone could set the clock back a few seconds together. It's a more effective tactic than you might think. In fact, resetting the clock happens all the time in football and basketball games. When something is off with the timer, they simply set it back a few seconds and resume play without taking it personally. You can do the same: Hit your own pause button when necessary, and cherish the freedom that comes when the opinion you value the most is your very own.

And one final golden nugget, **assume positive intent**. When someone's message delivery, either in person or electronically is subpar, assume the best and respond in the same manner. Bring them up to your vibration, rather than give them power to bring you down to theirs. And when you do, listen closely, because you'll likely hear the roar of the Sherohood (Recall, She+Hero+Sisterhood = Sherohood) cheering you on from behind the scenes!

What's at Stake?

Allowing someone to take your power and give you doubt. When you begin to give power to your doubts, you doubt your power. Hold your power close! It's yours and only yours to give or take!

Key Points

- Elements of both social conditioning and our DNA are partially responsible for why women take things personally.

- Removing the emotion and focusing on the true facts will help dissipate hurt feelings.

- You control your power. Stand strong in your power to prevent anyone from taking it.

- Assume positive intent.

Confidence Challenge Checklist

- ❑ Think back on a situation you took personally. See if you can re-frame it in your head.

- ❑ In your journal, write a different outcome for a past event where you felt something very personally.

- ❑ Watch for a future opportunity when you take something very personally and respond using the techniques in this chapter. Recognize how you feel differently and the duration of time it affects you.

- ❑ Compassionately coach a friend suffering from a situation she's taking very personally.

To condition and claim my confidence, one action I commit to is:

_____

_____

_____

Chapter 7
Rumination Amputation

Imagine your average workday. Picture yourself at work. Think about how you get around. Maybe you commute to the office on a bus or train. Maybe you drive in, then walk from the parking lot, to your desk, to the break room, to the restroom, back to your desk, then later to the coffee machine.

Maybe you work from home, with a very short commute between bedroom and office. Maybe you teach yoga and are constantly *in flow*. Maybe you have clients, patients, or students and you get in a ton of steps while engaging with them.

Now imagine that throughout your day, you carry a big, heavy rock. You're hauling it everywhere you go. Car, Uber, scooter, desk, couch, restroom...and repeat.

At first the rock is only a little disruptive. It distracts you mid-sentence as you discuss this month's revenue projections. Then someone catches you staring at it as they wait for you to respond to their question. When you visit the bathroom you have to strategize a place to set down your rock. It becomes even more inhibiting. You have to read the same sentence three times, you lose your train of thought in a meeting, you miss a reporting deadline, all because that darn rock keeps distracting you.

It's got to stop. I mean seriously. It must go away. It becomes clear that for you to maintain your job performance, and your sanity for that matter, you must go to the pond outside, heave the rock into the water, watch it sink out of sight, and walk away. Simply walk away, and never have one more moment of distraction, disruption, or discomfort because of that rock, ever again.

You do it. And it's liberating! It gives you closure. You walk back from the pond destined to never see or think about that rock, ever again. Ahhhh, freedom! Way to take charge! What a relief to return to your focused, productive life.

Wouldn't it be amazing if, just as easily, we could discard other things, like thoughts, that weigh on us like that rock – that ruminate and churn in our heads, over and over again?

- The negative words spoken in a meeting that keep re-playing in your head like a stuck movie reel, or the bad review that keeps flashing in your mind like a lightning bolt, impossible to ignore.
- The indecision about which direction to take a high profile project, or a high stakes move that will impact your career.
- The thoughts that keep you awake at night and distract you consciously and subconsciously.

Wouldn't it be cool if you could ditch those thoughts as readily as you made the rock vanish into the pond? Well, I'm thrilled to tell you that you can. You need not be imprisoned by thoughts that ruminate and hold you back from peak performance. Dismissing unproductive thoughts, the unwelcome thoughts that persist worse than garlic breath after lunch at Olive Garden, is a very important skill, and the men and women who succeed with it have more fulfillment and progression in their careers than those that allow the ruminating thoughts to win.

Ruminating is like letting someone live in your mind rent-free!

You can even think of the word like this: ROOM-I-NATE. Would you let a guy named Nate live in your spare room without permission or even paying his AirBnB deposit? Of course not! Any heavy thoughts that take up real estate in your mind must be evicted to create space for the guests you want to be there; the productive and creative thoughts that support fun, innovative thinking.

Luckily, you can prevent Nate from taking up that space in your mind (and from depleting your power, too). Let me share the example of my girlfriend, Mireya.

Oh, how I love Mireya! She's such a rock star, particularly at work. Mireya's in a male-dominated industry, at a male-dominated company in a male-dominated department, the only woman on a team of nine men. She's petite, pretty, and blond. She's intelligent and strategic and innovative. She does excellent work and often finds herself in team meetings. And she's generally soft-spoken! At lunch I asked her what she does to ensure that she's heard in those meetings. Especially when there's a lot of talking and talking over each other.

Most meetings, Mireya told me, had balanced communication. But when things got contentious and voices rose, she had to make a conscious effort to speak up. Sometimes she'd leave invigorated, because her idea was chosen, or a project she ran was praised for its success. On other occasions she'd leave feeling deflated. Her idea had been shot down. She said something that didn't come out quite right. Someone directed a hurtful or rude comment her way.

I asked what she did in those moments. "I'll reflect on what occurred and what was said and see if there's any valuable feedback I can take from it," replied Mireya confidently. "And then I drop it and move on."

"Really?" I asked. "Just that easily?"

"Pretty much," said Mireya, and for two very specific reasons. "One, it doesn't serve me whatsoever to keep dwelling on those thoughts. They kill my self-esteem, they make me question my next decision, and they bring me down. They serve no purpose. Two, I know the men on my team don't sit in their offices thinking about how their feelings were hurt, or worrying that so-and-so is no longer a friend. They shrug it off and get back to work. So I do too."

Rumination Elimination

What Mireya said makes so much sense. It might be slightly difficult at first, yet practicing the art of *not ruminating* improves your performance so much faster than letting the weight of the "rumination rock" weigh you down. If you're as qualified and capable as colleagues who seem able to unload unproductive thoughts simply by flipping a switch, know that what they can do, you can do too.

Here are some tips to stop ruminating.

Kick 'em off your couch

I came home from work on a Monday evening having had a really rough morning. It began with my boss all kinds of fired up over something I could not control. I greeted him pleasantly: "Good morning, Tim." And the first words out of his mouth were a loud and nasty, "Well, no, Jamie, it is *not* a good morning!" He proceeded into a rant that I let bother me for the *entire day*. I couldn't concentrate, I lacked my normal energy level, I had to take deep breaths, I couldn't wait to go home.

Of course, when I got home, still thinking about his rant, I walked into my living room and had a jarring vision. I literally pictured him, my boss, sitting there – stretched out on my couch, his feet on my ottoman, drinking my wine and petting my dog.

Oh. No. He. Didn't.

Get your hands off my dog, buddy. And that's when I caught myself. I laughed, thinking how ridiculous it was that I had let my boss make himself at home in my space. Then and there, out loud, I demanded that my imaginary intruder leave. "You are not welcome here anymore. Get to stepping, sir! Leave!" And so he did. I returned to work Tuesday morning and laughed to myself recalling our imaginary encounter from the previous evening. (The power of our thoughts in action!) I greeted him as if nothing had happened; and lo and behold, his greeting matched mine.

So, identify the thoughts that have a stranglehold on you and invite, or demand, them to leave. If spirituality is your thing, get your higher power involved and invite them to take over. "God, these thoughts no longer serve me. I'm handing them off to you now."

Set a timer

After a particularly rough breakup, I saw a therapist. "I'm just so sick of being sad and not feeling like myself," I cried to her one day. One of her coping ideas really stuck with me.

"Jamie, set a timer," she said.

I looked at her quizzically. I'm all about timing and measurable results, so with great intrigue I listened for more.

"When you feel the waves of sadness come over you, set a timer. Maybe it's for an hour, maybe it's for 20 minutes, but set a timer. Feel what you need to feel. Process what you need to process and when that timer goes off, you're *done*. Go do something else. Ride your bike, go to the grocery store, watch a re-run of *Friends*, (Now we're talking!) or call a friend to focus on her and nothing but her. For the time being, you're done being sad."

Hopefully, this saves you hundreds of dollars in therapy fees because, I tell you what, it works. An hour? Are you kidding me? I'm not wasting a whole hour this way. Okay, though, I'll give it 20 minutes. And I did. I've used this technique ever since for thoughts that keep spinning. I set a timer. I think deeply about them and when the timer goes off, I change my own channel and go do something else.

When you find yourself stuck, pull out the timer on your phone, set it, focus only on what you've been ruminating about for hours, days, or weeks. When the timer goes off, go for a walk, call a friend, blast your favorite song. Do something else. Give it a shot!

Write down all possible outcomes on Post-It® Notes

This technique comes in especially handy when you're making a big decision, or when something in your life feels like it is spinning out of control and you're afraid of the outcome.

Grab a fresh stack of Post-Its® and write one possible outcome on each note. You can even color-code, using neon orange notes for positive outcomes and pastel green for negative ones, or whatever color palette pleases you. Force yourself to come up with positive outcomes that outnumber the negative ones, even if only by one. Stick them on a wall or surface where you can see all of them at the same time.

Two things will happen. First, the act of writing down those outcomes will open you up to the good things that can happen. They don't all have to be realistic. (Maybe a unicorn will swoop through the office and dust your manager with magic rainbow energy right before he writes your review!) Have fun with it, and be creative about the many outcomes you hadn't even thought of yet. Second, getting things down on paper helps calm the storm inside your head. Pen to paper is a calming ritual. Sometimes it helps to brainstorm with a friend.

Then, when the situation's actual outcome occurs, compare it to your notes. Did your worst nightmare come true? Did you faint before you could gasp the first word of your presentation on the new equipment protocols, or did your manager commend you and say, "Great job!" in front of your whole team? After the outcome has occurred, either select the note that matches your prediction or write a new one to describe what actually happened. Then rearrange your Post-It® Notes from the wall into a stack, placing the note that best describes the actual outcome on top. As you do this exercise over time, watch as your Post-It® Note collection grows, and see which color winds up on top most often. My forecast is that your worst nightmares hardly ever occur, and over time, as you see not-so-bad or even good outcomes rise to the top, you'll ruminate less and be more confident in positive outcomes.

Have a trusted sounding board

One of my favorite co-workers will always be Jessica. Jessica and I were the two women on an otherwise male executive team of nine. She and I had similar thinking patterns, and we had each other's backs 100% of the time. Women supporting women. Holla!

For the most part, our executive team functioned and communicated well.

Like any group, especially at a company in accelerated growth mode, there were moments of frustration and, well, irritation. In front of colleagues we were professional and composed. Behind closed doors we were candid with one another and occasionally used private meetings to vent or get something off our chests. We were trusted sounding boards for each other.

If you have to let a frustration spill, be sure to do so in a private, safe, protected setting with someone you can unequivocally trust, lest it come out in a way that will hurt more than help you and, God forbid, come across as gossip. Find that sounding board, often better when he or she is external to your workplace, and use it reasonably.

Write down what you learned

Focus on what you gained. Back to Mireya, my soft-spoken, rock-star friend you met earlier. After a meeting that left her feeling defeated, what did she do? Instead of spending the rest of her day steaming, stewing, sulking, she reflected on what she learned and took away from the experience, going so far as to write it down while it was fresh on her mind. She got it out of her head and on paper. She could refernece it later if she so chose, and in the meantime, let it go.

Take advantage of opportunities like this to better prepare you for next time. Preparation leads to confidence and confidence increases your performance. Focus on the *right* thoughts. Leave those that don't serve you behind.

Finally, here's what to do if all else fails. If you try the five tips above, maybe even added a few of your own, and still feel imprisoned by those darn thoughts stuck on repeat, as a last resort, get your markers ready and follow these steps.

Find an actual rock. Maybe it's in the parking lot, maybe it's part of the building's landscaping, maybe it's in a potted plant at your house. Next, take a Sharpie to that rock and write down the thought that plagues you. Heck, find a whole bed of rocks and go crazy, writing one thought on each rock.

Now find the nearest body of water. You know what to do next. Launch that sucker as far as you can! Throw that 'rumination rock' as if you've won an Olympic Gold medal for shot put. Catapult that rock with the force of the entire Sherohood behind you. See ya later, rumination! Have fun swimming with the fishes.

What's at Stake?

Awarding mental energy to some idea, worry, or person that does not deserve an award in the slightest way. Save that space in your mind for inspiration and creativity to help you be an even more enlightened, lighter you!

Key Points

- Ruminating can feel like you are imprisoned by your own thoughts.
- Breaking free is essential to free up your mind for things that are more productive and beneficial to your performance.
- Prioritize releasing them by inviting them to leave, setting a timer, and/or getting them down on paper. Talk them out with a trusted friend to help alleviate their burden. Make ruminating thoughts tangible and then physically let them go.

Confidence Challenge Checklist

❑ Are you ruminating on anything right now? Repeat after me: "Get to steppin', negative thoughts that don't serve me!" Kick them out of your "house." Physically kick your leg to reinforce your commitment to making them leave.

❑ Talk it out with a trusted friend and then commit to moving on.

❑ Start listing out possible outcomes on Post-Its® and grow your collection.

❑ Help a friend who's stuck in rumination incarceration by sharing these tips.

To condition and claim my confidence, one action I commit to is:

_____

_____

_____

Chapter 8
The Beauty of Difference

I have a request, my reader. If you can help, I'd sure be appreciative. For years I've searched high and low for something, asking friends and colleagues. I've been on this quest since email became a standard means of communication. Maybe you, my reader, will finally connect me to the answer.

Will someone please, please, please invent a new font? A font that will serve to allay misinterpretation of emails, text messages, and social media posts, and avoid miscommunication? Let's find a designer and name it...the Sarcasm font. We could all select Sarcasm font in any situation when we're joking around. No semicolon-hyphen-parenthesis code to indicate a sly wink, and no emojis (not necessarily appropriate in workplace emails anyway).

My, oh my, would it alleviate so much unnecessary drama and worry! Away with churning self-talk about the imagined implications of an email or text. See ya later, hurt feelings thanks to misinterpretation and needless heated retorts! Sarcasm font would banish so many hidden issues from our digitally driven society. If you hold the solution to this problem, please get a hold of me, stat!

If there's one thing marriage has taught me, it's that men and women observe, think, process, and communicate very differently. My husband and I can experience the exact same dinner party, sitting at the exact same table, with the exact same people, and join the exact same conversations, and yet our recollection afterwards varies wildly. Not in a contentious way, more in a way that fascinates me. Although we share similar cultural origins, are of similar age, grew up in comparable socioeconomic circumstances, and share an appreciation for higher education, he and I have such different life experiences and different patterned brain activity. It's bonkers how our interpretations of a shared event can diverge, yet what we learn from each other when we compare notes. It's not that one of us is right and one of us is wrong. (Well, maybe *one* of us is right more often than the other. See, I need the sarcasm font here!) It's really that *both* our unique takeaways are accurate.

Now transfer this from a social setting to a business setting. Let's say the guests at the dinner party were customers, my husband and I, business partners. Wouldn't it make sense for both of us to be there listening, interpreting different cues, then later trading perceptions of the discussion? Wouldn't that be a more efficient way to solve our customers' challenges than if only one of us had gone to the meeting? It sure makes more sense to me!

It's encouraging to me that inclusion and diversity are becoming much more of a corporate priority. According to an article in *Business Insider*, women make 85 percent of all consumer purchasing decisions. This equates to $7 trillion in consumer and business spending. So why are corporate boards' male to female ratios not more reflective of who's making purchasing decisions? Imagine how much more robust of a solution results when people with a variety of thought processes and life experiences come together.

Based on my professional life experience as the lone (or outnumbered) woman in an ocean of males, I conclude 98% of workplace gender contests stem from one singular place. The frequently visited Land of Miscommunication.

Countless books, videos, thesis studies, comedy movies and Netflix series have been crafted around miscommunication between genders. And while gender factors in workplace communication are not the main focus of this book, this chapter presents some of the insight I've gained in this department through personal experience and observation.

The stories I can tell!

Like the story I shared in my Introduction – the time I was sent out to an oil rig for the first time as part of new hire training. I emailed the company man, Bob, in advance detailing the safety gear I planned to wear. I asked him to confirm that I had everything I needed to be allowed on-site. His eight-word reply to my query: "Just don't be wearing them stilettos out here."

My reply to his reply? "Well, my stilettos are steel-toe, so I'm sure that'll be fine." (Perfect opportunity to use Sarcasm font!) Was I fighting fire with fire? Meh, maybe. Really I was standing my ground and using a little humor to deflect his attempt to intimidate me. I'm pleased to report that it worked. I showed up wearing the proper steel-toed boots (accented with pink piping, of course) and Bob didn't mess with me. Rather, he took me under his wing and showed and taught me everything I needed to know.

I decided to make a hobby of studying gender differences at work. They sure are fascinating! I've essentially been the subject of my own experiment on numerous occasions. Some common male versus female stereotypes, we've all heard before. Men speak far fewer words per day than women. Women are more emotional. Guys don't stew as much. Women are more thoughtful. Some of these stereotypes I've seen validated over and over. Others haven't been proven quite so consistently.

When I dove deeper into statistically-based, quantitative studies on gender differences, what I typically found was that for every study proving one side of the story, there'd be another scientifically sound research project that proved the complete opposite result. I also realized the parallels between being the only woman at work with whatever is the defining characteristic that makes you unique. The discomfort or intimidation I felt throughout my career as the only woman, or one of a very few, is often present in situations where a person has a defining, differentiating characteristic, like age, race, etc. The lessons I've learned, and what I'd like to think of as wisdom gained, are actually far broader than tips for surviving a gender imbalance.

Imagine you're the only millennial in an office of Generation Xers, or the only boomer in a sea of millennials. When you're the only one in a group representing your ethnicity, culture, physical bearing, (height can be a key differentiator in the athletic world), education level, native land, or social class, you may feel a heightened sense of awareness that you're not like the others. This can (although certainly doesn't have to!) decrease your self-assurance or self-esteem, inhibit your confidence, and cause you to suppress actions and words that might be shared freely when in the company of others who are more like you.

Some men at work tried to intimidate me and make me stumble. Others acted awkwardly simply because they'd never experienced working with a woman, let alone a young one with a college degree that could very well catapult me to their boss one day. Do I pull out her chair? Do I open the door for her? Can she take a joke? Just how off-color can the joke be before it's inappropriate and HR writes me up? So many awkward moments – if I chose to let them be so. Offering light-hearted guidance was important. "That's so nice of you, but I've got it," as

I pulled out my own chair. "Great, thanks!" as a door was opened for me. I was usually able to move an interaction past an awkward moment by letting it pass and moving right along to the next conversation or order of business.

It ultimately boiled down to me conveying my own self respect with flexibility per the situation.

Even though I was more outnumbered than a Raiders fan at a Denver Broncos game, I had to acknowledge that they were learning, too. For men more on the "woke"[1] side (before that was even a slang word), it wasn't a big deal. For others, it was a matter of getting used to an evolving order, because the company wasn't going to back away from diversity, and senior leadership frequently reinforced that point. The realization that made things much less frustrating for me and far more productive was this:

Men and women are hard-wired differently. Embracing and working with our differences, rather than against them, leads to more fruitful and less frustrating results!

I stuck out worse than a cowboy at a CoverGirl convention given my gender, age, industry experience, technical knowledge, and formal education level. All of these differences were obstacles to fitting in or winning credibility. Yet we all have to start somewhere! And some people embrace differences whereas others struggle. Some are intentionally closed-minded about people who don't think, look, or act like them. Or, I believe, they haven't taken a step back and realized that the best decisions and the greatest progress come when people of diverse backgrounds and life experience collaborate – and contribute ideas rooted in their unique life experiences. They choose to be intimidated by the unfamiliar, rather than curious about it.

Embrace Differences!

We each have a pair of eyes that see things with a personal filter based on what we've seen before. It can be a lot of fun to have an Indian man, a millennial white girl, a Harvard-educated Latino, and a college dropout 20-something who is the chief strategy officer of his self-made business, all collaborate on a project. The innovation! Can you even imagine how much more rich and creative, the ideas would be surfacing from a group like that, as compared to a group that shared the same gender, age, ethnicity, education level, and economic background?

---

1   Woke means a person is consciously awake.

Years ago I learned the term *cross-gender enrichment*. It refers to the better, more comprehensive decisions and outcomes that result when both genders contribute. A man's life experiences are different from a woman's. Of course. That's not to say that one is good or bad, right or wrong. They're just different. The blend of viewpoints, opinions, and ideas is more robust. What an amazing gift we give each other at work when we share and collaborate for a better solution! How invigorating and synergistic (total business buzzword) to incorporate as many backgrounds as possible when an important, or even minor, project is in the works.

Let's Talk About Stereotypes

Back to the question of good old pure gender differences. Who's in the right and who's in the wrong? It's an impossible question to answer because the question itself is not accurate. It's not a matter of right or wrong, or even good or bad.

It's a matter of respecting each other, honoring where we are, and embracing the strengths of others, rather than exploiting weaknesses.

Nobody wins when we can't work together, and everybody wins when we do.

Many of us are repeatedly challenged by "typical male/female stereotypes." Stereotypes, by definition, are flawed in that you can never lump ALL people into one category or another. There are always exceptions. However, there is some truth to stereotypes and knowledge to be gained. We'll address some gender-based, common workplace stereotypes here because there is opporunity in what we can learn from them. We benefit by creating more awareness around them, exploiting any advantages they hold and eradicating any bias we may unknowingly carry. It's important to talk about them, not to play the blame game, but rather to become mindful about them, learn from them and appreciate the advantages that gender differences can offer. So let's have fun with it, be able to laugh at ourselves, enhance advantages and mitigate disadvantages.

We'll look at five common stereotypes here and you'll be asked, true or false? What does your experience tell you?

Stereotype #1: Women talk far more than men in everyday situations. TRUE or FALSE?

I've found when men get on a subject they like and know well, they can talk circles around anyone else. When I was with the paint company, I couldn't come up with more than a few paragraphs worth of verbiage on automotive refinishing, or the car show I'd attended for work the weekend prior. The men I worked with, however, could have easily talked for hours, maybe the entire day, about primer and sealer and clearcoat (yawn), or the craftsmanship behind a certain metallic flake finish (which was pretty impressive, I must admit, but I had no ability to discuss it for hours).

When someone is truly passionate about something, it doesn't matter if you're male, female, or any other gender identity. I've found that just about anyone can talk endlessly. For these reasons and more, I'm not inclined to believe a controversial claim published by Louann Brizendine of the University of California, San Francisco's Women's Mood and Hormone Clinic, in her 2006 study *The Female Brain* – namely that women utter three times as many words as men each day. Her: 20,000 words, said Brizendine. Him: 7,500. A follow-up study the next year placed women and men about even in daily word volume.

Incidentally, the movie, The Female Brain, found on Netflix, is worth the watch! Very insightful.

Studies suggest that men, different from women, bond simply by being in each other's presence: Watching or playing sports, or sitting together in the backyard. When in each other's presence can just *be*. They can foster a bond without the same word exchange that women use to achieve a similar bonding result. My brother-in-law Danny and his buddy Matt went on a seven-hour road trip, fourteen hours out and back, to pick up some restaurant equipment. Matt had just broken off an engagement and wanted an excuse to get out of town. When the two returned, my sister asked Danny how Matt was coping. "Oh, I don't know, he's fine," shrugged Danny.

"What about the break-up?" my sister inquired.

"Um, not really sure. It never came up."

Her eyes grew wide. "Never came up? You spent *fourteen hours* in the car with each other and it never came up?"

"Nope," said Danny, casually shaking his head, "Never came up."

I find this unbelievably entertaining. Two women in this scenario, one fresh from a broken engagement, would have analyzed things 31 different ways before hitting the state border! It's what we do for each other! It would be therapeutic, and we'd bond over the conversation.

A Dos Equis beer commercial pokes fun at this male condition. Dad and son are in a fishing boat and the dad, in a very heartfelt way, says, "Son?"

"Yeah, Dad?"

"Son, I want to tell you something. If you ever have any questions, you call 877-522-5001," Dad says as he reads the customer service number off the Dos Equis bottle in his hand. The son, now emotional, responds, "Dad, I've always wanted to hear you say that." The commercial is named, "Special Moments." And there you have it. Best to go in with an open mind, embrace differences, and have a sense of humor about it than fight the natural states of our being!

Stereotype #2: Women are better multi-taskers.

TRUE or FALSE?

There is a membrane in our brain connecting the left and right hemispheres called the corpus callosum. It's a bridge across the two. Many studies show (though a few differ) that a woman's corpus callosum has double the bandwidth of a man's, suggesting the female brain is capable of exchanging double the information between left and right sides. The conclusion is that women are naturally better equipped for multitasking.

Historically, it is theorized that in the days of cavemen and cavewoman, men had one critical job that required singular, undeterred focus: hunting. As the physically stronger gender, men were the designated hunters. They stalked prey in order to feed their families and keep the species going. Distractions were a threat to survival. Succumbing to a distraction could result in the hunter's family going hungry and, defeated, he would have to return to the homestead empty-handed. His female companion, exhausted from a long day of tending the fire, picking berries, nursing the baby, and minding the toddler, would be about to pour herself a glass of red wine, because that's what pairs well with red deer meat, of course. Apprised of how his day went, she'd turn to him and say, "You had ONE job!" No caveman wants to hear that! So he eliminated all other distractions such as sounds and hunger and fixated on slaying that darn deer to ensure the longevity of his family and his relationship. The only tinder back then was the kind for starting a fire, not the app for finding a new mate!

In a modern workplace environment, I've found the multi-tasking ability to be especially female-forward when talking on the phone. When I'm on a call with a male customer or colleague and we're talking about, for example, a certain file he needs to open on his computer, I've learned to stop talking. While he's clicking around to find the folder, I'll only distract him and challenge his singular focus on that task, prolonging it and possibly flustering both of us in the meantime, if I don't keep quiet. When a woman is on the line, however, she and I are easily able to continue our conversation as she performs the same task.

It took me a while to recognize this. For some time, I misinterpreted what was happening when the man on the line stopped responding to me. At first, I thought he'd lost interest, or didn't want to speak to me, but I figured out that wasn't it at all. I lost his attention temporarily because he shifted focus to his search-oriented task - finding the file. He hadn't lost interest permanently, though, and picked right back up with me once the task was complete. Lesson learned: Stop my chattering while he's searching!

Lesson learned: Sit there in a silence without discomfort, now that I understood and embraced our difference. Give him space to focus, complete the task, and THEN carry on the conversation. It was a huge ah-ha for me. Are there exceptions? Sure. But over and over, I've observed single-task focus to be a male-forward attribute. It's not right or wrong, good or bad. It's just simply *different*.

On the flip side, the female brain's greater ability to absorb and interpret multiple stimuli in parallel can also be a disadvantage – such as during an over-the-phone job interview. Studies show men do better in phone interviews because women thrive on additional visual cues from a live conversation. They help women respond better. Men don't need as much input and have more confidence in voice-only communication. Success Tip: Always request a video or in-person interview over a phone-only interview.

A caveat to multi-tasking is that it promotes lower efficiency. Articles published by Psychology Today suggest that, each time you switch tasks, you lose one-tenth of a second of productivity. In one day, that can equate to an overall 40% loss! No matter how broad your corpus callosum bandwidth, be aware that multitasking has its limitations.

Stereotype #3: Women tend to have hurt feelings and hold grudges more than men.
TRUE or FALSE?

Well, yes, there's a reason I dedicated an entire chapter to not taking things personally. Dudes certainly tend to shake things off better and move along faster. I can attest to past guilt on this one, too, admitting to hurt feelings or holding a grudge unproductively. When some negative shade is thrown my way, verbally or digitally, over email or social media, I first assess the source. Then I consider if I played a role in provoking it. I respond (or not, depending on the situation), and move on. The faster I shake things off and move right along, the better off I am. At Walt Disney World, I have no patience to wait in the regular line. My time is important to me! I'll take that Fast Pass all day long. The same holds true in my professional life. On to the next ride, because standing in a long line of grudge is preventing only me from getting on the ride.

Sometimes letting things go is far easier said than done, yet it's a skill certainly worth practicing. The journey will lead to satisfaction, once you're able to move along instead of letting trouble interrupt progress like a flat tire forcing you to pull over. And if letting it go is a struggle, start instead with 'Let it be.' It's still there, but it's going to just *be* and that's okay.

Stereotype #4: Men make decisions faster.
TRUE or FALSE?

A study demonstrated male-pattern thinking tends to be more linear and isolated in one brain hemisphere. A woman's thinking pattern, said the research, is more of a web-like pattern dancing across the corpus callosum (hopefully your favorite new membrane!). The study found straight lines connecting synapses in the male brain, diagonal lines connecting those in the female brain. And indeed, while my experience has shown that overall men reach decisions faster, women will factor in more details to influence a more robust decision. Women tend to consider a higher number of potential scenarios, asking additional questions such as, Have you thought about this? What if that happens? How will it work when other departments get involved?

Remember we talked earlier about neuroplasticity, or brain plasticity – the brain's ability to change and reorganize in response to life's circumstances. Women's brains can be conditioned to link linearly as well. I was part of a group of women who planned an entire girls' weekend, including booking flights, making hotel reservations, and putting down deposits on vineyard tours in Napa Valley, in 17 minutes flat. That was some swift linear thinking! I've also seen extremely well-executed business plan pitches and revenue forecasts delivered by men and women alike. Both did a fine job assembling information on the fly and organizing myriad details. We're certainly equipped to respond to our environments.

The important implication is that no two of us thinks exactly alike. Something that appears very obvious to you may take someone else a little longer to process. It's not necessarily an indication of higher intelligence or strategic thinking. The other person's wiring is simply different. Yet it does present an opportunity to incorporate someone else's thought process in order to enrich our own.

If you find yourself stuck making a decision, and your web-pattern thinking is taking longer than a spider weaving away in order to capture his dinner, a simple tool can force linear thinking: a timer. Consider incorporating a timer during deliberations, whether you're part of a group reaching for consensus, or working alone. Agree on terms, start the timer, and when the sand in the hourglass is gone, so to speak, votes must be cast for each person's decision. Count them up, acknowledge the winner, and move on.

Work together, not against each other, and everyone will be much happier!

Stereotype #5: Men and women have different languages.
TRUE or FALSE?

Have you ever noticed how guys use criticism, sarcasm, and teasing as a façade when they're actually complimenting each other?

Tim pulls up to Scott's house in his 2002 pickup truck. Scott greets Tim with a firm handshake, perhaps the one-armed hug plus strong double-pat on the back, and says, "Hey, man, you still drive that piece of sh*t?"

Tim returns the taunt playfully. "Yeah, she does the job better than the Domino's driver who's obviously been showing up here every night! Been hitting the pie pretty hard lately, huh, Scott?" Referring, of course, to the extra pounds Scott might or might not have packed on since he last saw Tim. And they both laugh, probably push each around another a little, then proceed inside.

Imagine Tim and Scott are women. Would we ever, in a gazillion years, greet each other this way? Referring to how awful one's car is or teasing that the other's looking heavy (gasp!)? Oh my gosh, NO. 100 times over, no, never. In my experience with other women who don't engage in catty behavior, our greetings tend to be much more congenial and come from a place of genuine truth. "Your hair looks fantastic." "Your heels are phenomenal." "Your last social media post was on point."

The approaches are totally different, and it's totally okay. They have a language. We have a language. And our two languages often don't always translate directly. Women can certainly give men a hard time, though maybe not with the punch a man would bring, and men tend to interpret a *little* smack talk from women as funny and complimentary. But when a man tries it on a woman? Picture Scott greeting his friend Sarah in that same manner, making fun of her beater car. Imagine Sarah going at Scott as hard as Tim did, giving him a hard time about his six-pack relocating from the vicinity of his abs to the refrigerator. Google Translator doesn't quite have this one figured out.

As a woman in business, I've had to translate "guy-speak" to understand the intended meaning of a sarcastic comment that came my way. After initially thinking *WTH?* or nursing hurt feelings in silence, I often realized that what I interpreted as a shot was actually intended as a compliment, falling into the category of you-only-tease-the-people-you-like.

This is where having a sense of humor is helpful. Everyone's tolerance and thresholds are different, and you have to honor yours. Personally, I enjoy witty banter and have a generally dry sense of humor. When I get a compliment in guy-speak, as long as there is no disrespect, I assume the giver of the "compliment" means well, it's just that he's unaware how guy-speak doesn't always jump gender boundaries. If a line has been crossed or a barrier pushed too far, though, I'll speak up right away and say something like, "Uh-uh, can't go there, buddy." I usually receive a sincere apology on the spot. Then we all move along.

(Note: Maintaining your boundaries and self-respect are absolutely paramount here. If someone has crossed a line and made you uncomfortable in a way you're not comfortable handling on your own, first, do what you need to do to get to a safe place. Then report it to your manager or take whatever step your company's harassment policy dictates. Don't remain quiet if it's impacting you.)

On the lighter side, when my friend and business colleague John broke his thumb, he asked me to take his place on a 65-mile charity bicycle ride for the American Association of Diabetes. He and I had ridden together on a team the summer before. This time, though, it was a last minute decision. I hadn't trained for it.

So I hesitated when John practically begged me to ride for him. The event was scheduled for the weekend after I'd returned from my honeymoon. Clearly my time had been occupied by other things that summer!

I rationalized it in my head. It wasn't a timed ride; it was for charity. What was the worst that could happen? I thought. *Well, I won't set any record for speed. I only have to commit to being on a bike for a few hours and help John honor his fundraising goal.* Ample training or not, I agreed to the ride and John was very grateful.

On ride day, as predicted, I was not fast whatsoever. As I approached a rest stop, *way* toward the back of the pack, there was John waiting to greet me. I rolled in, already exhausted, trying to summon more energy to finish the remaining 21 miles. John marched up and delivered some straight up, ill-timed guy-speak.

"Well, grandma was slow, but she's old!" he smirked at me.

I honestly don't remember if I responded out loud, but my inner monologue erupted. I saw not one molecule of humor in John's crack. I took it very literally and felt angry, irritated, and hurt. *You've got to be kidding me. What a jerk! I do this favor for him, both of us knowing that I was not prepared, and this is the greeting I get? What the hell, man?* Usually I can meet and match a sarcastic comment with one at least as spicy, but this time my tank was empty. I think I just shook my head a bit, took the water John had ready, and pedaled on.

It bugged me for the next five miles or so, then I truly had to let it go. If I wanted to reach the finish line, there was no excess mental energy to spare. And there was no way I was going to let John's stupid comment compromise my feel-good moment crossing the finish line – my only mental reward for riding that day in the first place.

Weeks later, I was telling my parents this story. When I got to John's punch line, so to speak, I wish I could've recorded Mom's and Dad's simultaneous reactions. At exactly the same moment my dad laughed and my mom, horrified, clicked her tongue with that "shame on him" maneuver all moms have. "That's so mean!" Mom exclaimed, while Dad, a retired firefighter and a guy's guy, chuckled: "No, no, no. It's funny! He was just having fun with you."

I paused to think about this, and also consider the completely fine and normal relationship John and I had both before and after the race. I realized Dad was right. John spoke to me as if I were one of the guys, not sensing our imaginary language barrier. He was just trying to be funny and tease me. In his way, trying to *help* me by offering some jest. I also acknowledged that when that exhausted, with a fading performance level, and confidence shot, my sensitivity level was off the charts. Had I been crushing that race, well, John probably wouldn't have made that particular comment, and even if he had I probably would have laughed, realizing he was playfully teasing me.

Two entire years later, John and I were catching up over coffee and I told him all I've just told you including my initial reaction and the part about my parents. John was mortified. "What? Oh my gosh, no! Jamie, I would never have said something mean to you! Especially considering your lack of training, I thought you were doing great! Oh, my gosh! I am so sorry." Obviously, I forgave him on the spot, and we both walked away with a lesson learned on communication!

So be mindful, my friends: An audience responds best when the language they hear is a dialect they know. And we each have slightly different accents and attitudes, so choose words and timing wisely and be open to different interpretations that may exceed the language you currently know. It's a learning opportunity.

When in doubt, enlist the help of a translator – a close friend of your opposite gender!

Summing It Up

What do you think? What differences would you add to the list and identify as opportunities to embrace the differences and work with them, rather than against? This list of common workplace differences could go on much longer. The goal of this chapter, however, is to acknowledge how brain anatomy and socialization affect communication and comprehension. No two of us are the same, choosing to be different. We are all naturally different and can choose to see the beauty and advantage in it. Nobody has a license to be mean or disrespectful. Yet we all have opportunities to broaden our own thinking about flowing with differences rather than fighting them. Perhaps doing so will lead to better ideas or solutions than you thought possible.

I choose (in most cases) to be fascinated, not flustered, by gender differences! If you're as intrigued as I am, I want to recommend two of my favorite books on the subject. The first: *Why Men Don't Listen and Women Can't Read Maps: How We're Different and What to Do About It,* by Allan and Barbara Pease. The second is by my good friend Caroline Turner. It's called *Difference Works: Improving Retention, Productivity and Profitability through Inclusion.* Both are excellently insightful reads.

My main takeaway from all of the gender studies and books I've read, along with first-hand experiences and observations, is that God had a reason for creating men and women as such different creatures. And that reason was not so He can plop down in His celestial La-Z-Boy, toss some popcorn in His mouth, and laugh at the entertainment provided by men and women attempting to co-work and cohabitate in harmony. Rather, that our differences present an opportunity:

Learn from each other. Respect each other. Support each other.
Make better decisions together.

We can choose to be frustrated by gender differences, or we can relish opportunities to see entirely different points of view. I prefer the latter. I also prefer to share the wine, no matter who's hunting and bringing home the meat.

What's at Stake?

The reward of embracing and working with differences rather than suffering in frustration and inhibiting productivity by resisting them.

Key Points

- Women and men are different. (Duh.) But, for real, our brains are actually wired differently.
- Embracing differences will leave you far more satisfied and productive.
- Awareness of differences in thinking and language is hugely helpful for effective communication.
- Mutual respect is paramount for everyone's success.

Confidence Challenge Checklist

- ❏ Pay attention to differences and identify what you see in your work environment.
- ❏ Brainstorm how to work with the differences. Learn from them.
- ❏ Have a light-hearted conversation with your team about gender differences and brainstorm the advantages.
- ❏ Embrace *your* key characteristics and define your unique contributions.
- ❏ Watch the movie *The Female Brain*, found on several video streaming websites. Great insight and laughs, guaranteed!

To condition and claim my confidence, one action I commit to is:

_____

_____

_____

Chapter 9

Speak Up and Win a Trip to Las Vegas!

As you know by now, I once worked for an automotive paint company. For about a two year peiod, Matt was my manager and he was awful. To keep my sanity, I often framed Matt's actions on the job as prime examples of what I myself would never do later in my career, when I progressed to management level.

Matt had just two direct reports: Myself and a guy whose name was, get this, Guy. So help me.

Don, who outranked Matt on the company organizational chart, forwarded me an invitation to attend a Women's Industry Network conference in Chicago. I loved the idea, and would need Matt's approval as a formality. When I did a little research before approaching him, I discovered he had not only known about the conference and not told me, but even worse, that he had submitted approval for *Guy* to attend instead of me – so he could speak on a panel about Lean Operating.

I was infuriated for two reasons. Why did Guy get to go to a women's conference while I got overlooked? And why should Guy get the slot on the Lean Operating panel when I had just completed a graduate level class on that very subject? I was even coaching customers on it! Grrr. I was incensed.

But my fury was beside the point. I knew what I had to do. I needed to speak up and stand up for myself. I was not going to let this go, nor let Matt get away with this BS.

I planned my timing and practiced my words and approached Matt. I calmly asked if he recalled that I was freshly schooled on Lean Operating. He approved all my classes so he 100% knew but acted surprised.

"Oh, no, you did? I must have forgotten," said Matt.

"And you also know that I'm a woman, and this is a *Women's* Industry

Conference?" (As much as I wanted to add some tone to this statement, I kept it neutral. Wasn't easy.)

Matt silently nodded.

"Don recommended that I go," I continued, indulging in a strategic name drop. "And I'd like to volunteer to speak on the panel in place of Guy. It doesn't really make sense for both of us to attend, given our budget. I'll be able to participate in the entire conference, not just the panel discussion, like Guy was planning."

After some moments of silence and staring, I was approved – and interested to later find out that Guy couldn't have cared less. "Jamie, it makes way more sense for you to attend this than me," he said. Right?!

A few weeks later, I attended the event. The conference was amazing and our Lean Operating panel was such a hit that all five participants were invited to the national conference, on a company-paid trip to Las Vegas a few months later.

So who knew that by speaking up, you could win a trip to Las Vegas?!?

The longer term prize, of course, is affirming the value of speaking up. It's a clear demonstration of standing up for yourself and showcasing your self-worth. The people whose opinions matter, the ones whom you respect, will recognize your power. And of all the people on that list, the most important one is you!

Think of speaking up, using your own real, organic voice box, as a top-tier, Level One workplace skill. It's essential to career success. Remember the Gifts of Confidence back in Chapter 2? Confidence gives you a voice. Sure, you can demonstrate your contributions electronically via email, Slack, or the company intranet. Yet contributing verbally, in a group setting, is a critical and killer way to up your game. When you find the courage to share the brilliance inside your head, you feel your own value rise. The more you practice, the faster you'll recover if your contribution may not be the most earth-shattering idea ever. Big deal. When you show no remorse by moving along, you'll carry everyone else to move right along as well.

A quick note for introverts! You don't have to be the loudest one in the room. So here's some empowered-woman-to-empowered-woman straight talk: You may not use "But I'm an introvert" as an excuse to not speak up.

Yes, those zany extroverts can sometimes overtake a conversation and may actually put themselves at a disadvantage with their own voluminous talking. Saying too much can dilute whatever really important things they say. But we'll let them worry about that as they network with ease at the next industry happy hour. Introverts have a hidden advantage over the extroverts, though: When you speak, people will listen. I know saying the right thing is important to you. Please know that the vast majority of the time, what you say will earn you respect and appreciation around the table. You are a thinker and you are smart. People will value what you have to say. Even a calculated but off-target response gets you on the board, and you have to get on the board in order to play the game. It's your turn. Play the game and have fun doing it!

Top Ten Tips for Speaking Up

Let's verbalize our brilliance and show 'em what we've got. Here are ten tips to draw out that inner monologue, create visibility and build confidence in speaking up!

1. **Think through it**

    Preparation will serve you well. Rare is the meeting that you have no prior knowledge of what will be discussed. Take some time, even a minute or two, beforehand to think through how the conversation could go and where you can contribute. Meet with the organizer ahead of time, even casually popping into his or her office and asking for their thoughts on the meeting. Offer some of your thoughts right then. The feedback you get will give you time to revise, if need be, and extra confidence that you're on the right track.

2. **Speak up early**

    Don't let anxiety build as you sit there in silence. The longer you wait, the harder it will be to contribute, and the more likely it is that someone else may "steal" your thoughts. The one contribution that puts no points on the board for you is, "I was going to say that!" Say something early, even if it's just, "Clare, will you repeat the question? I want to better understand what you're asking."

3. **Try a question**

    If you can't think of a response to someone else's question, come up with a thought-provoking one of your own. For example: "How will this most directly impact the people we serve?" "How will this short-term objective affect our long-term goals?" (Or long-term objective, short-term goals. Whatever works.)

4. **Enlist an ally**

    Who else in the meeting can support you? One of my favorite examples of ally enlistment happened between Molly and Courtney. Remember Molly, who channeled her confidence and got that promotion? Well, she embodies the Sherohood in more ways than one. In a meeting with eight other engineers, Courtney, likely the smartest person in the room, was struggling to speak up. Molly knew Courtney had the answer. Instead of letting her sit there in silence, Molly helped coax it out of her, demonstrating excellent leadership characteristics in the process. For everyone to hear, Molly declared, "You know, Courtney and I were talking about this earlier. Courtney, will you share with everyone else what you shared with me?" That was the little assist Courtney needed. Out came her ideas, and she wowed the group with her suggestions. Yay, girl power! And both Molly and Courtney gained visibility.

Along similar lines, you and an ally can make a before-the-meeting arrangement to support each other if others talk over you. When you're having trouble getting a word in edgewise, make eye contact with your ally, who may already sense what's up. She can tell the group, "Hey, Melanie had a really great point. I don't think everybody heard. Melanie, will you repeat that, please?" Absolutely fantastic! The ally just cleared the way for Melanie to speak up and be heard. And again, both gain visibility

5. **Raise your hand**

   When a lively conversation has ensued, you may have to get a bit bold to interject. "Put on your big girl pants," like my friend Dana says. Raising your hand and making direct eye contact with the person currently speaking sends a silent message that you're next.

6. **Name names**

   When you want to add something, call out the person currently speaking by saying their name, then pausing to confirm they heard you. "James." (Pause until James returns your eye contact.) "I think your point is valid. I would add that my forecast shows a 5% increase in our revenue stream if we make certain adjustments." Damn, girl. James will certainly look your way for more input in the future.

7. **Point to your notes**

   While contemplating your words, scratch out some speaking notes on a notepad or piece of paper. Sentence fragments or bullets work well. Hold up the paper, or slide it out into the center of the table. Point to key words to gain attention, then say them out loud. Writing them down helps you organize your contribution, pointing to them directs the group's attention, and saying them out loud means you're speaking up. Well done!

8. **Cut in**

It's not always advised, yet when you have a particularly talkative talker on your hands, you may at some point have to interrupt. He'll have to take a breath sooner or later. That's your window to jump right in, perhaps prefacing your words with, "Excuse me. Could I have the floor?" Others in the meeting may silently thank you.

9. **Cite stats**

Here's a great fix if you're having difficulty garnering respect because someone thinks you're "too blond," "too bubbly," or "too young." Simply being friendly and enthusiastic can be unfairly judged as flakiness. Thankfully there is a stop-them-in-their-tracks solution I can sum up in one word: Statistics.

Commit a few industry stats to memory – Google up some numbers and learn the context around the data. And share with authority. Not only do you *sound* smart, you *are* smart because you've taken the time to dig into numbers and data. It's an almost surefire way to earn credibility and silence your naysayers. Showing you can rattle off something like a statistic I lifted directly off of the Solar Energy Industry Association website, "As of Fall 2019, nearly 250,000 Americans work in solar - more than double the number in 2012 - at more than 10,000 companies in every U.S. state. In 2019, the solar industry generated $18.7 billion of investment in the American economy." A little of this can take you a long way. Choose something relevant to your role and your audience. Commit a few stats to memory and you'll be able to use them repeatedly.

ProTip: Make sure it's a stat and a subject that's genuinely interesting to you. Learn the context around it. It will help with the natural flow of the conversation as well as any follow up questions.

10. **Remember why you're at the table**

Sometimes you might need to give yourself some tough love. Your inner voice may just need to say, "Suck it up, Sister!" I promise that if you use the tips above, speaking up gets easier. I also promise this skill is way too vital to ignore. Your career may depend on it. Always keep in mind that your employer chose you. They specifically selected you over other candidates and are paying you to be there. You wouldn't have been invited aboard if someone didn't think you were smart, competent, and clever. Prove them right! You've earned your way in. You've come too far to sit there quietly and allow someone else to surpass you simply because they can speak up. You earned it, so do it!

How to say No

As women, we tend to take on a lot. Generally speaking, as the more nurturing, people-pleasing gender, we want to help and do as much as we can. The risk in doing so, however, is that we neglect ourselves and allow other priorities to take precedence over our own.

Part of the struggle between yes and no is that saying no can feel like we're personally denying someone, even offending them. While we are humans with heads and hearts, capable of infinite thought and love, our calendars have finite capacity. Time is one thing no one, not even Elon Musk, can buy more of.

A calendar is an unfeeling organizational tool; it won't care how you use it. Leverage it to say no. Recently I've discovered the beauty of time-blocking my calendar. Before a new week begins, I reserve time for appointments, responding to emails, working on reports, etc. I also block in flex time, which I reserve for whatever I deem most important at that moment. Flex time is a legitimate appointment I make with myself.

Time-blocking allows you to turn down new invitations without guilt. "I'm sorry, my calendar is time-blocked then."

You can suggest an alternative time convenient for you – or just say no and offer no explanation. A simple, "I can't do that right now," might be OK, too. Circumstances will help guide your response. Remember, though, it's your choice!

What if your manager wants you to perform a task or attend an event, that creates difficulty for you, yet complying is part of your job description? You won't necessarily be able to say no – but you do have options. Let's say your calendar is booked, or you were planning to work on a separate project. A good response starts with two specific words, "Yes, and..." Then cite the commitments you're already working on and ask your manager, "What's the bigger priority?"

For example, you're asked to submit a Performance Plan Update (PPU) earlier than usual, by 4:00 pm today. You were planning to work on a Women's Empowerment Group (WEG) project. You can respond, "Yes, I can do that. I had dedicated that time to make progress on the WEG. What is the bigger priority?" Ideally, you get a straightforward answer to your straightforward question. "Oh, okay, yes finish that first." Or, you may hear something like, "I really need the PPU first." Either way, you can respond accordingly.

Success Tip: When you speak up and say no to something, remember what you are simultaneously saying *yes* to in the bargain.

By saying no to one request you may very well be saying yes to your higher priority work duties or healthier eating choices. You know how many times I've been teased at work dinners for choosing a healthy option? Tons. I'm saying no to their peer pressure and yes to my own values and self-worth for how I take care of my body. They're not taking that away from me. No way.

In saying no to one thing you maybe be saying yes to your kids and pets. To your club soccer team. To your quality of life. Time marked for yourself. You can reframe a no from negative to positive by remembering what other priority you're honoring by saying yes to it. You're protecting it. It ultimately boils down to what's more important to you and honoring that.

Ask for What You Want

What's the worst that can happen when you ask for what you want? Seriously. Getting comfortable with directly asking for what you want is huge! At work, in personal relationships, or anywhere, it will save a whole lotta time, and it's the most logical way to get what you want. You can't expect anyone to read your mind.

As you get in to a habit of this, you'll quickly learn that it's fairly standard to hear a mix of responses, some that affirm your ask and some that deny it. Both can be good things. You'll become more comfortable in not taking the outcome personally and experience that sometimes hearing a no is a prelude for hearing a yes to something else.

The next section of the book goes deeper into this, as does Chapter 14, which covers high-stakes communication. In the meantime, here are five rapid-fire Pro Tips for Asking for What You Want:

- *Write up what you want and why you deserve it.* This will help get your thoughts organized. Bring a hard copy to your "ask meeting." It will help calm nerves and demonstrate that you're serious. Afterwards, be prepared to follow up with an email summarizing what you discussed.

- Have a *practice conversation* with someone who will play devil's advocate with you – someone who will push back and ask tough questions. You'll be even better prepared.

- Set the scene for collaboration with a *positive tone*. Starting on the defensive sets you up for failure. Go in on the proactive, positive side and keep your tone in check no matter how the conversation goes. Remember, as humans we naturally mirror others. Transmitting positivity can generate reciprocal good vibes.

- *Timing* can be everything. Be thoughtful about the time of day you choose. The one that is the least busy/stressful for both parties is best.

- *Labeling the meeting* is important too. Book a meeting on your decision maker's work calendar and call it something like "Strategy Session about Career Development." If it's not your first exchange, maybe state the subject more boldly: "Discuss increase in compensation." This is your judgment call, though, as personalities and specific circumstances will dictate the details.

I once heard a representative from the Women's Forum say one reason for the continual gender gap in compensation is because women just don't ask for the same money men do. We have to ask to get what we want and what we deserve.

A friend just shared her success story with me over coffee. Her company had made an acquisition, doubling the assets she managed. She recognized that, because of this, she was no longer getting paid market rate. After writing a carefully crafted, well-researched letter, she prepared to present her "ask" to the board. She practiced, she stayed positive and professional, and scheduled the meeting for a time when she knew her boss, the CEO, would be present and focused. She asked for more than she expected, assuming they'd meet her somewhere in the middle. Her strategy worked! She got what she wanted and then some. Atta girl!

Bring in da No's!

A moment ago I said a no can be merely a prelude to a yes. Hearing a no is sometimes associated with hurting feelings, taking a personal offense, or seeing nothing but a dead end ahead. Here are four reasons why one should set aside the sulking to celebrate instead!

First, a no means you spoke up – you asked for something big – and that's awesome! Keep it up! You can only have that which you ask for, and if your success rate on this is 100%, you're not asking big enough. Congratulate yourself for having the courage to ask in the first place.

Second, a no today doesn't mean no forever. It could mean "Not right now." I coached my sales teams on this all the time. Maybe the manager you've identified as your lead is too busy with other things and this is not a priority at the moment.

Maybe a new manager in that role, or a change in company priorities or policy, could turn the no into a yes. While a no can be frustrating in the moment, if it's really important and you keep pursuing it, you might eventually get your yes. A no can be an indication to change course, not cancel the whole trip. Consider that:

Rejection is redirection.

Third, a no might be protecting you from a bad outcome or setting up a better one. In the moment, it might be tough to see. "No, you can't have that promotion." *Because I have a better one in store for you.* "No, you can't work with that client." *Because I want you on a different project that will be a better leadership opportunity.* From a spiritual perspective, I've heard God telling me 'No' a whole variety of times. Sometimes I figure out the "why" later, sometimes I don't. Yet I must trust in a bigger, better, more beautiful – if sometimes mysterious – plan, and be thankful for another opportunity to celebrate my weakest virtue: good ol' patience.

Lastly, there's always a lesson within a no. Could I have approached that differently? Did I choose the right words? The right timing? Did I really have the information I needed to present the comprehensive plan and its benefits? The answers may just be the bridge you need to turn that no to a yes.

As a general rule, think about two things when you hear a no. Ask if the outcome you sought is worth pursuing further – and imagine a better yes!

And keep in mind that NO is simply a grammatically incorrect acronym for 'Nother Opportunity!

The Art of Disagreeing

At last we've come to one of the best and most crucial workplace skills of all: disagreeing.

You remember I confessed to a huge crush on Supreme Court Justice Ruth Bader Ginsburg. RBG. She is one of my all-time favorite Sheroes for a multitude of reasons, one being her finesse in disagreeing. As she so eloquently put it,

"You can disagree without being disagreeable."

She rocks at disagreeing. RBG has an extraordinary ability to thrive in disagreement, to be assertive without being aggressive. She was close friends with fellow Justice Antonin Scalia, a pillar of the Court's conservative wing. The two interpreted the United States Constitution in vehemently different ways. They held intense, contentious debates! Neither concealed their opinions, nor backed down when challenged. It could be uncomfortable and heated. There were stalemates when neither would retreat. RBG flexed those disagreement muscles harder than the winner of the Tough Man Contest and never flinched. Simultaneously, though. RBG and Scalia had the utmost respect for each other and were best friends. At Scalia's funeral, RBG delivered the eulogy for her dear and respected friend. She shared one of her favorite quotes of his. "I attack ideas. I don't attack people. If you can't separate the two, you need to get a different day job." Well said, Justice Scalia, well said.

Disagreeing can be SO uncomfortable. What can be even more uncomfortable, though, is biting your lip and suppressing your ideas. It can feel like a bowl of lava bubbling in your stomach, on the verge of eruption. People who express disagreement poorly can make the other party feel they've been personally devalued or invalidated, if they don't know how to put up their confidence shield. Yet disagreeing with confidence and finesse, like RBG does, is a very effective way to communicate your opinion, especially when you feel outnumbered in a discussion, or like a lone salmon swimming against the resistance. Productive disagreement takes effort and guts, and is certainly attainable when approached in the right way.

What You Can Control

When you're standing out there on the disagreement firing range you have no control over the critic who's taking aim. You can't control others, their words, their delivery, or their ideas. Say it with me: "I cannot control others." What you can control, however, is your own reaction to and interpretation of what is said to you. You can certainly control the way you deliver contrary information, ideas, and suggestions. So rather than focus on what you can't control, home in on developing the courage to disagree diplomatically and productively.

So how do you disagree productively in a contentious environment? Start with what you already know. Do not take things personally. Try to remove whatever emotion, tone, or superfluous signals you could be unintentionally sending, and focus on the factual content of your idea. There have been times when I know my opinion or idea sounded perfectly logical in my head, yet when I verbalized it, it came out defensive or whiny. Dammit. Not my proudest moments and certainly not the way to project confidence.

The good news is that through preparation and practicing, you can train your brain to communicate in more neutral tones.

One of the main ways to cut your odds of looking like an attacker, and convey that you want to remain on the same team, is by speaking in a neutral tone at an appropriate volume. It frames your response as logical and organized. Is this easy? Maybe not at first. It takes practice. How successful you are will likely depend on how your day is going, where your confidence level is that day, and who's disagreeing with you. Concentrating on what you can control rather than what you can't – and we have full control over how we project in the moment, even if we have to go scream in a pillow later. Maintain a level-headed persona and earn respect for keeping your cool

When someone else is arguing hotly, resist the urge to match the escalation. Use it as an excellent opportunity to demonstrate leadership characteristics by staying in control, keeping your cool and silently inviting them to meet your vibration, rather than sink to theirs. And, by all means, high-five and fist-bump later with anyone who noticed and appreciated your mad skillz. Atta girl!

Tips for Disagreeing

The rewards of disagreeing well and the risks of NOT disagreeing are both significant. If you react poorly every time someone disagrees with you, you'll find yourself invited into fewer meetings and asked to contribute less often. Being left out could stifle advancement in your career. On the flip side, when you're too agreeable, you might be pegged as a me-too player, going along with other peoples' ideas without offering many of your own. Fulfill your responsibilities by sharing your amazing ideas and creative views, even, and especially, when they may differ from what's already been presented.

Mustering the courage to disagree gets easier and feels a whole lot more natural when you have resources to do so. Use the following tips to achieve RBG-level status for productive disagreement.

Word and tone choices are everything

When presenting a differing viewpoint, begin in ways that are neither argumentative nor suggestive of stepping into the ring with Rhonda Rousey! If you want to be contentious, you could certainly lead with, "You're wrong." "That's a bad idea." "My idea is much better than yours." If you want to err on the side of collaboration, however, consider sending better signals.

If you're not yet comfortable directly saying, "I disagree," insert one very important adverb.

"I politely disagree." (Pause.) "And here's why…"

Something about inserting the word "politely" makes it just that: Polite. Respectful. I use this one a lot. It's a great way to disarm. It implies harmony between the two of you and doesn't put anyone on the defensive. Sometimes I change out the word 'politely' with *respectfully*. "I respectfully disagree." Years ago, when I read the book, *Men are from Mars, Women are from Venus*, it taught me that women want to be loved and men want to be respected. So even in a moment of disagreement, as long as someone feels respected, you're likely clearing a path for moving forward together.

Try these clear, unaggressive expressions when you want to soften what could be a bold and polarizing statement. Or when you're a bit intimidated to share a unique idea, yet committed to doing so as you convey confidence and respect.

"I have a different idea."
"I have another idea."
"Have you thought about it this way?"

Be inclusive

If your meeting has a high intensity level, or you're particularly intimidated by someone, you can deflect by deferring to a group that's not even present. Let's say you work for a nonprofit, and the meeting is to debate new standards that will impact the people you serve. Instead of directly disagreeing with someone else's opposing idea, you can shift focus by saying, "Let's consider how the (children, homeless, refugees, etc.) might feel or interpret *our* messaging if we go with that idea." Notice you used the word *our*, not *your*, in that statement. It's inclusive, of course. You're demonstrating your alignment with the team, and simultaneously opening the group up to other ideas, to reach a decision that will best serve those affected. Go you! You're such a woke strategist!

Negotiating 101

In particularly heated meetings, you may want to employ some Negotiating 101 tactics.

- First, acknowledge and confirm agreement on the end goal that everyone wants to achieve. **"I think we can all agree that launching a successful campaign in order to reach 35,000 people is our common goal."** Pause and look the others in the eye while nodding your own head. Get their buy-in. Once you've disarmed the group by achieving agreement on something, the campaign goal in this example, move on to your next statement.

- **"And having that shared goal in mind I believe we need to consider _____ as an option."** Using "and" not "but" and "consider" are very powerful, persuasive choices. They support cohesion among the group and virtually assure continued conversation.

Phrases that pay

These phrases disarm aggression, encourage continuity, and allow you to share your ideas, popular or not, in a way others will perceive as accretive and valuable, not offensive, disrespectful, or condescending. You'll be amazed at the agreements you can reach when you frame your disagreements well!

"We could also agree that our beliefs and opinions are always evolving, as are the circumstances around our launch. In light of that, I want to suggest that _____."

"I believe we have the responsibility to evaluate all angles."

"It's important for us to hear all sides because that's how we make informed decisions and advance the most comprehensive, well thought out plan."

"I think we can all agree that none of us has a crystal ball and there's room for uncertainty."

Practice your statements ahead of time. If you need to, make a cheat sheet. Take a screenshot of this page and keep it on your phone. Test out your disarming statements and see how they go! Remember the risks that come with keeping your valuable ideas and creative views locked up inside. They're just too high for you not to give it a shot!

The Benefits

When you disagree productively using strategic, disarming words and a neutral tone, you will likely achieve several results.

First, you'll shift your own mentality away from contentiousness and toward collaboration – away from unhealthy competition and toward contribution. You'll be adding value rather than regretting saying the wrong thing to the wrong person at the wrong time or not saying anything at all!

Second, there's a good chance the disagreement gets acknowledged and even appreciated as a positive contribution. You'll see yourself as helpful rather than obstructive and banish the self-doubt that can arise if you feel you're attacking the person rather than simply disagreeing with what they have to say. You'll see yourself working proactively rather than defensively, making important progress, and gaining confidence.

Finally, what's really neat about instilling a culture of welcoming disagreement is that it becomes a very fluid and natural part of communication. Whether the environment is personal or professional. You know it's really starting to work when an absence of disagreement feels like something is missing. Offering disagreement can now simply be thought of as a contribution to help reach a more comprehensive decision. It may even feel like a violation of communication rules when people hold back their opinions. So consider it your mission, your duty, your *professional responsibility*, to make your opinion heard! Flip the paradigm on its head – and make disagreeing the norm rather than the exception.

Wouldn't you agree? And if you don't, I sure hope you'll tell me! In a respectful, level-headed manner, of course!

Who's the Bravest of Them All?

Remember Brave-ah-na, the feeling first described way back in the introduction of this book and defined in the quote at the beginning of this chapter? Next time you see an opportunity has arisen to achieve Brave-ah-na, know that there is a fail-safe technique for motivation to get there.

You know you want to. You know you need to. You know you must speak up. You must stand your ground. Stick up for yourself, yet you're still a bit afraid.

It's time to shove that fear aside!

So, as you ready yourself, Brave-ah-na in your reach, your go-to technique is this...Picture an imaginary person staring up at you. And that imaginary person is your daughter, your future daughter, your niece, the little girl you used to babysit, or even the 4-year-old version of you.

Can you picture her as she looks up at you with her big, beautiful eyes? Her little hands are clasped with anticipation. She's quiet. You have her full attention and she's waiting to see what you do. She's waiting to see the example you set for her to someday follow. She waits in suspense and with the hope that she'll see your bravery in action, so that she too can be brave. Just like you.

So if you're struggling to do it for *yourself*, do it for *her* and in the name of the Sherohood at large.

And get ready, girlfriend, because the euphoric feeling of Brave-ah-na awaits you on the other side!

What's at Stake?

Girl, everything! Speaking up is a crucial skill for creating visibility, sharing original thought, demonstrating your value, and solidifying success in your career!

Key Points

- There's no turning back. You simply have to try and try again. A misstep is still a step and will likely be far less awful than you think.
- You get to say yes to something you prioritize when you say no to something else.
- You must ask for what you want.
- Disagreement is a means of reaching a better solution and can be done in an agreeable and collaborative fashion.

Confidence Challenge Checklist

- ❏ The next time your inner monologue is prompting you, give it a shot and speak up!
- ❏ Share your speaking up experience with a friend and celebrate your success together.
- ❏ Take the Rejection Challenge – Every day for one week, ask a question to which you expect to hear "No."
- ❏ Disagree! Use the phrases provided in this chapter to insert your valuable opinions and ideas in the next planning meeting.
- ❏ Ask for it! What have you been wanting yet haven't mustered up the courage to ask for? Follow the preparation steps and ask for it. No matter the answer, it's now on the record. You know the outcome and that's much more than you knew before!

To condition and claim my confidence, one action I commit to is:

_____

_____

_____

Chapter 10
The Magic of Making Mistakes

For several years I've belonged to a wonderful organization in Denver called the Women in Oil and Gas Association, or WOGA. WOGA's mission is to "encourage and empower the next generation of women leaders" in the energy industry. Our bi-monthly luncheons feature great speakers and alternate between technical topics and the Lean In Series – the latter inspired, of course, by Sheryl Sandberg's Lean-In movement. Recently a WOGA board member and friend, Lia, asked if I wouldn't mind assuming speaker duty, and offered a list of topics in the Lean-In category. I could pick any one I liked.

One topic on the list stood out.

It's Okay to Make Mistakes: Courage to rise after making a mistake; getting out of one's comfort zone.

I had to laugh. My inner voice spoke up: "Mistakes, eh? Did Lia offer me this topic because she thinks I make a lot of mistakes? Or maybe that I'm good at making mistakes? Ha! What's really behind this?" Good thing I know not to take it personally!

When I reported this to Lia, we had a good laugh. "No, I thought of you when I saw the 'courage' part," she smiled. Ohhhh! Funny how the positive things others see in us are sometimes hidden from our own view of ourselves. Now I was flattered and thought, "Great! Game on!" This chapter is a reprise of on the talk I presented to the incredible women of WOGA.

Taking the "Ache" Out of Mistakes

Why is there a backspace key on keyboards? Why is the shortcut CTRL + Z so frequently used? And why do pencils have erasers? Yep, you guessed it; because people make mistakes.

We *all* make mistakes. They're part of life. Just as he who is without sin is free to cast the first stone, none of us can say we made it through life mistake-free! And thank God! In the moment it occurs, a mistake might not feel like a place of growth, learning, nor a steppingstone to something better. Yet when managed properly, it can serve as gunpowder to shoot you forward. Mistakes can be catalysts to help you see challenges in a whole new light and become a stronger, more confident woman.

As surely as you'll encounter bad weather, traffic, and that difficult co-worker, mistakes are going to happen. The more we learn to work with them rather than against them, though, the more transformative they become!

Here's how to turn gulps ... into gifts.

Re-Framing from Bad to Good

As you learn to re-think and re-frame mistakes, you'll find that making them is not so much a sign that you did something wrong as much as a signal that you're on the right track. True story. Let that sink in. Mistakes are how you learn. Good judgment and decision making comes from making mistakes and reflecting on them – evaluating what turned out unexpectedly and how you can do better next time. When your focus shifts to what you learned instead of what you lost, it preserves and even bolsters your confidence.

Wisdom is knowledge you can gain from making mistakes.[1]

2004 Nobel Prize winner Frank Wilczek professed, "If you don't make mistakes, you're not working on hard enough problems. And that would be a mistake." Oprah has insight on mistakes as well: "Failure is a great teacher, and, if you are open to it, every mistake has a lesson to offer." She also advises, "Learn from every mistake because every experience, particularly your mistakes, is there to teach you and force you into being more of who you are."

Or as a ski instructor once told me, "If you didn't fall, then you weren't trying hard enough." Falling is only a failure if you don't get back up.

In his book *Tribes*, the bestselling author and marketing guru Seth Godin has this to say about being wrong:

The secret to being wrong isn't to avoid being wrong!

The secret is being willing to be wrong.

1 Ashley Fern, "Why You Need To Learn From Your Mistakes",Elite Daily, June 11, 2013, https://www.elitedaily.com/life/why-you-need-to-learn-from-your-mistakes

The secret is realizing that wrong isn't fatal. The only thing that makes people and organizations great is their willingness to be not great along the way. The desire to fail on the way to reaching a bigger goal is the untold secret of success. [2]

Mistakes and failures lead to dead ends only if you allow them to die off there. Instead of attending their funeral, plan a revival. Celebrate what you learned and what you'll refine the next time.

Our world has benefited from everyday products born from mistakes. I bet there are a few items you enjoy that you had no idea started out as mistakes. You'll be so relieved that they were not dismissed as dead ends.

Consider the lowly tea bag. In June of 1908, a New York tea dealer, Thomas Sullivan, cut his costs by putting sample pinches of loose leaves in tea-for-one sized silk pouches and sent them off to potential customers. They were perplexed by the little silk packages (you couldn't ask Siri for help back then), and decided to dunk them in hot water. The tea brewed, and voila! The tea bag was born.

Raw rubber, a 19th century sensation when discovered, nonetheless remained a curiosity of little practical use until 1839, when a broke and desperate inventor accidentally spilled latex mixed with sulfur on a hot stove. The result was a strong, pliable substance, impervious to heat or cold, that had never been observed before. By chance, Charles Goodyear had come up with the vulcanization process that wound up creating tires and Goodyear's success too!

In the current era, a famous mystical book series exists only because one editor's daughter liked it. The first volume in the series was the author's first novel, and twelve publishers passed on it. Only when Bloomsbury editor Nigel Newton's 8-year-old daughter chanced upon the manuscript on her father's desk – and begged for months to know what came next – did Bloomsbury decide to publish the book. Even then, Newton advised the first-time writer to look for a backup job. The author, as you may have guessed, is J.K. Rowling, and the Harry Potter books have sold 500 million copies worldwide – all because a little girl chanced to see what so many adult Muggles rejected! I sure hope Nigel Newton treated his daughter to ice cream on the company dime!

And the all-time king of productive mistakes was Thomas Edison, the 19th-century genius who gave us the light bulb, sound recording, electricity transmission, and so much more.

2 Seth Godin 2008, *Tribes,* New York: Penguin Group

Edison was a proud, self-proclaimed mistake maker. The way he framed them in his mind led to cutting-edge successes we all continue to enjoy almost a century and a half later. Edison has some brilliant quotes which capture his philosophy on mistakes. "Many of life's failures are people who did not realize how close they were to success when they gave up." Or, in my humble attempt to paraphrase the esteemed Mr. Edison, they simply stopped short. They threw in the towel too early. They didn't have the patience, tenacity, or courage to reach a breakthrough.

Edison tried for years to come up with a workable light bulb filament. The path to success was not so well lit! "I haven't failed," he said. "I've just found 10,000 ways that it won't work." *Ten thousand mistakes* – or, rather, steps toward the ultimate goal were made in order for artificial light to shine. I did the math on it. What does 10,000 mistakes actually feel like? Here's what I found. If you and I were working on a project and made just one mistake per day in pursuit of our end goal, it would take us eight years, two and a half months to achieve success. Eight. Years. The entire length of high school and college, including summer breaks! Can you even imagine? That seems like a very long time to have to wallow in our mistakes – unless we use the power of thoughts to frame them differently.

Take a moment to consider what Edison's self-talk and mindset must have been like. Do you think he told himself, "You poser. I can't believe you messed this up again. Why do you even try? You're never going to get it right!" Or was it more along the lines of, "Okay, in the midst of what didn't work here, what did work? How can I strengthen my theory about electric light using what I just observed? What do I know now that I didn't know before? And what I wouldn't have been able to learn unless I took the next step and tried? I am one step closer to inventing artificial light! Wow, this is so exciting, I might just reward myself with some keto-friendly ice cream!"

My theory, while not nearly as complex as Edison's, is that he went with the latter, not the former, and we're all still benefitting from his results today.

One of Edison's main takeaways is that mistakes are not dead ends or video game screens flashing GAME OVER. They're simply another step toward your destination. And maybe what you think is our goal today may evolve into something completely different tomorrow as you continue down the path.

I'm a big fan of alliteration to help remember key concepts, so I looked for a word in English that's a synonym for path or journey and starts with "M" -- so when I make a mistake I can say, "It's okay! Because I'm on my *Mistake fill-in-*

the-blank-with-a-word-meaning-journey-starting-with-m." Well, I was unsuccessful. So I ventured outside English boundaries and found that in Finnish, the word for journey is *matka*. Boom. Done.

When I make a mistake, does it warrant an apology, or mean I'm a bad person, or dumb? Absolutely not. *Instead*, it means that I'm on an exotic adventure: my Mistake Matka. Much better than a dead end or GAME OVER. And as one of the audience members pointed out, "Do you think it's a coincidence that 'matka' kind of rhymes with vodka? Because maybe that could help, too!" Ha! Sounds on point to me.

The Culture of Mistakes

Along the mistake journey, or matka, it is important to note that culture – a community's, or a company's – has a big influence on how mistakes are reacted to, viewed, and handled. A study that compared education in the United States to that in China and Japan found the Asian countries were more mistake-friendly. One variable measured was students' willingness to tackle tricky math problems in front of the class. U.S. students were far less likely to do so than those in China and Japan. Why? You might find it surprising that the study didn't correlate unwillingness to IQ, but fear of embarrassment. The U.S. students were unwilling to risk making a mistake in front of the class. They sacrificed an opportunity to learn in order to salvage their pride.

Let that one sink in a minute, because this is really important. There have been times when I've refrained from doing something because of the potential for embarrassment or failure. Was it a mistake to not to get up and sing karaoke at the company happy hour? Absolutely not. That was an excellent decision. But there was that project I shied away from because I didn't feel fully prepared. In that case, not only did I miss an opportunity to learn a new skill, I watched a colleague take it on and move ahead of me. Was that a mistake? You bet. One I vowed never to repeat.

Fortunately, we have all kinds of opportunities to stretch beyond our comfort zones and try new things. Depending on our company culture, we can extend ourselves, take risks, learn, and improve our own skill sets while benefiting the company too. Before we go there, however, let's revisit the study about students in the U.S. and Asia – and consider what made the difference in performance between the two groups.

As Chinese and Japanese students worked on problems at their desks, the teacher evaluated their answers. The kid who did the worst received special treatment. He or she had to go up to the board and re-do the exercise again and again until the answer was right. And here's the best part: the other students didn't make fun of the student at the board, instead they were asked to offer support and wisdom. It turned into a team effort. They helped guide him to the correct answer. Learning was collaborative and inclusive. The process meant the kid who at first couldn't get the problem right, later had it mastered with the assistance of classmates. Any initial twinge of embarrassment or shame soon dissipated as the underdog student was embraced by his or her peers, and together they worked toward a common goal.

Getting called to the front of the room for doing poorly might be considered punishment, yet it was actually a privilege and an opportunity for a true learning experience. And I bet that kid certainly got it right the next time.

That's much different from what I experienced in school. The kid who aced the problem was asked to show the rest of the class how it was done. The kids who struggled remained seated. They saved face, but missed out on an opportunity to learn, recover from a mistake, and collaborate with classmates.

Company cultures also create environments that support or discourage mistakes. I've seen both types, and observed profound differences in employee attitudes, aptitude, and longevity. At one extreme, I worked in what I can only call an extremely toxic environment. Not only were mistakes discouraged, they were flat out not tolerated. Higher-ups held nothing back in singling out individuals guilty of mistakes in a 'Reply All' email thread, or verbally on conference calls or meetings.

It was uncomfortable, deflating, and, quite honestly, scary at times. As I was one of very few women on our team, they weren't *quite* as harsh with me as they were with the men but it certainly didn't feel like any sort of special treatment. They could be pretty darn nasty. It was by no means pleasant for any of us to endure.

The company did offer above average compensation. On especially tough days I justified the awful treatment by telling myself I'd spend my generous disposable income on a spa treatment to make myself feel better. Boy, was I wrong! No amount of external pampering can compensate for, or erase, repeated hits to your self-esteem.

While working for this company, I got married. Now I came home to a handsome, caring face – a partner who looked lovingly into my eyes and asked the normal question, "Hey, babe, how was your day?" On a few occasions, in this safe place where I could let out a day's worth of bottled-up emotions, my response did not come verbally, but with tears rolling down my cheeks.

That was my wake-up call. I'd waited longer in life than most to meet my prince. No amount of money was worth the trade-off of being regularly brought to tears. That was not the woman nor the wife I wanted to be. My self-worth was better than that, and I sure as hell wasn't going to let this company erode it. I made my plan to resign. It was a mistake to stay as long as I had.

Later, while preparing to interview with a different company, I pondered what I'd learned from my mistake. How could I find out about the "mistake culture" at my prospective employer and avoid getting myself into the same unhealthy environment?

Both companies, the one I left and the one where I was interviewing, were in growth mode. Mistakes are particularly common in such environments, because you're working in uncharted territory and things are moving fast. You're building products, procedures, and policies the company needs to survive, figuring things out as you go. It can be messy. In order to know for sure, I decided to ask directly. (Ask for what you want and ask for what you need to know!)

At the interview I asked the CFO, "Dean, how are mistakes handled in this company's culture?" He paused and looked at me. "That's an intriguing question," he said with a smile. He thought for a minute and began.

"You know, in the boardroom, in strategy meetings, I'll tell you that it can get a little heated. We're not afraid to share our opinions, and we don't always agree. Afterward though, we extend an apologetic arm when called for. And there's always renewed confirmation that we appreciate our team members. If you're a team player and contributing to the company, well, we're a family here. We shake hands, or even hug it out – in an appropriate way, of course." He smiled and I smiled, satisfied with his answer.

I was hired. Yet it wasn't until I'd worked there a while that I realized how damaging it had been for me to work at the other company, where there was no room for error, where mistakes were not tolerated. Now that I was in an environment with room to test different things, report on findings, receive input, and pursue my projects, my creativity blossomed. I was in my element and I loved the environment and culture. I could take calculated risks, succeed, and be cheered on as a hero. I could also fail, face my team to review what went wrong, and quickly correct – without being berated, yelled at, or bursting into tears upon my arrival back home that evening. It probably took several months until I felt like the old Jamie was back. And I'll tell you, I did more in my new workplace, learned more and grew more professionally, than I had with any other company. It was invigorating, critical for my confidence, and paid dividends for my employer. Even though the salary was not what it had been before, there was value for me that I could never measure in dollars.

Staying at a job where mistakes are intolerable, or you're repeatedly on the receiving end of negative, non-constructive criticism, doesn't mean you're not tough enough. While at the toxic company, I did tell myself it was a good learning experience, and I could stand to grow thicker skin. In some ways it was true, but there has to be a threshold. There has to be a limit. When your self-esteem is crushed, you're no longer trying or learning anything new, strongly consider that it's time to look for a different opportunity.

Later I learned something that shocked me, but affirmed I'd been right to leave the toxic company: I wasn't the only one who came home and cried. Several men later admitted to me that they, too, had been brought to tears on occasion. I was floored. I had no idea while I worked there just how damaging such a work environment can be to anyone, regardless of gender identity.

So the moral of the story is two-fold. One, it was a mistake that I stayed too long in a toxic environment where mistakes weren't tolerated. And, two, cultures that embrace mistakes foster much higher creativity and are much healthier for your self-esteem and confidence.

What Holds Us Back

We're often held back by the possibility of making a mistake due to our not so great friend, fear. No fear, no risk, no mistake, no failure – yet no reward, either. Mistakes generate particular discomfort among the risk-averse. Any engineers in the audience? Raise your hands high and proud. Your brilliant minds build the roads, bridges, buildings, cars, and so many other things that make our lives wonderful. Thank you! But engineers are known to be especially risk-averse. They like formulas and exact figures. They like rules and laws and physics principles. At its worst, though, risk aversion can isolate you – restrict your travel to paths someone else has already laid and tested. Staying on the safe, well-blazed trail can stifle creativity and, more importantly, prevent you from possibly inventing the next big thing!

To get around this, there is a simple fix that requires no mathematical formulas or theories whatsoever.

Engineer or not, reserve time in your calendar to think outside the box. Block off time for imaginative thinking. In that timeframe, give yourself the freedom to think about a project in a completely different way – maybe some way that doesn't even make conventional sense. Try to break it. Or maybe test a formula with different variables, regardless of how implausible the calculation might be. Give yourself latitude to explore, experiment, do something imperfectly. Maybe even aim to make a mistake. (Gasp!) Trying these things activates a part of your brain that may have missed you! It may even create mental space for you to come up with a whole new theory, or to strengthen a formula in a new way. You can, of course, go back to doing what you do after a while, but please, at least give it a try. I'd so love to see you on the cover of Time, touting your new discovery!

We're also inhibited from risking mistakes and failure because of the transparency of society today. When it feels like you work in a fishbowl, any misstep liable to be highlighted and go viral, can make you think twice about going out on a limb. With managers and peers who are impatient for results, it sometimes rushes us into a mistake, not because we didn't know better, but rather because we succumbed to pressure. Consequences of such actions can hurt a reputation, reduce credibility, or possibly even result in job loss. All the more reason to surround yourself as best you can with safe, trustworthy people who will embrace mistakes, rather than use them against you.

Don't fret, though, because even if you do find yourself in a culture that hasn't caught on to the magic of mistakes, you can still chart your own course. Help is on the way! As long as you properly navigate mistakes, you'll be one step closer to success and one step further away from failure.

The Rewards of Mistakes

As we've heard from Thomas Edison, mistakes are stepping stones to knowledge and wisdom. They foster personal growth and guide us to a next step. Mistakes make us smarter.

Mistakes create opportunities for process improvement. I remember an old business case study about an American automotive manufacturing plant. When a car came off the assembly line, it went through a series of quality control checks. A Japanese automotive consultant visited the factory and asked why they did this final step.

"So that imperfections or mistakes made during manufacturing and assembly can be identified and fixed before we ship the car," the American answered. "Don't you do quality control checks, too?"

"No," said the man from Japan. "We do it right the first time."

Mic drop! This exchange, and others like it, were quite the wakeup call for the American auto industry to close the quality gap with Asian competitors.

Mistakes are blind spots that, once exposed, can lead to performance improvement. We all have blind spots, just like cars. When a mistake of yours is exposed, like submitting a report that lacks essential details, you can go back and fix it. You can think critically about how it happened in the first place. Next time, you'll improve by submitting a complete report the first time.

In the aftermath of mistakes, you can help others by sharing what you learned. This can be therapeutic given the right, supportive audience. Sharing the story of a mistake adds value and purpose. I've heard many a business leader, athlete, and even reformed criminals share stories of mistakes made and lessons learned. Humbly and generously, they're giving away wisdom so as to help others. Or, as Eleanor Roosevelt said,

"Learn from the mistakes of others. You can't live long enough to make them all yourself!"

In the comfort and safety of work, academic, social, or family value systems that support and encourage mistakes, you find more creative solutions and ideas. The Montessori education method is built in part around allowing children to commit errors and learn from them. The freedom to fail is an incredibly rich platform for creativity and innovation. People are more likely to thrive when free of judgement, retribution, or retaliation for "saying something stupid" or just proposing an inferior solution. There are no wrong answers; perhaps just some in need of further development. All groundbreaking ideas have to start somewhere. There are usually many iterations between a tiny, little seedling of an idea and the blossoming of a full-grown tree.

Not All Mistakes are Created Equal

We all know of athletes, celebrities, politicians, even companies who've admitted to making mistakes. The mistakes run the gamut from intentional to unintentional, from the easily fixed to the fiercely complex. Sometimes lessons are taken to heart; sometimes the same mistakes are made over and over. Not all mistakes are the same, yet there is a common system to address and learn from them.

Let's explore the four main types of mistakes as based on the research of Dr. Carol Dweck at Stanford University and a group called Mindset Works. They are High-Stakes Mistakes, Stretch Mistakes, Ah-ha Mistakes, and Sloppy Mistakes. I'll describe them here and then in the following section, propose a recovery plan.

We will start with what takes the prize as the biggest, most memorable offender and work our way down. When the consequences are significant and visibility is elevated, High-Stakes Mistakes are be extremely impactful. Here's an example. In August 2013, pro baseball player Alex Rodriguez was suspended for 211 games due to involvement with performance-enhancing substances. While the suspension was later reduced to 162 games, it cost A-Rod $40 million. He was later quoted as saying far more costly than the lost income was the hit to his reputation, possibly a future place in the Hall of Fame, "and a number of other things." It was a High-Stakes Mistake that cost him in more ways than one. High stakes, high consequences.

For anyone who is not a professional athlete, opportunities to make High-Stakes Mistakes come in other forms, such as when presenting large deals at work, pitching to an important client prospect, while taking a professional certification exam, or supervising a large safety operation.

High-Stakes Mistakes are typically performance-related. There is a measurable outcome. They occur within the boundaries of familiar territory. It isn't a freak accident when they occur because we've been taking intentional steps leading up to the error. There is time to prepare for the make-or-break moment. When your preparation comes to fruition as planned, it's a huge victory. If it didn't go according to plan, however, and a mistake ensues, it will be a huge letdown. You may reflect back and think, "I knew better."

In order to get ahead of the High-Stakes Mistake, it's critical to reflect on progress as you're building up to the big event and carefully consider potential obstacles or consequences to future decisions and actions. In the case of a baseball player who cheats with steroids or a corked bat, I can only assume that while he was achieving enhanced performance, he was ignoring a moral compass and the severity of the consequences of getting caught. In cases that you or I might encounter, the prevention fix is to build in checkpoints for big projects and reviewing progress with colleagues or trusted advisors is creating space for critical thinking that may very well stave off what could otherwise become a High-Stakes Mistake.

The beauty of the High Stakes Mistake is that while in the moment it may bruise our ego or be a hit to our career, it will also serve as an incredibly memorable learning opportunity. Oftentimes it's in the making of these mistakes that you achieve personal growth. You are strengthened and even protected from future High Stakes Mistakes. In the moment, it is challenging, yet after recovering from them, you may even look back fondly and thank them for getting us where you are now.

The second type of mistake is the Stretch Mistake. A Stretch Mistake presents an excellent learning opportunity without the sting that a High Staker will deliver. You can think of stretch mistakes as 'yoga for personal growth.' Get ready to get bendy! When you take on a new project or role in which your current capabilities must expand, you're creating space to make Stretch Mistakes. Stretching is how personal growth and career advancement are achieved. Those who eagerly stretch view these challenges as opportunities to learn new skills.

One circumstance ripe for a Stretch Mistake to occur is when you "get out over your skis," as a former boss of mine used to say, meaning that when you stretch too far, you could crash. (Note: Crashing involves putting numerous pieces back together and is far more severe and challenging to recover from than mere falling, for which our job is to simply get back up.) You want to protect yourself from a crash, so be mindful of a few things. First, if you start to sense a little thin ice, as if you're on the verge of making a mistake, trust your instincts. It could be that you took on too much, too soon. You may need to pause and assess. Review your resources and deadlines to see if you're being realistic. A brief pause may help to ensure that you don't lose control – and you can reengage before you get out over your skis, rather while still gliding along your path.

Inviting others into conversations about your new project improves your odds of success, whereas working in isolation increases the likelihood of Stretch Mistakes. Soliciting ideas and other points of view will often help your performance and help you advance in a de-risked, strategic way.

Stretch Mistakes are generally very healthy because they happen in a new place that starts out unfamiliar yet eventually winds up being natural, relaxing, and comfortable

A third type of mistake is the Ah-ha Mistake. Ah-ha Mistakes, like those mentioned at the beginnig of this chapter about the tea bag, tires and J.K. Rowling, are realized only in hindsight, meaning that by the time we recognize them, they're already made. We've already completed a task incorrectly. Ah-ha Mistakes give us no advanced warning like High Stakes and Stretch Mistakes, yet tend to be less severe, and can still teach us a ton.

Here is an example of an Ah-ha Mistake. I'll bet you a cookie that you'll be thankful it was made!

Legend has it that in 20th century Massachusetts, Chef Ruth was mixing cookie batter in her restaurant kitchen. Wanting to shake things up a bit, she added small pieces of chocolate to the mix, hoping they would melt and turn the batter brown. Well, much to her surprise, those bits, or chips as we call them today, baked up perfectly intact. Thus was born the Toll House cookie, or chocolate chip cookie. God bless Mrs. Wakefield for acknowledging the "ah-ha" in the moment, rather than tossing out those first Toll House cookies as mistakes never to fulfill their destiny of being dunked in a glass of almond milk.

Opportunities to pivot are born from Ah-ha Mistakes. Typically, they occur in low-risk situations and you may laugh at yourself for them. So before you discard the outcome, be like Chef Ruth and examine what you learned. Perhaps your mistake is actually an innovation that makes a situation better!

The final type of mistake is a Sloppy Mistake. Everyone commits Sloppy Mistakes. They occur frequently and are often so minor, we don't reflect or ruminate on them. Thankfully, we tend to move right along. Sloppy Mistakes occur when some mundane task goes awry for some non-obvious reason. We spill coffee, take a wrong turn, or don't override the auto-correct function on our texts, subsequently asking a manager out on a date when we meant to ask him for data. (Whoops!) We know better, and we usually do better. Yet thanks to a distraction or a change in priority, we make a Sloppy Mistake.

A Sloppy Mistake here or there? NBD (No Big Deal). But Sloppy Mistakes performed on repeat, present an enormous learning opportunity and should be heeded as a warning sign that our self-care is in jeopardy. At times in my own life when I've recognized an increased frequency of Sloppy Mistakes, it's often been indicative of a life imbalance. There was a time, for example, when my husband and I were involved in a personal project that was causing both of us great stress. As soon as our day jobs commenced, we were at it non-stop and losing sleep, glorious sleep. During this time, we were both making Sloppy Mistakes. It wasn't overtly apparent at first. Yet when I broke a glass while loading the dishwasher, forgot to feed the dog, and put the coconut ice cream away in the cupboard instead of the freezer, I had to acknowledge something was up. While the consequences of my Sloppy Mistakes were nil, they were a sign I'd taken on too much. My husband made some mistakes, too, none of which I'll divulge here as I'm positive he'd consider it a mistake to do so, Sloppy or otherwise!

If you find yourself making dumb, out-of-character mistakes over a period of time, hit pause and reflect on why. You owe it to yourself to do this. Is it a focus issue? If so, what's distracting you? Is it a timing issue? What's causing the hurry and making you feel so rushed? Is there any consistency in the time of day when mistakes are happening? Maybe your sleep or nutrition are off. Is a certain person consistently around when you make your mistakes? Perhaps it's an intimidation issue, and if it's happening at work, it might need to be addressed with a manager or via a direct conversation. Do you find that gadgets, smartphones, and Apple Watches, are helping you stay organized, or distracting you away from important details?

As a rule, Sloppy Mistakes are a modest irritant, with small consequences. What's behind them, though, might be significant. Something bigger could be going on. If you're not careful or don't address the root cause, Sloppy Mistakes could pave the way for High-Stakes Mistakes.

Treat a repeating pattern of Sloppy Mistakes as an opportunity for self-love. Take time to consider what's really bothering you and get the self-care you need. Maybe it's just an afternoon off, a massage, or a Girls' Night Out. Maybe something bigger is called for, like medical or behavioral therapy. Either way, be sure to acknowledge the situation so you can heal.

Let's look out for each other on this too. When the woman at work who normally has herself completely together, stumbles into work wearing two different earrings, and arrives late twice a week, maybe ask gently if everything's okay. That small gesture may be the catalyst needed for her to pause, breathe, and hopefully take the first step in getting things back on track.

Whether it's High Stakes, Stretch, Ah-ha or Sloppy, all mistakes are opportunities to gain knowledge and end up better off than you started. Being able to name each one and recognize them for their differences helps you understand what's on the line and how you'll prioritize, prepare, and respond. Mistakes are amazing gifts that while sometimes tough to deal with in the moment, can lead to surprising gifts.

Mistake Mitigation

At this point on our Mistake Matka, we've come to a fortuitous fork in the road. We know that mistakes happen to everyone; when framed properly, they reward us; and that a lot of good things can result from properly handled mistakes.

But here you are in a moment when you realize you've just made a big mistake. That mortifying, horrifying, terrifying moment when you know you've screwed up. There's a pit in your stomach and it's been at least 20 seconds since you've exhaled. What are you going to do?

If your superpower is to turn yourself invisible or sink into the floor, now might be a good time to use it. If, on the other hand, you face your mistake like the confident, sophisticated, professional woman that you are, thankfully you have a better way. You can use a system called PROWL, as in, prowling for a solution to mitigate your mistake into a stepping stone and keep moving forward.

PROWL is a systematic approach to navigating mistakes. It stands for:

Pause/Breath

Review

Own It

What to do

Learn

PROWL is not a time machine where you jump in a hot tub and erase what happened. It is, however, a way to cruise through the present more smoothly. Think of an old Fiat beater with bald tires and shot shocks. Now picture a brand-new Toyota 4Runner with performance suspension. When you reach the fork in the Mistake Road, PROWL is your 4Runner – and its GPS navigation will help you discover a better route.

Forget the beater, jump in the 4Runner with me, and let's ride into a case study. It's based on a true story of a High-Stakes Mistake made at work by two different employee personas, Spacey and Shero. Spacey did not follow the PROWL framework. Shero did. I'll let you forecast which one fared better!

Background

Simba Company provides around-the-clock data monitoring services for websites. Analysts at Simba assemble the data and generate reports which are delivered to clients every four hours. Each analyst manages two clients.

Scenario

It's 5:56AM on a Tuesday. The night-shift analyst has been on duty since midnight and has two hours to go. She's just putting the finishing touches on a report to be emailed to a client at 6:00 AM. The client is Twinder.com, a dating site which matches identical twins to other identical twins.

The analyst hits the send button and pats herself on the back, pleased that she submitted the report a few minutes early. She leans back in her chair to stretch and shakes her coffee tumbler. Time for a refill. She checks the clock to see how much time remains before her other client's report is due.

Ping! An inbox alert interrupts the analyst's thoughts. She glances at her screen. It's an automated out-of-office response from her *other* client, Twindling.com, Twinder.com's fiercest competitor. "That's odd," she muses. "Twindling's report isn't due for another hour. I haven't sent them anything. Why am I receiving an out-of-office reply from Twindling.com?"

And then she puts two and two together. "Oh, no. I sent the TwindER report to TwindLING!" Their direct competitor! And it has proprietary information!

This is bad. I made a HUGE mistake! What am I going to do?

What happens next depends on who's in the hot seat – Spacey, or Shero.

Spacey's Saga

Rather than honor the P for Pause that leads off in the PROWL system, Spacey starts freaking out, as her negative self-talk begins to spiral out of control.

"Oh my gosh, oh my gosh, oh my gosh! Ahhhh! This can't be happening. I'm such an idiot! I can't believe I did that. Why do these things always happen to me and to no one else?? That's it. I'm fired. I'm done. I may as well pack my things and leave right now."

Spacey loosely attempts the R in PROWL, Review, by re-reading the out-of-office reply from Twindling.com. It says the recipient is on vacation for three more days and all emails and reports will be reviewed and responded to upon his return.

Spacey talks out loud to herself in the empty office. "Okay, great. I can try to recall this email and no one will ever know." She dismisses the O in PROWL, failing to *Own* her mistake. She tries recalling the email and gets the return message, "Attempt confirmed."

"Well, what the hell does that mean?" Spacey mutters. Is the *attempt* confirmed, or did the *recall* succeed? Next she deletes the out-of-office response from Twindling and moves on to her next task, pretending her mistake never happened. Spacey skips the rest of the PROWL system — no W, evaluating *What to do*, and no L, reflecting on what she *Learned*. (Pro tip: Never count on a message recall. Even messages that confirm recall are not always accurate. Once an email is sent, it is safer to assume that it has been received and to prepare for the consequences of it not being recalled.)

She completes her shift and leaves the office before her manager arrives at work.

Spacey goes home and takes a nap, her standard, post-night shift procedure. When she wakes, it's mid-morning, and there's a text from her manager: "Call me as soon as you get this." Ugh. Spacey braces for the conversation looming ahead.

She is written up, demoted, and required to complete an online course on how to execute the PROWL method.

Shero's Solution

We'll rerun the case study with another employee, Shero, making the same mistake — sending Twinder's confidential data readout to Twindling. Shero's response, however, follows the PROWL methodology.

Here's PROWL in practice:

- **Pause and breathe:** Shero begins to feel butterflies in her stomach as the reality of the situation settles in. She pushes back from her desk and takes a minute to pause and breathe. The butterflies subside and she's able to continue thinking clearly. She doesn't resort to negative self-talk

- **Review:** Shero focuses on reviewing and assessing the severity of the situation. She thinks through her previous motions and considers how the mistake was made. Gosh, those email addresses are so similar. I must have typed the wrong one or the auto-fill populated it ahead of me.

I'm sure I'm not the first person who's done this, goes Shero's inner monologue. *Everyone makes mistakes. This IS a big deal, yet I'll get through it.* Her self-talk is positive.

Doing a thorough review, Shero analyzes what can she confirm to be true, and what is an unproven assumption. She opens her Sent folder and confirms that the email did, in fact, go to Twindling with the Twinder reports attached. Now she knows for sure.

- **Own:** Shero considers her options. She needs to contact her manager and explain what happened. Shero recalls a Confidence and Leadership Workshop she attended, where she learned what it means to own something.

"Owning it," she remembers hearing, "Means not making excuses, pointing fingers, or blaming others. It's admitting that I made a mistake. To own something is to manage the consequences, and most importantly, to communicate to the right person/people in a timely manner. Owning it allows me to control the situation and decide how I feel about it. It insulates me from others' ridicule or negativity because when I own it, I control the narrative."

Shero can hear her co-worker, Troy, saying to her after this episode, "You really screwed that up." To which she will respond, "It didn't go as anticipated, no. But I've implemented measures to fix it. I've spoken with management and received approval to proceed with my plan." Done, end of story, moving along. Owning it shuts down the drama.

- **What to do:** Shero devises a plan. Following company policy, she sends a message to alert her manager, Vanessa, and request a phone call.

Shero's phone rings a few seconds later. "Good morning, Shero, what's going on?" Vanessa asks.

Shero explains, calmly and using a professional, not defensive, tone. She takes responsibility *(Owns)*. She articulates what happened in clear, chronological order, makes no excuses, and presents one immediate solution, a comprehensive communication plan for both Twinder and Twindling, plus one long-term solution, a technology improvement to how reports are sent. Shero employs the kind of well-thought-out communication that results when you *Pause*, then think through *What to do*.

She concludes her recap by suggesting: "Vanessa, for the longer term, and we can talk about this later, I'd like to propose that instead of delivering our reports via email, we set up a shared dashboard where we upload reports and use automation to prevent cross-delivery to the wrong recipients."

- **Learn:** Vanessa is a good manager and reasonable person. She knows Shero is a good employee. Mistakes are very rare for her, and Vanessa tells Shero that she appreciates her being forthcoming. She also appreciates Shero's proactive nature in proposing a short-term solution and is especially impressed with her idea for a longer-term solution. "It sounds like you've already *Learned* from this experience. And a technology upgrade is probably something we should have implemented a long time ago. The only reason we know this happened is because you got the out-of-office reply. I wonder if it's happened before and we never even knew?"

Shero stays an extra hour that morning to make sure the agreed recovery plan is properly executed. She checks with Vanessa in person before leaving the office. Driving home, while admittedly still a bit frustrated by her mistake, she feels much better knowing her reaction demonstrated leadership and humility, not immaturity or dishonesty.

Vanessa reacted productively, too. When an employee approaches a manager and owns up to a mistake, the manager's reaction has a major bearing on the outcome. Had Vanessa exploded and reprimanded Shero, the situation would have gotten worse. After the "fire is out," an appropriate time will come for Vanessa and Shero to hold a bigger conversation about the situation. Vanessa's reasonable, calm response fostered a safe environment for Shero to confess. A more aggressive or accusatory response might discourage Shero from following the same protocol if a future mistake occurs.

As it turned out, by the way, Simba Company did implement a different process for transmitting confidential reports to clients. It prevented delivery to the wrong recipients, and worked so well it became a competitive advantage, allowing Simba to secure more clients.

Are there people who get away with mistakes they've covered up? Absolutely. Does it ever come back to bite them later? Sometimes. We have no means of predicting the future. But in the spirit of genuine confidence and trustworthy leadership, use PROWL as a tool to help you choose the right fork in the mistake road. Continue your Mistake Matka, holding your head high and with integrity intact.

Considerations

The saga of Spacey and Shero presents two extreme circumstances, one disastrous, one ideal. Most real- world experiences will likely fall somewhere in between – and hopefully closer to the ideal side when you follow the PROWL method. Other considerations that can impact the outcome include:

- Your organization's specific policies and prohibitions
- Personality types and management leadership style
- The overall performance of the organization – A struggling company may be more prone to volatile reactions when mistakes happen than one performing well.
- Volume of recent mistakes. Was it the seventh mistake this week, or the first in nine months?
- Self-talk. Positive self-talk will help keep you out of the panic zone. Negative self-talk is a nearly surefire way to launch yourself into a tailspin that will not serve you well.

Two Other Lifelines

Circumstances around mistakes will vary wildly. PROWL can help you calm the storm, while you enlist your best judgment. You know your colleagues and managers, your company and its processes, and can envision any potential consequences better than anyone else. Apply your intuition, expertise, and leadership skills to make good calls and communicate properly.

In the aftermath of a mistake, you can also phone a friend – literally. It's immensely helpful to talk through mistakes with an unbiased party who shares your sense of integrity.

Taylor Swift is Right

To complete your introduction to mistake mitigation using PROWL, let's end with a song – something to help us move along and not dwell on mistakes.

I'll lean on the lyrics of the oh-so-wise and visionary Taylor Swift. After a mistake has been committed, and after you've taken care of it properly, it's time to *shake it off*. Time to move on and go about your business. Learn from it? Yes, absolutely. Dwell on it? Heck, no. Shake it off, Sheroes! And do it with the level of T. Swift's swagger. Take satisfaction in knowing you're wiser than before, and better equipped and more empowered for next time.

Your creative, curious, innovative self can keep on vibing and thriving. Be a Mistake Making Machine! Listen to Albert Einstein, who said, "Anyone who has never made a mistake has never tried anything new." Old is older than yesterday's Insta feed. Embrace new opportunities, the risks of making mistakes, and the rewards that come along with it!

What's at Stake?

Your self-esteem! It's hugely at risk when you feel reprimanded and continuously wrong, when you deserve to feel rewarded and encouraged for getting one step closer to *right*. Stay creative with game-changing ideas and increased opportunities by honoring the Mistake Matka!

Key Points

- Mistakes happen to EVERYONE.
- There are different kinds of mistakes. Pausing to consider their root causes and their impacts will help guide you toward your next stepping stone and ultimately your solution.
- Use PROWL as a method to navigate the aftermath of a mistake.

Confidence Challenge Checklist

- ❏ What are you afraid to try? Identify it. Try it. Find excitement and satisfaction in the results, no matter what happens!
- ❏ Think about past mistakes. Re-enact the aftermath using the PROWL method. See if the results are different.
- ❏ Make a new mistake! Then identify it and use PROWL to respond to it.
- ❏ Find a friend and share what you learned in this chapter.

To condition and claim my confidence, one action I commit to is:

_____

_____

_____

Chapter 11
Sorry/Not Sorry

I spaced my friend's birthday. I talked overzealously with my hands, and spilled coffee on the gentleman nearby. Over appetizers at a friend's dinner party, I proclaimed my distaste for duck, only to find out that the main course was foie gras. I took a Sharpie to a wall in my sister's house. Or maybe that was my two-year-old nephew who took the Sharpie to the wall, and maybe that was *my* house. Ahhh, kids. Regardless, all these events warranted a sincere apology.

Most of us never intend to do things that warrant apologies. Yet we're all guilty at some point. Those two little words, *I'm sorry*, sure carry a heck of a lot of power. Sometimes they have the power to patch the fraying fabric of a relationship. Other times, they can actually put us at a hidden disadvantage – being more meddlesome than mending! We'll explore the distinctions in this chapter and what to do about it to ensure that you're communicating confidently and using your apologies astutely

To do so, I want to start by sharing the journey of one of my coaching clients as she worked to break her superfluous *I'm sorry* habit. She had what I would call a disturbingly high frequency of saying *I'm sorry*. Sarah said "I'm sorry" as often as the seagulls in Finding Nemo repeated, "Mine"! Occasionally a legitimate apology was called for, but by and large the *I'm sorries* flowed like beer at Oktoberfest. At even the slightest hint of an uncomfortable silence, Sarah used *I'm sorry* as filler. Sometimes she'd say it when she felt awkward without knowing why, sometimes simply because she couldn't think of anything else to say. It became a really bad habit – not as bad as vaping or ghosting, yet certainly one that could be just as deadly, professionally speaking.

To break her habit, Sarah and I started at the beginning. We addressed the difference between a personal apology and a workplace apology, and the "when to" versus "when not to."

The Apology Formula

A well-delivered apology, offered with sincerity, intention, and integrity, carries a lot of weight. An apology can be wonderful not only when a relationship needs repairing, but when you've caused inconvenience to others.

On the positive side, apologies benefit both offerer and recipient. When one humbly and sincerely extends an apology and the other accepts it and forgives, it can forge or deepen a bond. The two parties care enough about each other to set egos aside, listen, and strengthen their relationship. A situation with the potential to sever a relationship can be defused by a sincere apology.

On the danger side, the workplace environment can be a complicated maze of apology-powered dead-ends. At the office, overuse or unwarranted use of those two very important words, I'm sorry, can be more destructive than restorative. Too many unnecessary apologies can cost you special projects, important career advancement and even promotions, all of which will be explained here.

But first, let's look at scenarios worthy of an apology.

An Apology is in Order When...

- When someone has been hurt, physically or emotionally. And it's their call. If they felt it and decide to tell you, or you recognize it on your own, the right thing to do is sincerely apologize. When you let somebody down, hurt their feelings or break a promise, that stings. It's a perfect time for an apology.
  Note: Far more likely to happen in personal life than professional life.

- When you inconvenience someone. You were late, you forgot something important, you cancelled on them at the last minute. Or you caused a hassle or disturbance that affected, inhibited, or delayed them. In that case, say that you're sorry.
  Note: Likely to happen in both professional life and personal life.

- You get caught in a lie. I love this line about lying: "A lie is like a bald spot. "The bigger it gets, the harder it is to cover up." Lying is to be avoided altogether, obviously, but if you do it and get caught – or your conscience takes over – time to apologize. Lying will catch up with you at some point anyway. Don't make it worse by layering on additional excuses. Own it, offer an apology, and follow it up with, "I have learned my lesson." (Hear sprinkles of PROWL in there?)

Note: Lying can break out in both professional and personal situations – and both friends and employers have the power to "fire" you for lying.

So that's it! The top three scenarios in which apologies should be delivered. Are there other scenarios? Sure. More severe offenses such as cheating, stealing, or egregious missteps would qualify too, but those are rare situations. The three mentioned above are the day-to-day types that we as imperfect humans are far more likely to encounter. And along with the scenarios, there are several conditions that call for a special-order apology: First, when both sides share equal views regarding the value of the apology.

I invite you to commit to memory my battle-tested Apology Formula. An apology is appropriate when:

The Sincerity Level of the Deliverer = The Interest Level of the Receiver

Either both parties care about the apology, or neither is into it. When the parties have equal interest, each will feel valued and validated. Balance is achieved when people are on the same page. It leads to closure and both parties can move on.

Our personal relationships are built upon sharing experiences, being vulnerable, and exchanging emotional capital. We support our friends in ways that are appropriately different from the ways we support our co-workers. We tend to apologize more frequently in personal lives because, well, feelings. The bigger the feels, the deeper the hurt when something goes awry.

Relationships in a workplace environment, on the other hand, are about collaborating and relying upon colleagues to advance common company goals and maintain productivity. Sure, team building exercises can be fun and valuable, yet the point of work is to, well, work. It's a bonus if you wind up making friends at work and the culture is happy, but we don't have to be BFFs with co-workers. We build strong work relationships primarily through achieving tasks together.

What about when a situation seems to call for an apology, but the balance defined in the Apology Formula isn't there? For example, you think you need to apologize, yet the other party doesn't care. In this case, skip it. An apology will only work against you. Your good intentions notwithstanding, if your intended recipient doesn't want to hear it, honor that and redirect your energy into action. The only thing worse than not apologizing when it's called for is apologizing to someone who rejects your effort.

If the wounded party doesn't see your error as apology-worthy, save your words. No need for a verbal apology. Just fix the mess and move on. As mentioned earlier, a workplace environment is task-oriented. **Some people don't want words, they want action.** Tasks don't move closer to completion when unwanted apologies are happening. Often times, the best way to repair the thing that inconvenienced others is not to spend time apologizing for it, but to instead use that time to guide things back on course. Actions often speak louder than words, and that certainly applies here!

An Apology Formula imbalance you can't control is where you feel you deserve an apology, yet the party that wounded you disagrees. In that instance you have two choices. Address the situation, or let it go. It is a personal preference and will depend on the gravity of the error. You'll have to decide.

And lastly when someone else believes they deserve an apology, but you disagree. You'll have to decide what your main priority is and then choose the words and/or actions that move you closer to your end goal.

Another condition to consider: How often are you apologizing? As frequency goes up, perceived sincerity goes down. We know that sincerity is paramount for effective delivery of an apology. Overusing the words *I'm sorry* or *I apologize* dilutes their perceived truthfulness, efficacy and value. It's classic economics, really: The Law of Diminishing Returns. Too many apologies generate benefits inferior to the effort you put into them. When words that can carry a lot of power are overused, they can be knocked off their thrones faster than Daenerys Targaryen in *Game of Thrones*!

We use an expression in Sales: "Don't sell past YES." In other words, when the client agrees to move forward, don't continue to sell the proposition. Stop talking and start doing. The same goes for apologies. One solid apology will do. Once someone has forgiven you (or never felt the need for an apology in the first place), that's your signal to move on. When they get over it, you need to as well.

So if I do forget your birthday, or accidentally spill paint on your patio: oh, my gosh, do you have a huge apology coming from me! Yet if I need to correct a sales forecast, change the formatting in a report, or fix a customer presentation, I will do it sans apology. I will own my mistake and see it as an opportunity for improvement – a reason to be excited rather than defeated. I'll hold my head high, shake it off, keep on trucking, and save my apologies for the times when they are truly warranted.

Tread carefully where apologies may trap and unknowingly hold you back, particularly at work.

Remember Sarah, my coaching client who couldn't stop saying *I'm sorry*? As Sarah and I continued our conversation, this is exactly what we addressed next.

What Women Need to Know: The Risk at Work

Apologetic words used in the wrong context, especially at work and by women in particular, can hurt us more than help us. Studies show that overuse of the words *I'm sorry* is more common among women. In a fantastic book, recommended earlier, *Difference Works*, Caroline Turner explains that *I'm sorry* means something different coming from men. A woman says *I'm sorry*, writes Turner, to "express empathy, sympathy, or understanding of someone else's problem. We're not keeping score; this is about shared feelings." And, gosh, isn't that nice of us?!? But the danger lies in how a male listener interprets our gesture. As Ms. Turner's research shows a man may interpret *I'm sorry* as an implied confession of fault. In the unspoken rules of corporate culture, the woman just lost a point and comes off as lacking confidence and competence.

Deborah Tannen is a professor of linguistics at Georgetown University and author of *You Just Don't Understand: Women and Men in Conversation*. Tannen expands on this topic: "Women who apologize a lot may be well liked yet passed over for a promotion because they don't seem strong enough for the job." *Passed over for saying sorry, Sheroes!* In other words, you may be the most qualified candidate for the job, but if you're known for over-apologizing, that alone could prevent you from getting a promotion you deserve. Which makes me think of two more words. *Not anymore!*

Correcting a habit of free- flowing I'm sorrys could be the bridge between your current role and your future promotion.

The Risk to Your Confidence

Earlier we discussed body posture, and how it impacts your confidence and other peoples' perceptions. Now let's tie that thinking to the subject of apologies.

I want you to think for a moment about the posture you assume, how much self-assurance you project, when you offer a sincere apology. It's a humbling experience, right? Feelings of shame and guilt often accompany it and come along as unwanted baggage. It can be awkward. Since our bodies reflect our words, I bet you can easily picture the apologetic posture. Sloped shoulders, eyes cast downward, and head in a submissive tilt. It's a portrait of plummeting confidence. We feel awful, and it makes next steps seem that much heavier and harder to take.

Now, let's switch gears and think about posture when something exciting or invigorating happens, and you feel gratitude for it. You perk up in these circumstances! Opportunities to learn and generate new ideas are exciting. When you're feeling thankful, you're energized. Now your posture straightens up. You feel and appear taller. You make eye contact again and your face shows enthusiasm. Your mindset shifts to a place of higher energy and productivity. It's much easier to move forward. Resistance subsides.

Exchanging an apology for gratitude is just one substitute. Instead of responding as defeated and deflated, invite in excitement and thankfulness for the opportunity to learn something new. **The next time someone points out a mistake you made or a shortcoming, instead of responding with I'm sorry, express gratitude by saying, "I didn't know, thank you!"** And see how it shifts how you feel in the aftermath.

What to Say Instead

The rules for professional apologies are nothing like those of the board game Sorry!, where flipping over the wrong card can set you back a few spaces. In our world, having a good handle on apology substitutes will only propel you *forward*!

When deciding whether to apologize or choose alternative words instead, recall the three scenarios discussed previously. Did your mistake physically or emotionally harm someone? Did you inconvenience an individual or a group? Did you lie to someone, or misrepresent something? A brief, sincere apology is warranted, along with action to move forward.

Yet if the action you took fails to tick any of those three boxes, if it was just a mundane mistake that anyone could have made, then absolutely no apology is necessary.

Should you own it? Of course. Should you fix it? Yes, but that doesn't mean you have to apologize. Everyone makes mistakes. In a professional setting, let he or she who is without a mistake cast the first stone. It is a completely normal part of behavior, especially when you're building, creating, or updating something. Yet small mistakes so often seem to be the catalysts for unnecessary apologies! So let's replace the submissive, unwarranted words, with more powerful, more confident, more-likely-to-get-the-promotion words instead.

I'm Sorry Alternatives

With strategically chosen words, you can re-direct what initially may have elicited an apology into a simple acknowledgment instead. You may even wind up driving an opportunity for improvement.

Here are some common phrases that tend to elicit submissive language in the form of apologies.

- You're late.
- Your performance wasn't what I expected.
- I found mistakes in the project you submitted.
- You missed the point of the exercise.

Now, instead of responding with *I'm sorry*, possibly followed by effusive word salad (the kind you can visualize accumulating all around you when you wish it would just evaporate), give these succinct, suitable alternatives a test drive:

- Thank you for waiting for me.
- Thank you for pointing that out.
- I'll get right on it.
- I see your point.
- That's a good point. I'll consider an adjustment after I review the numbers. (A personal favorite.)
- Let me try again.
- Oh, good to know! I'll give it another go.
- I agree. I'll make a correction.
- That's interesting.
- Tell me more.
- I hear you.

These are all perfectly acceptable responses, all legitimate options, and all give you ways to ditch the old *I'm sorry* and preserve professionalism and ownership. Sounds like a good demonstration of leadership to me!

When you're in a managerial role, an *I'm sorry* can be equally as self-damaging. Owning your mistakes projects strength, whereas submissive *I'm sorrys* can make your subordinates question your authority or sincerity. Instead, respond using one or more of these apology alternatives. (The last three options are useful when a team member approaches you with a complaint or excuse, such as, "I can't understand why I have to do this." "This isn't fair." "I'm not feeling up to it today.") Your direct reports should feel heard and acknowledged, yet not tempted to discard their respect for you, or belief in your leadership. It's important for you to justify and maintain the respect that comes with your position on the company organizational chart.

Another acceptable alternative, for both managers and their teams, is to answer a challenging question with a question. Respond with clarifying questions, or requests for suggestions about how to do things differently or better.

- Walk me through that again? I want to make sure I'm properly capturing what you're saying.
- We all bring different lenses to the conversation; I'd like more details on how you see this.
- What would you suggest?

Even though it's natural to respond defensively to a perceived verbal slight, be extremely careful to stay in a positive, or at least neutral zone and be mindful of tone of voice. Stay professional. Stay positive. Maintain upright posture! It can be challenging when you feel attacked. I promise you, though, the more you can remain professional while responding and standing up for yourself or appropriately representing your position, the more satisfied, successful, and respected you'll be afterwards.

And honor the ear to mouth ratio:

It's no mistake that God gave us twice as many ears as mouths!

Listen twice as much as you speak, and focus thoroughly on what you hear.

No Need for an Apology: Case Study

Let's meet Monica, a manager asked to create a forecast for next year's marketing budget.

Being the go-getter and problem solver that she is, Monica is excited to take on this special project, even though the facet of marketing she currently handles is the social media channel, much different than a forecasting project. She thinks: "What a learning opportunity!" She sets up meetings with members of the promotion, pricing, event production, and advertising teams, collects their inputs, and assembles the budget forecast – knowing full well she's working without a crystal ball and her work is merely a useful estimate.

When Monica presents the forecast to her peers, it is very well received. The other team brainstorms collectively and offers ideas and suggestions that Monica hadn't thought of. They point out an error in a formula Monica used to calculate the Q2 advertising budget. Overall, her forecast is thorough and well done, and after making the suggested tweaks, the marketing department implements it as a strategic guide for the year ahead.

Despite there being a few gaps to fill and a formula that required fixing, Monica was succesful with her project. Should Monica have apologized for her misses? Of course not. Fixing shortcomings is the iterative part of the process. Is a man likely to apologize when he miscalculates as Monica did? Doubtful, according to Carol Turner's research. Was anyone physically or emotionally hurt? Nope. Did Monica inconvenience anyone with her minor errors? That's a 'no' as well – it's not an inconvenience for teams to collaborate on an improved product. And did she lie about anything? Not at all. With a trifecta of nos, the nos have it. Monica need not apologize. She owned her work, fixed it, and moved on.

Imagine, however, the moment when whomever found the error in the advertising budget formula spoke up: "I see here that the Q2 numbers have been subtracted when it needs to be added." Monica's knee-jerk response might have been, "Oh, *I'm so sorry*. Let me take a closer look." *No-no-no*. No need. One error within a complex spreadsheet, especially when it's in draft mode, is a pretty normal, reasonable mistake. The better response is simply to state, "Let me take a closer look." An inappropriately delivered apology may cause the team to question her confidence and, as we learned earlier, be interpreted as a sign of weakness. Worse, it may cause self-doubt on Monica's part, and she could hurt her case further by assuming a defensive, slumped, apologetic posture. Her power would be sucked out of her and it would impact her performance for the duration of the meeting.

Look at Monica go, though! She took on a special project, brought in other teams, and stretched out of her comfort zone to make things happen – all while soliciting feedback, offering no unnecessary apologies, and making adjustments accordingly. Atta girl, Monica!

Introducing: the I'm Sorry Slayer

This chapter began with the journey of Sarah, whose challenge was to cut back on the compulsive apologies. Upon talking through when to apologize and when not to, alternative language to use, and how over-apologizing could put her career at risk, Sarah was incredibly motivated to break her *I'm sorry* habit. She wanted to make a "no fail" commitment to change her behavior and increase her confidence. So as a final action item, we brainstormed tools she could implement in her life to catch and eliminate her treacherous tendency.

Thus the I'm Sorry Slayer was brought into being.

The I'm Sorry Slayer is a fictional character whose black cape and scythe are a badass complement to her long hair and spiked heel boots. Envision a female superhero version of the Grim Reaper. Our new advocate the I'm Sorry Slayer shows up every time Sarah and her friends catch each other spouting unnecessary apologies.

To acknowledge the arrival of the I'm Sorry Slayer, Sarah and company now shout out her name right then and there, the way you used to yell "Jinx!" as a kid when a friend said the same thing as you. Or they make a slow, arc-shaped motion with their hands, starting in front of the face and gliding down toward the waist. A back-and-forth slicing motion. Go ahead, try it yourself! Pass your hand in front of your face and down to your waist and envision the words *I'm sorry* sliced cleanly in half!

Since Sarah introduced the I'm Sorry Slayer into her life, I'm pleased to report she's done exceptionally well. On occasion, the Slayer will make an appearance, yet her sitings are rarer all the time. Today the I'm Sorry Slayer mostly lurks behind the scenes, because Sarah and friends have drastically reduced their unnecessary spouting of apologies. It worked for them and it can work for you, too. So be sure to slay those apologies like a boss! Lest you let them slay you!

What's at Stake?

Submissive language leads to shrunken posture which projects the exact opposite of confidence. It can literally cost you an invitation to work on a special project, credibility in the workplace, even a promotion! Stand tall, proud, and confident by keeping those *I'm sorrys* at bay!

Key Points

- Proper use of *I'm sorry* in the right circumstances is essential for successful personal relationships.
- In business relationships, misuse of *I'm sorry* can negatively impact your career.
- Use alternative words for acknowledgement and suitable responses.
- You are your most important audience. Keep in mind what happens to your posture when saying *I'm sorry*. Compare the effects to positive alternatives.

Confidence Challenge Checklist

- ❏ Grab an accountability partner, yet don't change a thing about your behavior. Count how many times each of you says *I'm sorry* in a given day. Actively work to reduce that number.
- ❏ Pick two phrases from the list of alternatives in this chapter and say them repeatedly until you commit them to memory.
- ❏ Call yourself and others out by introducing them to the I'm Sorry Slayer. Put the back-and-forth slicing motion to work to reinforce that you're cutting out the *I'm sorrys!*

To condition and claim my confidence, one action I commit to is:

_____

_____

_____

Chapter 12
Relatability at Any Height

Not long ago, I had a single-day work trip to San Francisco. The CEO and I flew out early in the morning to meet some very high-powered investors atop a skyscraper overlooking the bay. The views were as stunning as the feedback we received. After a late lunch, feeling good, we returned to the airport for a flight back to Denver. As I entered the TSA security line, I noticed an unusually tall man, I mean close to seven feet tall, up ahead of me. He was well dressed, bald, and had to literally duck his head to pass through the metal detector.

He seemed like someone I'd seen before. I turned my CEO and mouthed, "Kareem Abdul-Jabbar?"

Wide-eyed, he nodded. Yes, it was in fact the six-time NBA MVP and former L.A. Laker. A legend in many regards! "I'm going to see if I can get a picture with him," my CEO whispered.

Celebrity sightings intrigue me, yet I never want to be the person who asks for an autograph or a selfie. I was scarred in my early twenties when my sister and I got into a disastrous "May-I-take-a-picture-with-you?" situation with, of all people, actor Ian Ziering — Steve Sanders from *Beverly Hills, 90210*. I don't want to bag on Ian, but let's just say he was none too pleased with our innocent request and it made an impression. I never wanted to put myself through such discomfort again! But that's a story for a different day.

Back to the security line at SFO airport. Upon clearing the metal detector, no ducking necessary, I found myself pulling my heels back on as I stood right next to the big bald man towering over me by exactly two feet, standing at 7' 2", as I later looked up on Google. The airport wasn't very crowded, and Kareem was traveling with just one companion, not a huge entourage. While my CEO trailed

193

behind, still emptying his pockets trying to figure out why the darn metal detector kept beeping, I decided to strike up a conversation with Kareem. Rather than go for the tired selfie request, of course, I decided I'd make a valiant attempt to say something unique – something Kareem might not have heard from the thousands who approach him in public.

I thought for a minute, came up with my little quip, practiced it once in my head, caught his eye, and spoke up.

"You think after I put my heels back on, I'll be as tall as you?" I said in a jovial tone.

I silently laughed to myself. I was kind of proud of my repartee. To be honest, every time I've told that story since, I receive at least a tiny giggle, if not an outright chuckle. Kareem, however, looked up, or rather down, at me as I smiled at him, expecting an equally amusing comment in response. I was already experiencing a high from what I imagined would be a forthcoming exchange of pleasantries with a former NBA star.

With a stone face, though, Kareem looked me square in the eyes and simply uttered a short, dry, "No."

One short, tiny, game-over word: No. No attempt to reciprocate whatsoever. Ouch, not the relatable guy I'd expected.

I felt as deflated as a pierced basketball. My inner monologue rushed along at a mile a minute. "Well, sheesh, I'm sure the guy's been hounded his whole life, but wasn't that a little harsh, Kareem? Maybe a courtesy laugh? A wink? Something?" Maybe I shouldn't have said anything at all. My intentions were good, though! I was just trying to connect and maybe give the guy a laugh. I wasn't asking for a picture, let alone an autograph or a cameo on my Insta account. I tried for a quick, fun exchange, yet I was swiftly and distinctly shot down.

My smile faded. I re-directed my energy to zipping up my adorable black bootie heels. I *love* those heels, by the way.

And just as my defeated self was about to move on, Kareem looked down at me and spoke again. This time he was a little more loquacious. "Hey." He paused while I met his gaze.

"You think if I comb my head, I'll have hair like yours?"

He gave me a bit of a smirk, which I returned, adding a small giggle. Yes! Kareem was with me again, on the relatability playing field, or court, I guess, in this case. I felt as good as if I'd dunked on a break-away steal.

"You could certainly give it a shot," I replied. (Like my basketball reference? Give it a *shot*?)

We both laughed a bit and our exchange came to a natural close. I turned to walk toward my gate. As I did, my CEO walked up and, with boyish wonder, asked Kareem if he could take a photo.

"No, man, sorry, I don't do that," Kareem said. (Relatability foul!) But then he reached into his attaché case and handed my CEO an autographed card. (Relatability 3-pointer!) I can't speak for Kareem, of course, but at that point, all parties appeared satisfied and we merrily went on our respective ways.

Can You Relate?

I can't even imagine the amount of unwanted attention anyone that tall receives, let alone a 20-season NBA legend recognized around the world. I quite enjoyed our exchange. I use it here as an example of how quickly and unexpectedly anyone can shift from unrelatable, to relatable, and back again.

Being relatable is a liberating skill to practice and master. It's about being able to connect with someone regardless of if, and especially, when you have seemingly little to nothing in common. It's the ability to bridge your differences with natural conversation and meet at a place that cultivates a productive conversation. It's helped me in so many ways as I established rapport with customers, co-workers, and colleagues. I find the experience to be so enjoyable. It's an opportunity to practice a confident delivery style, and it certainly makes a positive impact in the conversations and meetings that follow.

Relatability is almost synonymous with finding common ground with another person. And no matter how different two people may be, there is always some mutual interest or connection to discover. You're a person, I'm a person. You're a woman, I'm a woman. You went to school? I went to school! You had a first job, I had a first job. You like Italian food, I like Italian food. Actually, pasta isn't really my thing, yet I do appreciate a good eggplant parmesan with marinara sauce. But see? There are almost always commonalities – you just have to be open to looking and listening for them.

It wasn't until about six weeks into a new job that the receptionist and I figured out that not only did we go to the same high school in Toledo, Ohio, five states away, but she was in my youngest sister's class! Insta-relatability!

The ability to be relatable improves your confidence in any situation, regardless of whether you know another soul! There are three easy and effective ways to up your relatability game, and they all tie into how you start a conversation.

1. Ask a good open-ended question.
2. Share an interesting fact about yourself.
3. Offer a fun fact, intriguing tidbit, or provocative piece of information.

Let's look at some examples.

Relatability tends to be especially important in two scenarios: when you first meet someone, or when you're spending one-on-one time with someone. (Whether it's on a road trip with your boss or a first date with that new guy.) Avoiding awkward silence can feel just as important as not over-talking – or word-vomiting because you're nervous and telling a story as special as the time you spilled ketchup on your white blouse at an academic honors ceremony, then had the stain covered in bird poop as you ran out to your car for your Tide Pen. Maybe not the elegant opening you envisioned.

Up Your Relatability Game

Enlist Technique 1 from above. Ask a good open-ended question guaranteed to help avoid awkward silences. Get the other person or people talking about themselves. Everyone loves talking about things that get them excited: work, family, hobbies, life stories.Simply start with just one good question, listen well, then follow up with additional questions that build on what you just heard.

Fun fact about listening: Do you know what the anagram is to L-I-S-T-E-N? When you rearrange the letters in listen, do you know what it spells? The next sentence contains the answer so pause here before proceeding if you want to figure it out!

When you rearrange the letters in listen, it spells S-I-L-E-N-T! How crazy is that? It cannot be a mere coincidence! So remain mostly silent while listening and show you're paying attention by inserting the occasional, "So I think I just heard you say…" And know that if you're someone who tends to word babble, pausing to *listen* will allow you to harness words that may have otherwise spilled out uncontrollably.

At a networking event or a dinner party, here are some open-ended questions to get the conversation started and relatability flowing:

- What kind of work do you do? (The most frequently asked question, and a slightly tired one, but it works!)

- What inspired you today?
- What was the best part of your day?
- What's the happiest news you've heard in the past week?
- What fun projects do you have going on?
- What are you doing for (<u>Insert upcoming holiday here</u>)?
- Red or white?
- Heard a good podcast lately?

Say you're on a roadtrip with a work colleague, this technique can get you at least half-way to your destination.

For a great open-ended starter question, try: *Tell me about your journey to the role you're in now, and don't leave anything out. I love details. What was your very first job?*

Follow up with additional questions like:

- What did you love about that job?
- Was there anything you hated?
- What did you learn from your manager's leadership style?
- Which of your roles has been the most rewarding?
- What got you excited about that job?
- Where do you see your next adventure when it comes to work and professional accomplishments?

I must point out that these questions should not be delivered in rapid-fire synchronicity in the order listed above. Weave them naturally into the conversation during the appropriate pauses, and remember to listen for interesting responses you can further dig into.

If the other party has relatability skills as good or better than yours, you'll get conversational questions in return, and a relatability tennis match is on. I'll hit the ball to you, you lob it back to me, I'll swing a light backhand your way, and so on. Or the other person could catch the question ball you lobbed, hold onto it, and just keep talking. They may talk about themselves the entire time! But even if that does happen, I'm willing to bet that if someone sent them a Survey Monkey link the next day to rate *your* reliability, you'd score very high. Good listeners make a very relatable impression. You can make another person feel good, important, and invigorated as they reminisce about the highlight reel of their career. Simply ask a good, open-ended question and listen with genuine interest to the response.

In a book I recommend called *Captivate: The Science of Succeeding with People*, Vanessa Van Edwards, a self-described "human behavior hacker," tells a funny story about the time she took a two-week vow of silence to become a better listener. During that time she attended a conference. While there she honored her vow. She made herself understood by holding up pre-written notecards to anyone wanting to speak with her. After the conference, Vanessa received an email from someone she'd encountered there. The woman wrote that she couldn't stop thinking about their incredible conversation (a "conversation" in which Vanessa had spoken not one word!) and invited her to coffee in a few weeks. Wow – those are some impressive listening skills. Simply by being a completely silent listener, Vanessa made a really positive, memorable impression on someone who recalled it in retrospect as a full two-person exchange.

Beyond listening, other ways to be relatable revolve around curiosity for others' hobbies and interests, and showing willingness to listen to the excitement in someone's voice when they talk about them. I must confess that neither golf, nor hunting, nor NASCAR interest me in the least. Yet in the male-dominated industries where I've spent my entire career, *hours* of my life have been spent listening to others' stories. And I like it! It gives me a peek into their world, and we wind up working better together because of it. My innate interests lie elsewhere. What I *am* interested in, though, is learning what makes somebody tick and watching them perk up when they talk about it.

The ability to stay present in someone else's story is a gift, and everyone involved gets to untie the bow. I consider every opportunity to hear someone else's story a chance to practice relatability. It's also fun to subsequently brighten someone's day by proving you remember their passion. You might see an article about the latest NASCAR test track or Tiger Woods latest swinging technique of a 3-iron (Or was it a Wood? What's the difference again?) and forward the link to someone you know will love reading it. It's not about you. It's about them. Relatability goes up when you relay something of value to someone who values it!

That's the side of relatability where you initiate conversation and ask productive questions. The side where you make the effort to demonstrate genuine interest. But what about the sharing side? When you offer others the chance to see a genuine side of you? Sharing is caring, after all. Revealing fun, lighthearted facts or stories about yourself could intrigue someone – or at least make them appreciate that you thought enough of them to engage in such a conversation.

Creating awareness around what brightens *your* day, and talking about whatever that thing is, can increase your relatability, too.

I now invite you to focus on Technique 2 from the previous list. Share an interesting fact about yourself.

Pause for a moment to think about your "things." What are your things? What professional topics, outside interests, or leisure pursuits instantly perk you up when you talk about them – or when someone asks you about them? Hobbies, sports, job, kids, adorable new puppies, vacations, chili cookoffs? Think for a moment about what your things are. You likely have more, but let's start by writing your Top Three Things here:

Thing 1 _____

Thing 2 _____

Thing 3 _____

I'll share one of my things with you and how I've put it to work. My college football team, the Ohio State University Buckeyes, (already mentioned once) is definitely one of my things. Any day of the week, in or out of football season, I love talking about my Buckeyes. I get so fired up (in a good way) every time it comes up! On the morning that I had a meeting with a big customer in Denver. I stopped on the way to their office to buy a dozen Chick-fil-A breakfast sandwiches. After pulling away from the drive-through window, to keep the sandwiches warm in transit, I placed them in my red Ohio State casserole tote (all true fans have casserole totes).

I joined up with my co-worker who was accompanying me to the meeting. He eyed my casserole tote. Although he didn't show it, I'm sure he was secretly envious. I nodded at the tote and told him, "This is either going to earn us even more business, or get us kicked out if David's a University of Michigan fan." (Michigan, of course, being our fierce rival.) I was kidding. Sort of.

Well, as luck would have it, David, upon greeting us, noticed my tote and said, "Oh, Buckeyes! My wife's family is from Ohio. They're die-hard fans and I tend to cheer for them, too." I looked at my co-worker and winked as he playfully rolled his eyes. Boom! Relatability success, because I shared a little piece of what makes me, me.

When I originally started use the 'Three Things Technique,' I actually had five things and used them more socially (in my dating life) and found their use to be so effective in that realm that I incorporated them into my professional networking activities too. My five things were: Nutrition, travel, relationship dynamics, religion/spirituality, and sustainability/clean energy. I used them in methodical rotation, casually serving them up to drive conversation.

I utilized my five-topic list to level up my conversations beyond the open-ended questions listed earlier. So if you're looking for the Advanced Level, this is it. Eventually, one of my five things, energy and sustainability, wound up steering my career path directly toward it, a place where I knew I belonged because of how easily the conversation flowed and how fascinated I always was to learn more.

It's so important to actively work on relatability because it will lead you to your natural habitat, where you won't struggle to fit in.

While you're in the process of finding your people, prioritize using Techiques 1 and 2 to get you there faster. If you yearn to feel a sense of belonging and purpose, practice relatability by starting a conversation with someone you don't know, ask one really good, open-ended question. Listen. Achieve relatability. Then, ask a question about something that is interesting to you. "Do you like talking about quantum physics?" And you'll instantly be able to gauge how relatable you two are to each other.

It's a bit of an art and a science. There's no exact formula. It doesn't have to be perfect. Simply get in practice mode, and reward yourself for giving it a shot.

Finally, here's Technique 3 from my list: offer a fun fact, interesting tidbit, or provocative piece of information. And they don't have to be profound – sometimes useless trivia is fine!

In this relatability department I have four ideas for you.

Idea 1: Sign Up for a Subscription

Subscribe to a "Random Fact of the Day" email list and share your newfound knowledge. Start a conversation with, "Hey, want to guess today's trivia fun fact?" Everybody loves a good fun fact and they serve as great ice breakers, too.

You can set up fun facts as questions or teasers and give others a chance to respond before revealing the correct answer. Here are some random facts from www.triviagenius.com. Each is followed with examples of additional questions you can ask to demonstrate the the idea in action.

- Out of Twinkies, Cracker Jacks, Fritos, and Hershey Kisses, do you know which was the first junk food item? Survey says...Cracker Jacks! What's your favorite junk food?

- Do you know what prompted Samuel Morse to invent Morse Code? To get a hold of his wife faster. Wow, communications have certainly come a long way! I bet Morse would be blown away by Snapchat and Tik Tok! What's your preferred method?

- Do you know where the most expensive coffee in the world comes from? Indonesia! It costs more than $500 per pound! What kind of coffee drinker are you? 7-11, Starbucks, or French Press?

There are a million more examples, of course, but if you're talking to someone who has ever eaten junk food, communicates, or drinks coffee, chances are they will find these fun facts, well, fun and intriguing too. With each question, you also learn something to warm up your next visit or communication. You can make a note of their favorite coffee or junk food and bring it to your next meeting. (Once I learn a detail like this, I store it in my phone, in the Notes section under Contacts.) Give it a try! Watch your relatability grow faster than a marigold. Marigolds, incidentally, are one of the fastest blooming flowers, most often taking just five to seven days. Tell all your friends!

Or, maybe better yet, come up with some news or random facts relevant to the industry in which you work. Be sure to make them positive – Upbeat Angela is way more relatable than Debbie Downer. News or random facts are conversation starters you can use to "warm up the crowd," so to speak, and get the conversation flowing. Others might be very relieved that you took the lead, and took the burden off of them!

Idea 2: Use Tech Support

Use technology to increase your relatability! Doing a little Facebook creeping, er, professional research, on someone's social media accounts prior to meeting is an excellent way to start to get to know them. If the person intimidates you, this will also help allay your nerves when you see them as a real person, out on a boat with their family, at an outdoor concert or posting an article about a business topic that's important to them. They're in to rock climbing? Cool, so are you. Boom, relatibility achieved and you haven't even met yet.

Once you've made a contact, record a note or reminder in your phone of an important event that's coming up for them. For example:

- In your smartphone's Contact Info, add to the Notes section that your boss's go-to coffee drink is a Grande Americano with a little bit of steamed milk, and his wife's name is Jill.

- Your girlfriend's daughter's 5th birthday is coming up next weekend. Put a reminder in your phone to text her Happy Birthday that day.

- Your customer is going on vacation to Hawaii and you won't see him for at least another month. Put a note in your phone so you'll remember to ask about his trip the next time you see him.

- Your out-of-state coworker's mom is having foot surgery next week. Make a calendar note to reach out a few days later and ask how she's doing.

With just a little effort and planning, your relatability will soar. You'll have a lot of fun testing out new ways to start conversations, sharing interesting facts, sparking excitement in someone, or sharing an exciting interest of yours. The conversation will generate contagious energy and is an enjoyable way to learn interesting and random facts about the people who surround you.

Use technology to help you remember important details. I'd be a hot mess without the calendar and contact info I've stored in my phone! Simply having the courage to ask one tiny question, or offer one fun fact or positive piece of news can give you all the momentum you'll need.

Idea 3: Memorize the state capitals

Or re-memorize them if you need to recall what your 4th grade teacher once drilled into your head. Hear me out on this one. How does memorizing state capitals make one more relatable? Because everyone is from somewhere. When you meet someone, ask where they're from. You'll be relatable right away when you bust out with, in your humblebrag way, "Oh, you're from Arkansas? Little Rock is the state capital, right? Did you grow up near there?" Or, "Oh, the Northwest...I hear Washington is a lovely state. Olympia is the capital, correct? Or is it Seattle? I can never keep them straight!" State capital memorization is a really beautiful technique to show that, one, you listened to their response, and, two, you know something about where they came from, a place near and dear and familiar to them. Watch them light up when they see you know a little something about them and care enough to mention it.

Here's a bonus geography challenge: Set a travel goal. My friend Christine is out to hit all the National Parks. My friend Stacy wants to climb every 14,000' mountain in Colorado. My sister has seen almost every zoo in Ohio, Michigan and Indiana! I'm working on all seeing a baseball game at all the Major League ballparks.

Travel is fun, you learn a lot, and it ups your chances of connecting with someone. How neat and easily relatable when you share experiences others can relate to, even in a tiny way. ("You've been to Yosemite? Oh, my cousin just went hiking there.")

And if you really want to challenge yourself, in addition to memorizing state capitals, aim for a longer term goal of visiting all 50 states. Imagine how much you'll learn and the color you could add when you ask someone, "*So where are you from?*" "You're from Las Cruces, New Mexico? The pecan capital of the country, right?" "Kansas City? More water fountains per capita than any other city, I believe!" Or while you're working on your list, try, "I haven't been there yet, but it's on my list! What's a must do?" Enjoy the smiles and laughs that follow.

Idea 4A: Watch ESPN

If sports are your thing, SportsCenter's Top 10 is quick, it's interesting, and it's uplifting. It's a prime source of relatability fuel. Many people love to talk about sports. What I like about sport news is that it's positive. There are *always* winners and a lot of feel-good stories about the perseverance and dedication it took to get there. So imagine yourself using sports to up your relatability score:

"Wow, did you see that game-winning dunk Jefferson made in last night's Nuggets game?"

"Did you see UCLA come from behind against Texas A&M? Biggest comeback in 27 years!"

You *don't* have to be an expert. Just a few timely or exciting tidbits will do the trick to break the ice and quickly connect.

Idea 4B: If Sports Aren't Your Thing, Watch *Some Good News*

As an alternative, watch John Krasinski's YouTube Channel, *Some Good News*. There's enough bad news out there. Be the person that struts your relatability and share something inspiring, engaging and heart-warming.

What's interesting to you? What challenge can you think of that would allow you to relate to just about anybody? Brainstorm and add to the list!

In Summary

Being relatable is about being curious, being a thoughtful listener, and giving others the opportunity to get excited about what excites you. Enjoy the journey as each conversation is an opportunity to find people with whom you can naturally relate and work or collaborate with in a way that feels organic, safe and unforced.

And if all else fails, grab those heels, flats, or flip-flops and *stand tall in your power!* Regardless of how you measure up while standing next to Kareem Abdul-Jabbar, your confidence is contagious, and others will certainly relate to that!

What's at Stake?

Shallow conversation, or no conversation at all, isn't going to advance your career. With just a little bit of (really fun) effort, increasing your relatability increases your visibility – and helps to foster opportunities in your career.

Key Points

- Relatability is the ability to quickly connect with another.
- A small phrase, sometimes even a smile, is enough to get things started.
- There is no exact formula for what to say. The key is to have a few go-to ideas up your sleeve and use them in rotation.
- Demonstrating relatability is an easy way to make someone's day.

Confidence Challenge Checklist

- ❑ Commit to memorizing three good open-ended questions and practice with people you already know or someone new.
- ❑ Write down your three "things."
- ❑ Pick an avenue for acquiring fun, random, and useful or useless facts.
- ❑ Grab a shy or introverted friend and practice on each other!

To condition and claim my confidence, one action I commit to is:

_____

_____

_____

Chapter 13
Mentors, Allies, and Champions

I'm so excited to write this chapter! Partly because the importance of a good mentor is immeasurable, and also because creating your network is an essential piece to achieving the career success you deserve and desire. If I could name one strategy that influences your career path more than any other thing, it is this. It is thrilling to be surrounded by people who teach you, inspire you, and demonstrate the type of leadership characteristics to which you, yourself, aspire.

As we've seen in other chapters, confidence and positive energy are contagious. You'll know you've found the right mentor, ally, or champion – MAC for short – when that person lights a spark inside you.

Common questions that come up about MACs include, "How do I find a mentor?" "How do I initiate an alliance?" "Why do I need a champion?" "What does having a MAC really even mean?" Those questions and more will be answered here. The magic of mentors will be explained as well as how this relationship is not only a gift to you, the mentee, but a gift to the mentor, too.

I'll start by sharing how I connected with my most trusted mentor, a man who at first could not have seemed more of a mismatch.

On a cold and rainy morning in Denver my alarm went off at 5:30am – particularly early. Dreary days being very rare in Denver, it would have been so easy to hit the snooze button and roll over at least three more times. But a friend had invited me to attend the South Denver Metro Chamber "Captains of Industry" breakfast panel. It started at 7:00am and took place a decent distance south of home. I grudgingly slid out of bed and began my routine. I drove to the breakfast, arriving just six minutes before it began, and greeted my friend.

Her cheery smile immediately made the dreary day seem less so. She motioned to the seat she'd saved for me and I sat down, meeting my tablemates and shaking hands with them.

The panel discussion began as breakfast was served. The "Captains of Industry" were five distinguished men and women, each representing a different business sector important to Denver. There were representatives from healthcare, tech, economic development, construction, and finally a gentleman from the oil and gas industry.

When people picture an oil executive from Central Casting, they picture Jack. He was white and in his 50s, silver-haired, sharply dressed, with a rather austere presence and an all-business demeanor. Jack drew my interest; I worked in renewable energy and sustainability. On the "green" side of energy, we viewed those who extracted fossil fuels as the dark side. We were natural opponents, more fierce than college rivals on football Saturdays.

Jack's contributions to the discussion reinforced the stereotype in my mind. He was abrupt, sardonic, confident in his ways, and wise in his industry knowledge. He minced no words, told it like it was, and didn't seem to care if anyone agreed or not. His primary purpose in being there wasn't to make friends, but to share facts and details about industry realities and forecasts.

When Jack spoke, I could see some audience members were taken aback by his sarcasm. I, on the other hand, found it entertaining, raw, and intriguing. I remember wondering if this was typical, or if Jack was having a bad morning. Either way, I had to meet this guy. I reached into my bag to make sure a business card was poised and ready to go.

After 45 minutes the panel offered closing remarks and the breakfast plates were cleared. Tablemates exchanged cards and bundled up before heading out into the rain to get their workdays started. I thanked the friend who'd invited me and walked to the front of the room where Jack was standing. I was fresh out of grad school: blond, bubbly, and passionate about saving the planet one carbon footprint at a time. I was admittedly intimidated and nervous as I approached Jack, but seized with too much curiosity to stop. He was so different from me, and I felt compelled to uncover what made him tick.

We made eye contact and I extended my hand. "Hello, Jack. My name is Jamie Dandar and I really enjoyed hearing what you had to say today." Confidently I received the hand he proffered and shook it firmly. Jack looked at me a bit quizzically. He smiled and in a softer tone than he'd projected as a panelist onstage, said hello, and asked what I did for work.

"Well, this should be good," I thought to myself, ready to spew my green-and-clean credentials.

"I work on the green side."

"Hmmm," said Jack. "That sounds really interesting. How might I help you?" The whole room had been surprised, perhaps even shocked, by some of what Jack said in the discussion. Now it was my turn to be surprised one-on-one.

I replied that I wasn't yet sure, but I'd bet him a cup of coffee we might be able to figure it out.

Again Jack smiled, and was that a small chuckle I heard under his breath? "Send me an email and let's get something on the calendar," he said, and handed me his card. "You'll have it in your inbox later this morning," I said, exchanging his card for mine. "Have a great day, Jack."

When I walked outside that cold, dreary day somehow seemed a bit brighter. I was more than surprised. My encounter with the fossil-fuel enemy had not only left me unscathed, but with a pending coffee meeting! And no regular meeting, either: a meeting with an intimidating big shot, far senior to me, a white-haired male executive from none other than the dark side.

I was absolutely thrilled.

Fast forward to present day. Jack and I were laughing over lunch, reminiscing about our first encounter. In the ten plus years since that day, I've been so honored to have Jack as my mentor, trusted advisor, influencer, champion, project partner, and friend – a friend I can unequivocally trust and rely upon every time.

Jack's influence and guidance lured me over to work in the oil and gas industry, an industry about which I had so many misconceptions with regard to environmental impact and how much it actually works alongside green energy. I was interviewed on a radio show with Jack. I produced an industry-related video with him, and had Easter dinner with him and his beautiful wife Diane. It was Jack who gave a toast at my wedding; at whose retirement party I spoke; and with whom I've had infinite lunches, coffees, and conversations – all because I didn't hit snooze on that rainy Denver morning.

With Jack I won the professional-mentor lottery. The dividends of a great mentor relationship are unsurpassed. As with co-workers, good books, and socks, it's advantageous to have more than one. Mentors come in all varieties and having a small, diverse portfolio at hand will serve you well.

The Importance of Mentors

Before we dive into finding a mentor, let's examine why they're such an integral part of your success.

Good mentors are beacons, voices of reason, and guiding lights.

Some are willing to play a therapeutic role in your career: like a therapist, they'll listen and help. (While they don't take insurance, they don't charge either!) A good mentor is accessible and won't leave you hanging on hold. They're not a sounding board for drama, necessarily, yet they will listen and ask questions to help you see things from a different point of view. They'll likely share experiences of their own that might be relatable and applicable to your situation, or spark curiosity in you. They'll almost certainly offer advice, support you, and possibly advocate on your behalf. They'll share resources and steer you toward opportunities of which you were unaware.

Whether you're just starting out your career or are a seasoned professional, you'll face challenges and unknowns. Myriad resources are available to help you reseach and navigate those circumstances, such as internal databases of courses and resouces offered by your employer. Externally, of course, YouTube, white papers, more databases, websites, and, heck, maybe even Pinterest, can connect you to a lot of answers. But mentors, mentors add color and depth that exceed what you'll find on a website or in a video. You'll learn so much from them by listening and observing.

Another mentor, John, was a phenomenal visionary. His brain worked in ways that astounded me. Every time we talked, I learned something new. Conversations with John left me with lists of things I wanted to look up and further explore. He really helped expand and stretch my mind in ways it hadn't previously known.

As you're going about your career, mentors are helpful at many times, and two in particular. When you're working on a new project, and when you're itching to take your career to the next level or in a new direction.

You'll want someone you can connect with on a regular basis, you can bounce ideas off of, and who will help hold you accountable for self-imposed deadlines. You'll want to feel as though you and your mentor can easily pick up where you left off. "How did your presentation go?" "What happened with the manager that you were having communication issues with?" "How's your interview prep going? What questions do you want to practice?" A good mentor knows enough about your life to ask such questions, have continuing impact, and be relevant.

While mentors do not have to be local to you, whenever possible meet in person. A lot can be accomplished over video chats, phone, email, and text..Yet I still maintain that even in the midst of all the tech options, there's still nothing as effective as an in-person meeting. Studies show that bonding occurs when handshakes are exchanged, and two people are physically in the presence of each other, something that cannot be accomplished over Zoom!

Mentors will allow you to talk out ideas and solutions, and create space for original thought to flow in a safe, judgment free zone. Something you may not have in your regular business environment. Mentors are voices of reason and confidantes. They have your best interest in mind and want to see you succeed.

Finding a Mentor

Anxious to get the mentor party started? Let's look at how to acquire mentors. It can be really fun. There's a variety of ways! Here are a few ideas of where to look.

- Many industries and professional environments have **formal mentorship programs**. Places to look include within your own company, at chambers of commerce, trade associations, women's organizations, alumni networks, and even at hobbyist organizations. The mentor and mentee are matched and, to help foster the mentee's development, given a specific rubric to support the regular exchange of information.

- Less formally, you can meet potential mentors at **networking events**. The South Metro Denver Chamber event where I met Jack was one such event. I'm sure the Chamber had others such as golf tournaments, happy hours, or charity events. You can network at trade association events when the association has no formal program. Ask colleagues and managers within your company what industry groups they belong to. See if you can tag along with them to an event to check it out and perhaps join.

- Sign up for a virtual event ideally where you can see the mosaic of faces also attending. Pick out a few names from the mosaic and find them on LinkedIn. Reach out to the people who spoke during the event either via the contact info they provide or LinkedIn. And speaking of LinkedIn...

- **LinkedIn** is truly your BFF for networking to find a mentor and for a whole host of other reasons. Let's say you're new to a role, company, industry, or city. Search LinkedIn for others in your industry who hold higher titles. Reach out and introduce yourself, saying that you're new and want to connect with people who might be able to share wisdom. They may or may not respond but keep trying until you find someone who does. I did this when I was promoted to a newly created position in my company. With no example to follow, I turned outwards for advice and guidance. I reached out to someone who had experience under the title that I had just acquired. "May I bend your ear for some advice?" I asked on LinkedIn. He responded that sure, he'd love to connect, and we quickly set up what turned out to be a useful, educational call.

It's important to connect with people who've been in your industry for a while. Leaning on their experiences will serve you well as you get a feel for the industy's history and significant events. It's also important to connect with both men and women. As we've seen in this book, genders see things in very different ways. It's really helpful to learn a point of view different from your own. Gender, of course, being just one variable.

In all major categories of your life, mentors are such an invaluable resource. I rely on my parents for some things, Jack for others, my husband for his strategic insights, my friend Patricia who's amazing with holistic insight, and a woman at the top of her company – in the same industry as mine – whenever I need management or big-picture advice. I need different resources at different times and I'm intentional about lining up the right go-to mentors. My mentor list evolves over time based on ever-changing life circumstances.

How about you? How does your list look or how will it look? What areas are complete and where are there gaps to fill? Take a minute and fill in the table below:

Mentor within my company	
Mentor in the same industry, outside of my company	
Woman mentor	
Male mentor	
Highest up the org chart I can go to seek a mentor	
Freestyle – Who would be a good mentor?	

I've often been asked if mentorship is like dating. "Do I have to, like, ask my mentor out on an official mentor date?" "Is there a form that can be filled out?" "Will this be awkward?" "What if they say no?" While there is no romantic element to mentorship, you do have to ask for the appointment, and you may experience rejection...or not. But that's where the parallel ends. A clear professional line should be drawn and honored.

How defined the relationship is, is up to you. To maximize clarity and value, you'll want to name it so both of you are aware. A simple ask can make it official: "I really enjoy learning from you. May I call you my mentor?" In the case of formal mentorship programs, there will be a process and very clear labels for mentors and mentees alike.

When seeking out a mentor on your own, you may want to clearly state your purpose. At a networking event you can say, "I'm looking to develop my skills in product management, and I'm looking for a mentor. Is there anyone you recommend I should meet?" On LinkedIn, you may want to use a similar approach. A productive mentor-mentee relationship will develop organically as you meet repeatedly with someone and then, one day, find yourself referring to him or her as your mentor. They may be very flattered!

There are a variety of approaches you can take. Lean on the suggestions here and use what feels most natural to you. The main goal is for you to be inspired and enlightened by the relationship while simultaneously giving back to your mentor. This brings us to you, the mentee, and your contribution to the relationship.

How To Be a Good Mentee

As a mentee, you'll want to play your part. The general assumption is that a mentor does more of the "giving" in the relationship. Yet as the recipient of a mentor's time, wisdom, and advice, a good mentee will keep four things in mind.

1. It is up to you to establish the rhythm and cadence of your relationship. Strong relationships take time and consistency to develop. You'll want to be respectful of your potential mentor's time, so ask what a reasonable meeting frequency looks like. Send an email and take initiative in sending the calendar invite.

2. Show up on time and be prepared. What do you want to review with your mentor? Come prepared with questions based on the role you want your mentor to play in your professional life. What do you want to learn about him or her? What skill set do you want to develop that

he or she already has? What advice are you looking for? What project are you working on that you'd love to talk through with your mentor?

3. Follow up. Follow up. Follow up. This is crucially important. It confirms to your mentor that his or her time was well-spent. Following up also demonstrates respect and your ongoing interest and commitment in developing a relationship with your mentor. To follow up, do these things:

   a. Send a thank-you email (or even the occasional handwritten note!) the same day you meet or the day after at latest, highlighting what you appreciated in particular about your meeting and what action item(s) you're going to tackle.

   b. Do your action items. If your mentor mentioned an article you should look up, then do it and jot down a few notes you can reference during your next conversation. If they gave you a referral or a lead, follow up with that person.

   c. Let your mentor know when you've completed your follow-up tasks and how it went. If they gave you advice on a presentation, project, or forthcoming conversation with your boss, let them know how it went afterward and thank them again for their contributions and help.

   d. Generally speaking, it's simple. Be courteous and have integrity. Say thank you and share updates. Simple as that!

5. Be proactive. When YOU find an article, event, referral, or piece of information relevant to your mentor, send it to them! They'll appreciate your motivation and this establishes a really solid platform for EXCHANGING information. The best relationships are two-sided. While your depth of wisdom or experience may be on different levels, your willingness and eagerness to reciprocate, even if just sharing an update, should be fairly equal.

As many mentors will tell you, it's not a one-sided relationship. Jack's version of our mentor-mentee story is quite different. While I could write additional pages summing up what I've learned from him, I know he has learned from me as well.

Other mentor-mentee relationships are less formal and scheduled. In that case, I recommend a mentee take responsibility to reach out to her mentor with the frequency necessary for each side to feel a trusted relationship is developing. Maybe it's over coffee. Maybe it's a phone call. Maybe it's a quick "walk and talk" appointment, my favorite way to meet when I know I won't need to take notes.

What To Talk About with My Mentor

- When you have to vent, which we all do from time to time, a mentor outside your company may provide a professional, safer sounding board. Don't let the session sour into a "bitch fest," though, and make sure to talk about opportunities and positive options too. End on a high note!
- Current projects – the mentor's and the mentee's
- Challenges with projects
- Challenges or uncertainty about co-workers and managers
- Reviews of how a presentation or project went
- The mentor's work history, experience, career highlights and lowlights
- Current events or industry news
- Upcoming events that can be networking opportunities
- New people to connect with and meet, also known as referrals
- Career goals and aspirations

Remember "MAC" – mentors, allies, and champions? Mentors are the "M" in the mix. Next come allies.

Allies

Allies can help you light a meeting on fire in ways that blow away your fellow meeting attendees. Allies are there to support you out front, stick up for you, and promote you in outgoing, apparent ways.

One of my favorite allies was an amazing friend and co-worker, Kaci. Kaci and I were introduced by a Houston non-profit. We were both in Denver and shared an interest in starting a local chapter of that non-profit. As chapter leaders we got to know each other. Our leadership and work styles meshed incredibly well. With time, our jobs changed and we found ourselves having ceded our roles at the non-profit – but, long story short, we wound up working at the same company. Kaci was already there as vice president of sales and invited me in to interview for vice president of marketing. Wow, what a team we were! As the only two women on an otherwise all-male executive team and board of directors, Kaci and I had each other's backs like nobody's business.

We thought very similarly about strategies, tactics, and values. In meetings, especially strategic planning meetings where one of us presented research, findings, or ideas, the other would chime in support. If anyone challenged either one of us, we always advocated for the other. It was powerful and bracing. Our confidence was exponentially increased by our ally-ship.

Kaci once told me, "I love that you're saying the same thing to Heath that I am, yet in a different way and at a different time. I feel so supported and we're getting so much done! When only one of us makes a point, he'll listen but might still be skeptical. Yet when the other one of us jumps in, he thinks it's the best idea we've had yet, and wants us to implement right away! This is so productive!"

We had a blast at our jobs, supporting each other along the way. We also held very honest two-handed feedback sessions, each offering advice about how the other could improve or do something differently in future. It takes skills (which you'll learn in the next chapter!) to take criticism. Having those types of conversations with just anyone isn't easy. In a safe environment, as allies, we shared valued feedback, and our individual performance improved because of it.

To have an ally, be an ally. Who's that person at your company you naturally jibe with? Or possibly could if you put some intention behind developing that relationship? Once you have someone in mind, have a formal conversation about it. Name it to claim it, the relationship, that is and enjoy the advocacy, confidence, camaraderie and success to come.

Champions

Finally, the "C" in MAC: champions. A champion is someone within your company who supports you and looks out for you, another important relationship to prioritize and nurture. Champions tend to be seasoned veterans of the organization, or someone recently up and out of the role you have now. They'll wave invisible pom-poms and cheer you on, on the front-lines and from the behind the scenes. There's nothing particularly formal about the relationship you have with a champion, other than intentionally carving out time to have a conversation, and they're sure worth recognizing and thanking when they support you.

Here's an example. A major energy company held a woman-specific networking event. Top-performing women from throughout the company's global operations convened at the Houston headquarters to listen to speakers, learn in workshop sessions, and network. Top managers and executives attended as well. They wanted to meet the talent who had been granted these special invitations. So it happened that a vice president of business development met a business development manager from a small territory. They exchanged cards. After returning home, she sent the VP a follow-up email saying it had been nice to meet him and asking that he keep her in mind for any special projects in the future.

A few months went by. The territory manager checked in about every four weeks, sharing information about a new customer she'd acquired, or commenting on a project elsewhere in the company. One day the VP happened to visit the city where she was based and asked to meet with her. She jumped at the chance and soon found herself working side-by-side on a special project with him, just as she'd suggested in her email months earlier. Their first project was a success and soon after, he offered her a promotion. After talking it over with her current manager, she gladly accepted the new role, advancing her career. She did an excellent job staying on the VP's radar, and he became a champion for her.

Here's a pro tip. To develop potential champions for yourself, create rotating reminders in your calendar to make contact. When a reminder shows up in my calendar, I do a little homework so the email I send or call I make contains information relevant and interesting to the recipient. After I make the contact, I update my calendar so I know to reach out again in a set amount of time – and I make a note of what we discussed so I can pick up right where we left off. "How did that pitch to ABC Customer go?" "How did your son's soccer tournament go?" "How is the (insert major project they're working on here) coming along?" When the potential champion knows you took the time to think of them, and remembered specifics rather than sent a generic "Hey, what's new?" email, it goes a long way.

You never know when they might be in an important meeting when your name comes up. You can bet they'll be cheering you on with no prompting from you. Or they may offer your name as the person to be invited into an opportunity. Authentic third-party testimonials are among the most effective marketing tools. Testimony from a champion singing your praises carries a lot of weight and adds fuel to accelerate your career.

Summing It Up

Mentors, allies, and champions offer relationships to be cherished. Professional success rarely happens on an island. Incorporating MAC relationships into your career with intention and focus will elevate your knowledge and boost your confidence. Having a bad day? Call your mentor and talk it out. Presenting a new pitch or data review to colleagues? Give your ally a chance to review and critique your draft presentation, and if possible, make sure she or he is there when you're presenting. ("That's an excellent point, Madelyn. Could you tell us how you came up with that great idea?") Interviewing for a promotion? See if your champion is available for coffee to talk through your interview prep and strategize about follow-up.

Having someone who genuinely supports you, whom you trust unequivocally, and who has your best interests in mind will help you succeed at work like almost nothing else. And you'd be surprised how rewarding it is for them as well.

I mentioned that Jack's version of our mentor-mentee story is a bit different than mine. I know now that in the early stages of our professional relationship, when I thought he was giving, giving, giving, and I was taking, taking, taking, something much more balanced was happening. We were partnering on projects, he wrote letters of recommendation on my behalf for interviews, and I absorbed every detail he shared about oil and gas. Wonderful benefits for me – but something happened for Jack as well. The sardonic, grumpy, hard-shell exterior I first saw at the Captains of Industry breakfast panel one dreary morning developed a tiny fissure. In fact, it progressed to a darn big crack. Jack's ability to help me, and my eagerness to learn and express my gratitude, softened him in a way he says "was much needed, and is a much healthier place to be." Both our lives are enhanced and enriched for having the other in it. What a gift!

It's exciting to consider who might become your mentor, ally, or champion. These special and strategic relationships might simply be the catalyst for a better day – or jolt you to a life-changing promotion. Be curious, be brave, be good at saying thank you and following up. Be a good mentee, and your mentors may thank *you* for what you did for *them*.

What's at Stake?

Floundering, ruminating, wondering why others make things happen while you're stuck in churn cycle, feeling alone, and overall dissatisfaction. Ugh! Strong mentors will help you stave off frustration, see bigger visions than what you can see on your own, and steer you through exciting advancements of your career.

Key Points

- Great mentors are game-changers and share in the joy of your victories.
- Allies and Champions are particularly helpful in situations where you're struggling to find your voice, an essential part of career success.
- A good mentee shows up, follows through, and expresses gratitude.
- A symbiotic relationship results in a synchronized mentor-mentee commitment.

Confidence Challenge Checklist

- ❑ Identify one person in each MAC category -- mentor, ally, and champion – and invite them to coffee for a test run.
- ❑ If you're at the very beginning of a mentor search, keep a list of things at work that confuse or frustrate you. You'll want to find a mentor who has familiarity with these things.
- ❑ If your friends and colleagues have mentors, ask how they found them and what purpose they serve in career support and encouragement.
- ❑ Ask someone to commit to be your mentor and set up a regular plan for meeting.

To condition and claim my confidence, one action I commit to is:

_____

_____

_____

SPEAK UP, Sister!

Chapter 14
Transforming Criticism into Compliments

If I have kale in my teeth, I'm begging you to tell me right now! If you see my zipper is down, I implore you to share your observation. If my eye shadow wound up on my forehead or I have a typo in my PowerPoint, please do speak up! Sans mirror, I have only limited angles on myself, after all! Ah, the things others observe that we cannot see in ourselves.

While as individuals we're often trying our hardest to do our best, we never achieve our goals in total isolation. Other peoples' thoughts, opinions, and perspectives influence ours. Our individual blind spots can be bigger than those on a Chevy Suburban without a backup camera. Yet we can achieve 360-degree feedback by inviting the observations of those around us. Have you ever been parallel parking in a tight spot and had your passenger jump out to help guide you? Unless you have the fancy Lexus that will do the parking for you, many of us have certainly taken advantage of an extra pair of eyes. Why? Because they can see more angles than we can from our own driver's seat.

To humbly listen and learn about what others see in us can be eye-opening and beneficial. Many times, their observations or unsolicited suggestions can be helpful and positive. Other times, feedback can be harsh, hurtful, or critical. It can sting. It can rattle. It can kill our confidence. It can leave us feeling unworthy and defensive – but, and here's the secret, *only if we allow it to do so.*

Criticism can be hard to take, but criticism you reconsider and reframe so it has the effect of a *compliment* is truly a gift. You can turn the tables! The relief of learning something that could otherwise have hurt you in the future, and the joy of being turned on to something you hadn't thought of are just two of the gifts that can come from criticism. Criticism may enlighten you, and steer you onto an entirely different, *better* trajectory. Heck, you may even wind up thanking the messenger, no matter how heartily you might have cursed him or her in silence at first!

The journey to achieving that state of mind can be a tad bumpy! Understandable initial reactions to criticism include hurt feelings, a self-defeating state of mind, thoughts of incompetency, and a deflated attitude. And let's acknowledge that the criticism you take the hardest likely comes from someone untrained to deliver it as constructive feedback, nor with concern for how it lands. Sometimes criticism innocently intended to point out something you hadn't thought of comes out far more aggressive than planned.

My friend Rachel works in healthcare. She teaches a course on how to compassionately deliver criticism. Her students come out choosing their words more carefully and effectively. They're more mindful about timing, of privacy so others can't eavesdrop, and of focusing criticism on the *behavior itself*, not the person performing the unsatisfactory behavior.

I'm sure that when you deliver criticism, you do it sensitively, and take the time to consider these factors. And as you know, not everyone does.

You don't have much control over how others deliver criticism.
Yet you have full control over how you interpret it, what you do with it,
and how you move past it.

When someone's harsh, critical words land in a pleasant moment like a sneak attack, it can be very jarring. It can be hurtful, and make you want to sink through the floor. You may form a visceral response, feeling a pit in your stomach.

But, pssst!, here's the secret benefit. And it's a game changer.

When you put some intention into getting beyond hurt feelings and the disgust you feel toward your critic (it's not easy, I know), the core content of what was said may prove extremely useful, even insightful. Strip out the emotion, remove your own assumptions or inferences, forget your critic's harsh tone, and you might find that the criticism actually includes very valuable information. It could be a treasure trove even if delivered in a really ugly treasure chest.

Once this realization is in place, you have a powerful choice about how to handle criticism. You can take it or leave it. You can let it weigh you down. You can ruminate over it. (Although you know the benefits and methods of not indulging in toxic rumination.) Or you can consider it for a moment, and either incorporate it or toss it aside like an empty Mentos wrapper.

When you can pause to consider criticism and perhaps use it to your advantage, it truly becomes an opportunity for success. It's a rich opportunity for self-improvement when you can focus on the content of what your critics are saying. More on this shortly.

Why It's Such a Stinger

Your ability to use criticism to your advantage and interpret it as a compliment is a huge opportunity for valuable personal and professional growth. Why is this an important skill for professional women in particular? Because men tend to have an easier time with taking criticism. Looking again at data, studies show correlations between youth sports activity and social conditioning influencing how one handles criticism. From an early age, boys are more often yelled at by coaches who use criticism to motivate. When they're told they're slow, or can't catch the ball to save their life, or their swing is crap, it often motivates them to complete their wind sprints faster, or improve their fielding or batting average. When their flaws are pointed out publicly, it can fuel better performance.

Women often have different formative experiences. Even in sports, the language is softer. It's nicer and less aggressive. Women tend to be "critiqued" more than criticized. Encouragement is an effective motivator for women.

Think about the implications as we fast-forward to your present-day adult life. Think about how this conditioning might affect you in a professional environment. The more criticism you heard growing up, however, the better you handle it. Criticism is part of the job. You can hear it, learn from it, appreciate it to some degree, make adjustments when you find it to be helpful and, either way, move on. If you're not conditioned to receive criticism as a child, and if feedback was given in only very careful, gentle ways, it can affect how well you cope with it as an adult.

When you're on the receiving end of criticism, feelings can get hurt. There can even be pouting. After receiving negative feedback, a coping method might be to commiserate with a friend, "Can you believe he bagged on my presentation like that? Who does he think he is?" Or, "She totally cut me off right when I was getting to my point." Criticism tends to be processed as a personal attack, rather than an attack or oberservation of the behavior in question.

But look closer. Who is its source? What could be the motivating factors behind it? Are you a unique target, or is this fairly standard behavior, directed at others as well? Most importantly, is there validity to the criticism? Can you find value in it? Can others help you find it? Remember, others can see angles that we can't see on our own.

A present-day demonstration of men tending to have an easier time than women taking criticism is observed in social media.

I get a big kick out of the comments on posts made by Noah, my 17-year old cousin. Noah is a high school senior, quarterback of the football team, and a regular at the gym. He posted a beach picture in which he's wearing board shorts and no shirt. The comments from his buddies cracked me up, "Fat boiii, Dad bod really hittin, Where are your abs?" Just your average, funny, teenage boy banter. My cousin Brandi, just a few years older than Noah, posted a similar pic of herself in a bathing suit. The comments on Brandi's feed? "Cutie, Babe, ILYSM." (ILYSM = I Love You So Much). Very nice. All complimentary. No criticism.

Imagine, if you will, interchanging the two. What if Brandi's commenters posted: "Fat giiiirl, Mom bod really hittin, and Where are your abs?" I mean, seriously, can you even imagine?

When I asked Noah about his comments he said they were funny, interpreting them as acceptance and inclusion from his buddies. Had Brandi received them, her reaction would likely have been much different. Back to language differences we discussed earlier, there are clear distinctions between genders.

The words men use to show their approval are more caustic, even bordering on critical, and it's a learned behavior. Try it yourself. Look at your own social media feeds. Concentrate on friends who've just updated their profile pics. Compare the comments men get from those women get. I bet you'll quickly detect different trends for men, than for women.

So instead of allowing a negative comment or piece of criticism to ignite a tailspin of unhealthy self-deflating thoughts, let's transform it into an opportunity for elevation and improvement.

Six Steps Toward Transforming Criticism into Compliments

There is a concise, productive process for receiving and processing criticism. It takes some practice and may be easier to implement, at first, on a high confidence day. When confidence is soaring, criticism won't affect you as much as on a day that your self-esteem has already taken a hit. However, if you can channel your frustration into forward motion, this may be exactly what you need to prove your own resilience. You've got this, sister! Either way, the following steps will certainly give you an advantage and two solid, confident legs to stand on!

Six Steps Toward Transforming Criticism into Compliments

1. Receive, listen to, and process the criticism.

2. Dismiss emotion, tone, and delivery factors if they were anything other less than professional or even neutral.

3. Consider the criticism's core content rather than the person who delivered it. Reflect only on *what* was said, rather than *how* or by *whom*.

4. Evaluate whether it has validity and can be an opportunity for improvement.

5. Take action: If it is valid, implement it for improvement. If not, dismiss it.

6. Move on!

Women who know how to take criticism use it to catapult themselves to higher performance.

It's liberating and empowering to hear valid criticism of your work, strip it of any negative emotion, implement it, and use it as an opportunity for improvement.

Try imagining that most criticism you hear is offered with good intention. Remember *assume positive intent* from the chapter on not taking things personally. Appreciate that it may be illuminating blind spots. It's providing you with information you can use to pivot on a project and deliver better results. Why? Because you listened, absorbed, learned from, and acted upon the feedback that was given, rather than dismissed it because of someone's crappy delivery of it.

In my own career, I didn't figure this out overnight. Nor did I immediately take to applying the six steps.

At first, criticism in the working world caused me great discomfort. Throughout school, in sports when I was a kid, and even in my first job out of college, I received a lot of pretty darn good feedback… over and over again. As I advanced into higher, more competitive positions, though, the gloves came off and the tone of the criticism was sometimes new and different. I sometimes found myself an unprepared target, standing squarely on a shooting range.

Whether you work in male-dominated industries or not, as your career accelerates and you gain confidence, as you build up courage to express unique ideas and chart new courses, you're going to encounter criticism. When you do, pat yourself on the back – because it means *you're getting somewhere*. Way to go!! Congratulations! *Mazel tov!* This is an excellent sign. When you're excelling in your job and drawing criticism in the process, you're testing limits and boundaries that haven't yet been explored, and man, oh, man, is that exciting! You deserve to be commended.

At the moment you're feeling attacked, however, it may not feel so exhilarating. Let me give you a firsthand example of criticism delivered to me in phenomenally harsh and awkward fashion. It was a dig that I was not at all expecting and I really had to fight to get through the rest of situation.

Criticism Transformation in Action

A couple of months before I was scheduled to give a big, potentially career-altering presentation, I did a practice round before a focus group. On a Sunday afternoon, five carefully selected girlfriends (my future audience would be all women) came over for a sneak peek at the project I'd been working on for months. I was terrified and excited. I welcomed my guests by serving mimosas and snacks. I wanted to set up the right frame: the exercise was meant to be fun and upbeat, yet I wanted real, honest feedback about the information I was about to present.

I gathered the group in my living room and projected my slides on the flat-screen TV. I handed out notepads and pens and requested no-holds-barred feedback. I explained what I'd been up to, why I'd been up to it, and what I wanted to achieve with my future audience.

Part of what I presented was my own life story. It was a personal account interwoven with research, the ultimate goal being an impactful and powerful message to empower professional women starting out in their careers. I'd spent nights and weekends preparing. My living room audience would give me my first honest reactions. Talk about feeling vulnerable! I mean, these were my friends, of course, but my heart was pounding.

I started off. Things went smoothly at first. I saw nodding heads and thoughtful notes jotted. Intrigued, smiling faces were looking on as I delivered my material.

I reached the part of the presentation where I wanted to test out an audience exercise. I wasn't sure whether it would receive a cheer or a jeer, but here was where I wanted to test it out. Well, it garnered more of a jeer than a cheer. No big deal, though, I'd review later to see what improvements I could make. I'd rather find out now than later! My feelings weren't hurt, I didn't dwell on it, and I continued on.

And then, about two slides later, something happened. There was a shift. The energy in the room took a bad turn. Christina, a member of my intimate audience known for being particularly outspoken, interrupted me.

"Do you want us to hold our comments until the end or could we express them now?" she asked. Her tone was surprisingly aggressive. I was a little shaken.

Without allowing me to respond, she continued: "Because I am so *offended* right now, I cannot even *hear* you anymore." I glanced around the room. The others present seemed to be as surprised as I was by her words. Yes, of course, I wanted constructive criticism, yet this felt more like the prelude to a cafeteria table showdown in the movie *Mean Girls*.

Christina charged on with what I'll call an intense tirade. No exaggeration. She challenged the research I'd presented and criticized my ideas, going so far as to express disgust that I would even present them. She was incensed. And while I'd invited, even encouraged, criticism, I was not mentally equipped to field this attack. I was in shock over its intensity.

Yes, I had prefaced the presentation by asking for feedback, both positive and negative. What was happening in the moment, however, was really exceeding my expectations. I was at a loss for knowing what to do next. Christina's rampage was so extreme that, for a moment, I wondered if it was some sort of odd joke. Perhaps in a moment she'd interrupt herself, saying, "Oh my gosh, I am so kidding! I actually *love* what you're saying." But no. She went on sharing her unabashed, extremely critical opinions, and I was at a loss. Actually, and quite honestly, I was *utterly* devastated that all my hard work was being received – and savaged – like this. I had set out to provide impactful and powerful insight to help younger women. Christina's response was impactful and powerful, too, but not in the way I'd hoped. She was suggesting that I'd accomplished something much different than my goal.

My other audience members were wide-eyed, some with their mouths dropped open. They were silent until one interrupted Christina and volunteered a contrary, opinion, more supportive of me, and more what I had expected. Christina went at her, too.

Now I was in further disbelief, and actually becoming angry. It was one thing to criticize and attack *me*: I'd invited it, for better or worse. Being rude to a guest in my house, though, was a whole other issue. This had started out as such an exciting and fun afternoon (I mean, mimosas, for Pete's sake!), but was now spiraling into a hypercritical, venomous maelstrom of bubble-bursting – the bubble, of course, containing my hopes and dreams for the presentation.

I had previous experience handling hecklers in an audience, but that was a work-related audience. I had no experience catching sharp verbal daggers hurled at me by personal friends in my own living room. This was a level of criticism I'd never felt before. Believe me: *I felt it!*

After Christina reached the end of her declaration, the other, stunned, members of the group tried to retun the energy level back to where it was (my allies) by offering their verbal feedback. I slightly questioned if I'd lost complete control of my presentation. I needed a minute to process events, a self-awarded time-out, if you will. I was honestly happy to let everyone else talk for a bit, even if they went way off topic. I contemplated ending the afternoon. I wasn't sure if I wanted or cared to continue, feeling like I'd been punched in the gut and considering that I'd utterly failed in communicating the message I'd worked so hard to craft.

Yet after a few deep breaths, positive self-talk, and silent channeling of my confidence superpowers, I decided to take back the reins.

"Ladies, I love the conversation this has evoked!" I tried to say with as much genuine enthusiasm as I could. "I want to be respectful of your time. Why don't I get through the rest of my slides, then we can pick up more conversation at the end. Sound like a plan?"

"Oh, definitely, I want to hear the rest!" said one of my other audience members. The remaining heads nodded. So I continued to the finish, albeit with reduced energy than how I'd started. I powered up and made my best effort to carry on like Christina had never opened her mouth. While I continued, not cowering, Christina now stayed quiet, and the tension was admittedly palpable.

I reached the end, smiled, made eye contact with each of my audience members, and thanked them from the bottom of my heart for being there. They smiled back and clapped enthusiastically. A tiny yet surprising and welcome wave of euphoria (Brave-ah-na!) passed through me as I completed my test run.

Upbeat discussion followed. I received more feedback, offered now in a much more constructive way. Thankfully, the conversation continued with the exact type of feedback I'd hoped for: "Have you thought about this...? "Would it add value if at the end you said this...?" "I'd love more clarification when you talked about..." "I liked the part where you said...I wanted to hear more about *that*."

And I really, truly appreciated the impressions and ideas they shared. This was much more how I had envisioned the day.

What did Christina have to say at this point? Not a whole lot, inserting only the occasional head nod or "Um-hm." I did notice, however, that she continued to jot down notes and it appeared that she'd filled several pages. And then at the very end, she exclaimed with a huge smile and cheerleader-like enthusiasm, wildly different from the mean girl who sat in my living just moments earlier, "Well how do you feel?! You should be so proud of yourself!" This newfound energy felt incredibly foreign. Still recovering from her earlier comments, I didn't even try to match it. I politely smiled and nodded my head. Now it was my turn to not say much.

Everyone hung out for a little while longer for more snacks, mimosas, and friendly conversation. After they left, I gathered their feedback sheets and was just about to read over them when my husband came home. "How'd it go, babe?" he asked excitedly, having been an impromptu member of previous, informal practice sessions.

I looked at him. I was no longer in a place where I had to press on and could now process what had happened. My face fell. I let out a big exhale.

"Not like I thought it would." He gave me a supportive hug. I set down the feedback sheets and decided that my task was complete for the day. I'd give myself some space and pick it up later.

Several days passed and I resumed my project. I first read through all the feedback sheets, except Christina's. They were full of ideas and suggestions that were constructive and valuable. Then I reluctantly picked up Christina's, bracing myself to revisit the ugliness I had felt when she erupted at me.

As I took the time to read Christina's comments line by line (Step 1 in the 6 Step Process - Receive and process.), however, I was again thrown off guard, but in a much different way this time.

As I looked at the words, I first dismissed any implied emotion or tone (Step 2 - Neutralize.). I focused only on the words, rather the hand that had written them (Step 3 - Focus on what, not who.). I laid aside the harsh tone I'd heard in Christina's spoken words. I dismissed the defensive feelings that had washed over me. I didn't see her face, nor those of the other shocked audience members and I read her written notes rather clinically, as if I'd picked them up off the street not knowing a thing about the circumstances of how they got there.

At first, I noticed how thorough and articulate they were. The writer had captured a lot of detail.

"Huh," I thought, "This is actually chock full of really good ideas. There's some brilliant stuff in here (Step 4 - Evaluate for validity.)."

Focusing on the words and ideas, hearing only a flat, neutral voice behind them, I absorbed what I was reviewing in a completely different way than if I had allowed the emotion and the story of what had happened infiltrate my thoughts. I read and re-read the pages. And then, not be dramatic, but something truly *magical* happened.

My eyes were opened to an entirely different angle I hadn't considered. A better angle. A bigger angle. An angle that made my mouth drop open with excitement.

I set the sheets down and paused to process everything.

In the movie *A Christmas Story*, Ralphie gets his long-awaited Ovaltine decoder in the mail. Remember how excited he is to rip open the package and dive into the decoding, showing his delight with each suspenseful reveal of a new letter? Well, that's how I felt! My brain started reframing the presentation, considering impactful ways to change it, hopefully satisfying future audiences that much more! Poor Ralphie's decoder mission culminated in nothing more than a devastating letdown of an advertisement: "Be sure to drink your Ovaltine." For me, the decoding was going much better. Deciphering the code of Christina's criticism was paying off in amazing ways. It was truly an exciting shift! I was thrilled to return to my computer with renewed zest for refining my presentation (Step 5 - Implement improvements).

What a gift I received from this criticism! When we work on projects that are important to us, we're closer to them than anyone else. The danger is that your view can become myopic. Like the fabled frog in a pot of water that doesn't notice the temperature slowly rising, you might not notice things are going south for you until it's too late. Or perhaps you're basing things on your own life and experiences, and others might not resonate the way you expect. You may ask, "Who's right?' But in this case, I'd say it's not a matter of being right. Successful delivery of a message, report, or a proposal, is often a matter of connecting with your audience. Soliciting feedback in advance will help you achieve a higher success rate with your audience. The more feedback, both positive and negative, you process, the more inclusive and impactful your result will be!

I made some compelling changes based on Christina's feedback. I was pleased with my final product and, of course, I followed through with Step 6 - Move on.

So even though Christina's *delivery* was, well, um, really, truly, absolutely *sucky*, her content was fantastic. Since I was committed to making my message as relevant as I could for my well-understood audience, I traveled an uncomfortable path to get there, yet came out better on the other side. #winning!

Incidentally, when I delivered my revised, final presentation a month later, it was so well received, I was asked on the spot to come back again that same year. You, too, may endure a rocky road when stretching out of your comfor zone, yet when it's the journey, itself, that serves up an opportunity to discover improvements, well then buckle up! It is well worth the ride.

You might wonder what came of my friendship with Christina.

A month went by before we communicated again. One day her name appeared in my voicemail box. We hadn't spoken, messaged, texted, commented, liked, disliked, or anything since "attack day." I pressed play and listened intently.

"Jamie, my friend, you've been on my mind," Christina began.

She went on to very sincerely apologize and share that she had been triggered by something I'd said that day. The "something" had nothing to do with me, but she took it out on me, unfairly. Before hanging up, she kindly asked if she could take me to lunch to apologize in person and hug it out. Literally, that's what she said: "Hug it out." I paused and smiled. A welcome wave of relief rolled over me.

Our subsequent lunch, I'm pleased to report, was a civil meeting of two professional, mature women who are imperfect, forgiving, and able to accept criticism in a healthy way. While Christina never did share exactly what had triggered her, she sincerely apologized and even brought me an orchid to reinforce her *mea culpa*.

We're friends to this day and appreciate each other's ability to point out weaknesses or deliver criticism. We also made some new rules for doing so. Each of us gave permission to the other to raise a hand should criticism start to feel ugly and unproductive rather than constructive. The goal is to catch the criticism before it escalates, to the level we'd experienced in my living room, to where it becomes ineffective for both recipient and deliverer. Christina and I have a renewed and deep respect for one another, and believe it or not, she's one of the first people I got to bounce off new ideas.

Of course, not all criticism you or I receive will be as harsh as Christina's living room rampage. (Insert smile and exhale here!) In fact, most won't even be close to this. Every time you find yourself receiving unexpected criticism, when possible, take time to emotionally distance yourself so you can work through the Six Steps of Transforming Criticism into Compliments. Evaluate it at face value. If at that point you find it contributes value, great! Incorporate it. After all, someone may be pointing out the kale in your teeth, or that thing you didn't see. They could be handing you a missing piece for your puzzle. If you see no value, though, ditch it and move on.

We all will be on the receiving end of criticism we don't like from time to time. A very important point must be addressed, however, when it comes to respect and someone crossing a line. Under no circumstances should you tolerate someone yelling at you, berating or belittling you, or being otherwise verbally abusive. Toxic environments can do both short- and long-term damage to your self-esteem and well-being. They must not be ignored. If someone is continuously delivering criticism in a way that is disrespectful or verbally abusive, you'll need to address it directly with that person or his or her manager. If you're in a situation that borders on unprincipled, and is violating or upsetting you to the point that it inhibits your job performance and self-worth, take steps to ensure self-preservation and self-respect. Address the problem via safe channels. Give no one the power to tear you down.

Additional Tips to Navigate and Benefit from Criticism

On the flip side, there's a responsible way to receive criticism as well. How you react to criticism influences what happens next. Fighting fire with fire rarely douses flames. Remaining calm and professional, not escalating or pouting, possibly even thanking the critic, will help keep your mind in a constructive place and perhaps condition the other party to deliver the next dose of criticism more positively.

"Respond, but don't react," I heard Dr. Edith Eva Eger, a psychologist, tell Oprah on a Super Soul Sunday podcast. I believe that Dr. Eger is implying that it's fine to acknowledge, yet don't succumb to mirroring negativity. More words of wisdom from Dr. Eger include, "Our painful experiences aren't a liability—they're a gift." Transform that criticism into a gift and wrap it with a big bow if you're so inclined!

Trust me, you want feedback. You want people to show you what you've missed. Then on delivery day, you'll hand in a more complete product, not one with holes or leaks. And even though it may not feel like it, most people who give you feedback, no matter how harsh, care about you or your performance at some level. They're giving you information to support improvement, even if they do it in a savage way.

The only thing worse than receiving criticism is receiving none at all. When someone sees a mistake of yours yet doesn't share it, or keeps a better idea to themselves, that is cause for concern. It could be a sign that they may be attempting to sabotage you. So know that if they're 'knives out' that's better than back-stabbing.

Invite regular feedback. Welcome feedback even before it's given. Own the process of receiving it by inviting it early and often! Go on the offensive rather than the defensive. Get ahead of it. Do your work, and seek out occasional feedback from a variety of sources. Willingly share drafts of your work. Request input from managers and people who think differently than you do. If you're an introvert, ask an extrovert. If you're an engineer, ask someone in sales. If you're American, ask someone from a different culture. If security permits it, ask a friend or someone outside of the industry. I can almost promise you they'll point out something you've never thought of and you'll be better off for it!

Schedule your own reviews if management does not. I once started a job and was given zero feedback until my 90-day review, at which time my manager brought up things that had happened in my first week. I could have used the guidance then. *What was I supposed to do about it now?*

What I learned was to not leave my feedback destiny in someone else's hands. Based on what happened in that uncomfortable 90-day review, I made it a habit to send a calendar invite to my higher-up approximately every 30 days requesting a Strategy Review Session – feedback on whatever project(s) are most important at the time. In the Outlook invite, I'd name the event, *Q3 Sales Strategy Review*, using 'review' as a strategically chosen word. In the meeting, after we address the specific project, I ask, "What else? Anything else we should address? Any areas where you see an opportunity for improvement?" Invite additional feedback.

Stay in control by getting ahead of someone's criticism. Doing so allows the other party to offer criticism, but at the time and place of *your* choosing. This way, you won't be thrown off guard, and you're creating a boundary for the critic on how to deliver it.

Creating space to both give and receive criticism will likely serve you well. It will help prevent unspoken criticism from swelling up, then bursting out at a bad moment. Heck, you can use this technique in personal relationships, too! Create space for feedback before it becomes an issue. **And my favorite question to close feedback conversations is, "Are we aligned?"** It confirms you're on the same page and your performance is moving in the right direction.

A higher-up once told me he didn't care for the way I had handled a situation with Ron, one of my team members. This wasn't a scheduled conversation between the higher-up and me. It came up in the hallway between our offices. I listened; I recognized his point of view. I took what he said into account and said, in a neutral, agreeable tone, that I'd fix it. (Note: I did *not* apologize. I said I'd *fix* it.) Then, offering an opportunity for him to get anything else off of his chest, I asked in a friendly tone, "Anything else you want to discuss or address?"

"Nope," he said casually. "That's all."

Early the next week, I fixed the issue and reported back to him. "All good with Ron," I said. "Okay, thank you for taking care of that," he said. "Thanks for telling me about it," I said, and meant it with complete sincerity. Our communication was professional and direct. Had one of us chosen a different tone, timing, or words, the criticism could have gone in an unnecessarily complicated direction. Yet we each accomplished something: he needed something fixed; I fixed it. Problem solved, we moved along.

Criticism often precedes breakthroughs. We each process criticism differently based on social conditioning and experience. Who delivers criticism, the frame of mind of the recipient, how the rest of our day is going – they're all contributing factors. Keep in mind that receiving criticism is acknowledgement that you did something of note. You evoked a reaction or a response, and that deserves to be commended. Effective leaders don't sit around. They take action and risks. Doing likewise means you're challenging yourself, doing things you haven't done before, and stretching to learn new skills.

Luckily, there are effective ways to navigate criticism. Remember the six steps: Receive it, dismiss the emotional wrapping, consider the criticism's core content, evaluate its validity, take action or dismiss it, and move on.

The Greek philosopher Aristotle weighed in on criticism. He theorized that there is only one way to avoid criticism and that is to, "Do nothing. Say nothing. Be nothing." That, of course, would be so boring and underachieving! So not you!

Get comfortable facing criticism, and use it to your advantage so you can prove Aristotle right: Do something! Say something! Be something! And be criticized! Use criticism as leverage to improve your performance and accelerate your career.

I close this chapter with a final, profound question for you, my reader. I'm looking for your honest, unabashed response. Don't hold back and don't sugarcoat your words. Take a good look and please, I'm begging you, tell me ... do I have kale in my teeth?

What's at Stake?

Feeling you've been stabbed in the heart with criticism daggers tears down your awesomeness. Transforming criticism into valuable information that provides uplift for your own improvement and growth is the smartest response of all!

Key Points

- There's a social conditioning aspect to managing incoming criticism that can be alleviated when you reframe!
- Removing the emotion and focusing on the true facts will help advance you forward.
- Receiving criticism might wind up being among the best things that ever happen to you.
- Be a good steward of criticism by receiving it well. It is better to receive some than none at all!
- Greet criticism with gratitude, not a grudge, to make it work for you!

Confidence Challenge Checklist

- ☐ Think back on a situation when you were criticized and see if you can reframe it.
- ☐ Review past criticism to see if there's still an opportunity to learn from it and take action.
- ☐ The next time criticism comes at you, use the six steps in this chapter (Receive, Remove the Emotion, Consider the Content, Evaluate Validity, Take Action, Move On) to work through it and notice how you feel on the other side.
- ☐ Grab a friend and talk through a situation where she was criticized.
- ☐ Coach someone on how to give you feedback before the next opportunity for its delivery.

To condition and claim my confidence, one action I commit to is:

_____

_____

_____

Chapter 15
The Main Event: High-Stakes Communication

For a couple of years after grad school, I fulfilled my dream of working in renewable energy and sustainability, as you know. The gig went well until my employer failed to secure an expected funding round and was forced to make cuts. My department was let go. For the first time since I'd graduated from college 13 years earlier, I was unemployed. A single woman with a mortgage and without a job.

My mentor at the time, Jack, whom you met in Chapter 13, had by that point become a close friend. With a soft job market in renewables, Jack, the oil and gas executive, really took me under his wing. He opened my eyes to facets of the industry that enticed me to pursue an industry shift.

I became interested in a large oil and gas service provider that was casting around for a sales executive with my skill set. The company had a global presence and seven different business units. But most of the workforce had technical degrees and engineering or science backgrounds. I had only business degrees; on paper, I was not a logical fit. Nonetheless, I gave it a shot and found myself invited to an interview.

It would be a classic example of High-Stakes Communication.

I'll hit pause on the story of what happened in my oil and gas interview to focus for a moment on High-Stakes Communication. This chapter throws a spotlight on the art and science of successful communication in high-stakes situations.

Recall that our confidence gets rattled in two primary kinds of circumstances: when we find ourselves in unfamiliar territory, and when the stakes are high. This chapter provides further remedies – proven techniques to familiarize the unfamiliar and prepare you for High-Stakes Communication. They won't lessen the stakes, yet your diligent preparation will give you a shield of confidence and a "Yes, I can!" attitude.

Everything laid out in previous chapters culminates here. Now that you've acquired and practiced new confidence skills, your A game is teed up! You are ready for the main event.

A job interview isn't the only example of High-Stakes Communication. The groundwork we're about to lay also covers negotiating, pitching to investors, having a tough conversation with your boss, asking for a promotion or raise, or selling to a prospective customer or a partner. It will apply in moments of confrontation, conflict resolution, and change management. It applies to situations where you have high visibility and an opportunities to strut your stuff in front of important people. Even in networking situations, a little High-Stakes Communication thinking makes you that much more on-point and effective. Preparing for any one of the circumstances via the means suggested here will render a transferable skill set you may apply for your next high-stakes moment as well.

The goal of this chapter is not to overwhelm you with an A to Z list of questions that must be answered in advance of and in order to have a successful meeting, but rather to give you a variety of questions to help you prepare, to get your mindset in a constructive place and to add some flavor of your own. Some questions you'll be able to answer in advance, others are designed as thought-provokers regarding how different scenarios could unfold.

All are intended to get you good and prepared, to assemble an armor of protective knowledge, and to build confidence every step of the way.

When the High-Stakes Communication meeting does come you will be one heck of an ironclad, formulated, unstoppable machine!

Here is your High-Stakes Communication cheat sheet. Refer to this to thoroughly prepare for any important forthcoming conversation in order to strengthen your position and your confidence as well. We'll expand on these more later, but at a minimum, ask yourself these three quick questions.

To begin, the three important questions are:

1. **What is your goal?**

    How will this High-Stakes Communication impact you? What's the best outcome for you? This is a good question to run by a mentor, trusted co-worker, or respected manager. Articulating the answer helps ensure you're thinking big enough. Also, it creates space to acknowledge any fear standing in your way, address it, and ask for courage to supersede your fear. Comprehensive preparation will get you so ready, so fired up, that fear becomes a distant memory, discarded like an empty LaCroix can in the office recycling bin.

2. **What's in it for them and what will they want to know?**
How will the other side benefit from this conversation? Shift mindset from me to we or, said another way, you to them. Consider what's in it for them that would compel and encourage them to agree and collaborate with you. Put yourself in their shoes and ask what their goals, issues, wants, needs, and objections might be and craft your conversation around that. Knowing what's coming in advance is an excellent way to prepare. (Gaming out possible incoming questions is sometimes called the Ben Duffy Approach – Duffy being a legendary ad man and sales guru, and longtime president of a global ad agency. He aced his share of High-Stakes Communication.)

3. **How will success be measured?**
And how will you know you've achieved it? In the case of an interview, it's pretty straightforward: you get hired, or you discover that the job is wrong for you and you save yourself. In a high-stakes negotiation, will success be determined when both sides reach any kind of agreement, or when some specific concession is won? In conflict resolution, do you succeed by resolving the conflict, or by letting it go and moving on? All considerations are worth evaluating in advance.

You can only hit the bullseye when you've identified the target.

Or as Wayne Gretzky said, "You miss 100% of the shots you don't take." So take the shot, and know what you're aiming for. So let's prepare to take the shot.

Yes, preparation again: the gift that keeps on giving, the bridge that helps familiarize the unfamiliar. When the unfamiliar becomes familiar, fear subsides, and you reinforce your ability to stay calm. By preparing, you're simultaneously conditioning yourself to adopt a cool, collected, confident mindset.

When you start to doubt your power, you give power to your doubt. Yet when you're impeccably prepared you have no reason to doubt yourself!
As preparation goes up, doubt goes down.

Ninety-nine percent of the time, you can expect for High-Stakes Communication scenarios to play out a little differently than you envision them. Yet thinking them through in advance, and asking strategic questions, puts you way ahead of the game. And they may even turn out better than you imagined!

Team efforts enhance your preparation game, so invite others (throughout all levels of your company) to join you. By incorporating other viewpoints in advance, you greatly increase your chances of connecting with the actual person or people on the opposite side of High-Stakes Communication. Talking things out helps you surface ideas that might have otherwise stayed boxed up in your head.

Let's break down the act of preparing for High-Stakes Communication. If the previous three questions were the cheat sheet, this is the text book.

Here's the organizing principle: *Situation, People, Organization, Conversation.* Four departments, four phases of prep. Four quarters adding up to one championship game. Prepare this way and prepare to feel your confidence and your success climb.

The Situation

The Situation, simply stated, is the circumstance that lies ahead - An interview, negotiation, promotion conversation, etc.

When you've got a High-Stakes Communication booked on the calendar, ask these questions:

What is the collective goal? Getting clear on the answer to this question will help align everything else. First identify your personal goal, as already discussed. Now, what's the shared goal? If known differences of opinion or agenda lie ahead, what are the other people's goals? Frame a shared goal to achieve early buy-in and set yourself up for success.

Just how high are the stakes? What's riding on this? Where does the outcome rank on the importance scale? The greater its importance, the more time you'll want to spend preparing. How will you be impacted – professionally, personally, or both?

Who or what is your competition? Competition can be more than the company you're up against to win business, or the other candidates for the job you so badly want. Sometimes you might be competing against higher priorities. As a potential customer once said to me, "The service you're offering is important. It's just not important to me, right now. Right now, I've got bigger things to worry about." Having a clear picture of your competition will inform your strategy.

What considerations are there around timing? When is the ideal time to hold the conversation? Timing affects outcomes. Trying to hold a high-stakes conversation with people who are distracted or in a rush is a sure-fire way to fall short of the desired outcome. Are morning meetings more likely to start on time, while afternoon meetings get cut short or cancelled because brush fires break out and individual calendars unravel? It depends on the culture. One common way important meetings get derailed and conclude without decisions is when a key player has to leave the conversation early. Assess schedules and plan accordingly.

What facts do you already know? Have you verified them? I had a gentleman on one of my sales teams who was notorious for reporting information that was completely blown out of proportion. I acted on his false guidance just once before realizing I needed to "trust but verify" anything he told me, that is, double-check with another, more reliable source. I also like the phrase, "trust but triangulate," to avoid falling prey to false assumptions.

Consider all sides to the story, especially when your High-Stakes Communication includes conflict resolution. Perform due diligence to reduce the chance of misunderstanding. As they say, there are usually three sides to a story: what I say happened, what you say happened, and what actually happened, which is somewhere in between. Gather and confirm as much detail as possible before High-Stakes Communication.

What are the unknowns? What questions remain to be answered? The value of a good question cannot be emphasized enough. Eliciting the other side's thinking with good, provocative questions will always serve you well, and thinking through those questions ahead of time is essential. What does the other side want out of this? What's at stake for them? How will they be affected? What might they be concealing?

Before moving forward, it's imperative to uncover as many relevant variables as possible.

Now for our second key preparation phase: The People.

The People

This is probably the most important prep phase for High-Stakes Communication, because people are always the major wild card. You never know exactly how someone, possibly even ourselves, will react in the moment. Yet you can prepare thoughtfully by getting inside people's heads in advance.

Ask yourself the following questions.

Who is joining you and what is each person's role? If you will be flying solo in the high-stakes conversation this phase of preparation is especially helpful. If you'll be with colleagues, loosely script the meeting to plan out who will say what. Assign names to bullet points or sections. Figure out who will lead with what information, and designate someone as the get-us-back-on-track official, should the meeting veer off course. Be flexible about going off script if the meeting calls for it, and also mindful to honor the agenda and continue to work toward your desired outcome.

Role assignments help prevent colleagues from talking over each other. You're all playing for the same team, so work out how you'll support each other in the meeting ahead. And if this high-stakes conversation is with customers, prospects, or the media – any outsider – save insults, disagreements, or unnecessarily condescending opinions for when you're back at the office. Remember Family Dinner Rules: It's one thing to argue at the table in your own home, but in a public restaurant, act like you like each other!

Who are the decision makers? It is critical to identify the decision makers. Meeting success often hinges on their presence. Most High-Stakes Communication revolves around making a decision of some kind. Make it a priority to find out who has decision making authority. One person or several? Will some or all be present in the meeting? If some will be absent, plan a follow-up strategy to ensure you connect with them, get their input, and keep the conversation going or achieve agreement on a course of action.

What are the personality types of each person involved? Friend or foe? Introvert or extrovert? Analytical or expressive? Empath or unsympathetic? Try mapping the room ahead of time. Another question you can ask is, "What language do they speak?" What jargon or level of detail resonates with them?

If you want your message to land with impact, you have to speak the audience's language. If, as an extreme example, I speak only English and you speak only Spanish, we're going to struggle. If I have a genuine interest in reaching you, though, then by all means I am going to learn at least some Spanish. Comprende? If someone's personality type is quantitative and analytical – they like numbers, data, and charts – be sure to bring those things to the high-stakes meeting. (If they love stories or anecdotes, of course, bring those instead.) If someone is known for being a natural naysayer, cantankerous or downright difficult, consider taking an ally into the meeting as a buffer.

If a conversation gets overly heated, feel free to suggest taking a break. When the participants reconvene, guide the conversation back toward a positive tone and shared goals.

If the other person in a high-stakes conversation is known to be going through a significant source of stress, professionally or personally, SEC lawsuit or sick cat, it could compete for your attention. It might be appropriate to check with them on timing. When you do sit down to meet, give them a minute to get present with you by asking a light-hearted question. "How'd your morning go?" "How are you doing on time today?" "For how long do I have the pleasure of meeting with you?" All such pleasantries, solicitous yet businesslike, are likely appropriate and even welcome.

What do they have riding on the situation? You might measure the stakes involved in this High-Stakes Communication by estimating what the other side has riding on the situation. The higher the stakes, the more intense it can be, mentally or emotionally. This is a good time to take the high road and, as always, keep calm. Be respectful of where they are. If the result is hugely important to them but not to you, meet them at their level or somewhere in the middle, working toward collaboration.

Who else will be affected? For example, if you work with a nonprofit charity that focuses on children, how will they be affected by these high-stakes decisions? If you're making a decision that will affect customers, how do you anticipate they will react? You can either ask the affected group directly before your meeting, or really try to put yourself in their place. Either will lead to a more comprehensive solution and a better chance of success.

What does a shared win look like? There's a lot of room for creativity in this one. What does each side value? Value can be a key consideration: it can lend a lot of leverage in a negotiation. You can almost always identify things that one side values more than the other; some may not even have monetary value. Would the other side see value if you offered promotion through social media posts? Would dual participation in a volunteer day be interesting? Getting creative on this one increases the reward level of a shared win.

Now for the third of our four preparation phases.

The Organization

Almost as important as the people in your High-Stakes Communication: Get a feel for their organization, too. If you were to describe the organization as an individual person what words would you use? Bold, assertive, innovative?

Conservative, thoughtful, stable? How would you talk in order to get its attention? The questions in the section will help lead you to the answers.

What is The Organization's personality? Is the culture comfortable with conflict? Expert at collaboration? What communication styles have you observed among its workers? Is the vibe more formal or casual, more tense or more relaxed? Are there shuffleboard tables and dogs running around the office, or is there a strict dress code without so much as a messy bulletin board in view? All these are indicators of organizational personality that can help acclimate you to the environment.

How will The Situation affect The Organization's resources? This depends on the range of outcomes that can result from the high-stakes conversation. Is someone seeking a financial commitment? An in-kind commitment, such as borrowing employees for a volunteer day? Is this High-Stakes Communication about safety? Whatever the case may be, if a request for resources is involved, the person who has authority to make decisions around resource allocation should be present as well. Prepare to communicate effectively with that person and/or team.

What unique internal or external factors at The Organization might be influencing The Situation? Is this organization in start-up mode and strapped for cash? Is there pending legislation that could affect its products or policies? Has the political climate impacted operations? Is there a merger or acquisition pending? The point is to be aware and sensitive to anything going on in The Organization that could affect High-Stakes Communication.

What can and cannot be controlled? Of the unique factors influencing The Organization, which can managers control, and which are beyond their control? If legislative or regulatory action, or election results (factors beyond their control), impact the organization, be sensitive to plan around days when results are announced.

What are the short-term and long-term goals of The Organization? This question speaks to the overall impact your communication will have. Depending on what the organization wants to accomplish in the near or short term, the issue at the center of your high-stakes conversation may impact it. Having a grasp of this is important.

When you've focused preparatory energy on The Situation, The People, and The Organization, the fourth and final thing to turn to is the format of the High-

Stakes Communication event itself.

The Conversation

In advance of the main event, ask these questions about The Conversation.

How will attendees participate – In person, on speakerphone, or via webcam? Knowing the answer is important for two reasons. First, if you're bringing handouts, leave-behinds, marketing collateral, logo'd coffee tumblers, or pizza, you'll want to know how many are attending. (If most of your audience is on speakerphone, there's no point in supplying pizza for all.). Knowing the lay of the attendance land will prevent anyone from being left out.

Secondly, speakerphone or Zoom meetings will require different efforts to elicit feedback. Plan accordingly and know that they take more energy than face-to-face meetings. Plan for a post-meeting re-charge!

Do a tech check. Whether virtual or in person, do a technology dress rehearsal to ensure that you know how to make everything work and that it is actually working, that the systems are talking to one another. Have the IT support person's cell phone on hand and give them a heads up about your upcoming meeting.

Set the Agenda. Among your best tools to keep High-Stakes Communication organized, goal-oriented, and running on time: an agenda. Write one up in advance, share it with the team, and bring hard copies to the meeting. If prior meetings or communication have occurred, note it on the agenda so nobody's out of the loop about events that have already transpired.

An agenda is also a very effective driver for staying on task because, if you sense the meeting is going off-beam, you can point to the agenda and say, "Thank you, Bob, for those comments. I think that's something we should certainly address in a later meeting. For now, let's keep to the agenda. I believe we were about to conclude on bullet point number two."

Confirm the time allotted. This is a biggie. As a best practice, always confirm at the start of the conversation the planned ending time. When time is limited, it discourages tangents and helps everyone stay on task. And when people commit to a certain block of time – one hour, say – it's harder for them to duck out early muttering, "Sorry, have to go, I have another meeting." Confirm in advance by saying, "Okay, great, so we're all committed to an hour today. If anyone has to leave early, do I have permission to proceed with the rest of the meeting as planned?" By doing so you'll set yourself up for success by being able to move forward, regardless of a surprise exit.

Is there value in setting ground rules? If you know there's a big talker in the room, ground rules can be an effective way to mitigate unwanted hijacking. You might say, for example, "I want to be respectful of everyone's time today. I know we only have an hour, so I'd like to stick to our agenda. Is there anything anyone wanted to cover today that's not included?" Give others a chance to comment briefly, then keep moving!

If the high-stakes conversation has potential to be highly contentious, you can set helpful ground rules just by saying so. Name it to claim it. Call it out. "I know this is a highly sensitive topic," you might say as a meeting leader. "It can be complex to talk through, yet I feel confident that by showing each other respect and choosing our words carefully, this meeting will go well." Laying appropriate groundwork can prevent unforeseen bombs from exploding. Even if one does explode, you'll now likely have allies to give you cover and collectively work through it.

What happens immediately before and after? What mood will attendees be in when they arrive? Will there be a window for lunch or happy hour afterward? Of course you can never know for sure, yet having a notion of what their mindset could be when they get there, may help you decide whether to get right down to business or dedicate time for a little relationship building.

Can you summarize and agree to a goal? One of my favorite managers used to say in his thick Texas accent, "We don't have to all be on the same page, but we do have to be in the same book." It's always productive to start out by stating the conversation's shared goal, if possible. "Before we begin, I'd like to state what I believe to be the shared goal for this meeting. And I'd like to confirm that we're all on the same page." Depending on the vibe, you may want to try breaking the ice with a little humor, saying in the style of a wedding pastor, "We are gathered here today to . . . "

Anticipate what could go wrong. What scenarios could prompt everyone to feel as though they need to run for cover and assume battle stations? Somebody blows up, an unexpected piece of information surfaces, or the meeting gets disrupted by a higher priority. If disaster or even semi-disaster strikes, how will you respond?

Don't conclude until you've asked three important questions.

In order to ensure that all important variables have been identified and that the conversation is tracking in the direction you want, use these final questions before closing and concluding the meeting:

- Is there anything we haven't covered or that we've missed?
- Do you have any concerns that would prevent us from moving forward?
- Is there anything I haven't asked that I should be asking?

I've found that unless you're up against a flat-out liar, these three questions will surface any remaining details you need to reach agreement or make a decision about next steps.

How will you conclude?

What statement(s) will need to be made or questions answered in order to conclude the meeting? What will you need to know to determine next steps and to confirm that a decision has been reached? Identify what those are, clearly articulate the different possibilities and practice them out loud.

What will you need from everyone to end the meeting and move forward? What are the anticipated action items? How will you delegate them? Well before the meeting starts, visualize how you want it to end. If a written agreement is part of that picture, bring printed documents ready for signing. Even if they can be signed digitally, it's always prudent to have a hard copy on hand. Will a follow up email be expected with a bullet point summary? Take notes and follow through. Is sending a thank you note appropriate? Still a thing, especially with job interviews!

Plan for how you'll move swiftly at the close of the meeting and beyond to ride out your success, maintain the momentum you've ignited and to avoid back tracking later.

This may seem like a lot to think about before High-Stakes Communication takes place. Yet I promise that reviewing these questions thoughtfully is a lot less taxing than recovering from a high-stakes conversation gone off the rails.

If you find yourself stumped by any of these questions, connect in advance with meeting attendees. Depending on the state of your business relationship, send an email or make a phone call: "Jim, I'm working on preparation for our meeting. I'd like for it to be really successful. As part of my due diligence, do you mind if I ask you a few questions? I'd really like to understand where you're coming from and what the company's viewpoint is before we come to the table."

I've had a pretty good success rate with that approach. Anyway, the worst they can say is 'No,' which could be a clue right there for how the meeting will go. Either way, you're better prepared than if you hadn't asked.

When you're confident that you know The Situation, The People, The Organization, and as much about The Conversation as possible – you're ready for dress rehearsal. Invite co-workers to play the roles of the people you'll be meeting with and run through scenarios from best-case to worst. Yes, I know saying "role playing exercise" out loud is a sure-fire way to elicit groans of, "Do-we-really-have-to-do-this?" Yet role playing, bad reputation or not, is one more way to familiarize the unfamiliar and reduce the odds of some unforeseen curveball denting your confidence and success. Role playing prep can feel awkward or goofy in the moment, yet will translate to strength in familiarity when you are beyond prepared in the moment when you need it the most.

Bonus Tips

Here are a few additional tips to send you walking out of that meeting, pumping your fist with satisfaction. You'll be doing your touchdown dance in the elevator, because you scored and scored big!

Dress the part. Whether you've been a bride, a bridesmaid, or just a wedding guest, you know what head-to-toe preparation the bride goes through. From precise placement of every highlight and hair on her head down to the high-gloss pedicure. No detail is spared and the bride radiates on her wedding day. That glow starts from inside and is reinforced by the care she takes to present her favorite version of herself. Her confidence is undeniable. While going through that same preparation isn't exactly the protocol to follow her, that level of preparation and choice of confidence couture will work in your favor! For me, proper makeup, hair secured, well tailored clothes, pointed-toe patent leather heels and a fresh manicure bring it all together. Wear what makes you say, I look great. I feel great. *I am great. Look out, world, I'm ready for you!*

Take your notes with you. You've spent all this time prepping. Thankfully, this is not a closed-book exam. Take your research into the meeting. Remember the meeting survival technique we talked about way back in Chapter 3, where you increase confidence by making yourself appear bigger? In a high-stakes conversation, do that with your notes, neatly printed out and organized in a binder. Your laptop or touch pad works too, just be sure to silence alerts to eliminate distractions and maintain your focus.

Voice and Timing. Recall the voice features you can control to ensure a trip to Professional Palisade, while cruising straight past Timid Town. Uptick, also described as a high pitch to end your sentence, implies to listeners that confidence is wavering. Keep your pitch grounded and your volume consistent to hold your audience's attention on your great content.

The timing of your words is another consideration. When you're excited or frustrated, it can be tempting to interrupt another person. You'll be forgiven at times due to your irrepressible enthusiasm, but be mindful of talking over others repeatedly, somthing you'll easily be able to avoid while standing tall in your power.

Expect the unexpected. Mike Tyson, the champion prizefighter, said, "Everybody has a plan until they get hit." And your preparation will prevent you from getting launched out of the ring, even if you do get blindsided.

Be open-minded about unanticipated changes in direction. High-Stakes Communication might not always go as expected, yet preparation will undoubtedly build and help you maintain a higher confidence level for when the time comes – a professional tool you'll always have in your belt!

My High-Stakes Interview

I opened the chapter relating the story of a high-stakes job interview at an oil-and-gas company – for a business development position that I *really* wanted. Here is how this case of High-Stakes Communication turned out.

Although I had no industry credentials, my goal was to leave my interviewers unequivocally convinced that I was *the* candidate for the job. During my preparation I learned that I was up against another candidate who had previously worked for the company and was well-liked. I knew that if I wanted to "win" the interview, I couldn't just bring my A game; I had to dial it up to A++.

My preparation for that interview was insane.

I bought a beer for a buddy already in the industry and asked him to draw me a diagram of the equipment I'd be selling. "Tell me everything you know," I implored and he willingly obliged. I still have that diagram (Situation).

I printed out and committed to memory the LinkedIn profiles of all six men who would be interviewing me (People). I compiled a thick tab binder containing everything from the company's core values, to its competitors, to technical details of the product line (Organization).

I anticipated their questions, wrote my answers on notecards, and rehearsed my delivery out loud with a coach (Conversation).

I tried on the outfit I'd strategically selected for the interview a week beforehand, making sure it was crisply pressed and free of loose threads. And that if I started to sweat, the material and color would not betray me.

When my appointment at company headquarters finally rolled around, I was more ready for this job interview than an overworked, under-socialized, well-deserving mom heading off for girls' night out.

I sat down on one side of the boardroom table and faced my interviewers. No stranger to being the youngest in the room, nor the only woman, I was here in that situation again. And with no industry experience. The six men who lined up and sat down across from me were welcoming, yet not overly friendly. They began firing questions at me. My heart was pounding, yet the pen I held tightly in my hand ensured that I wouldn't shake. A 'power bracelet' wrapped my left wrist.

The questions ranged from, "Tell us the difference between a strategy and a tactic," to, "What do you know about Artificial Lift?" a service line with which I of course had zero previous experience. I responded honestly, saying I'd studied the process and equipment, on my own and with a friend in the industry. My voice was steady. Assured. Confident. I pictured the interview coach I'd worked with while rehearsing the answers I was now delivering in real time.

Then I shared that I'd already conceived and built a chart to guide my formal learning process should I be offered the job. I maintained a pleasant look on my face, not too smiley, and consciously avoiding RBF. Welcoming, friendly, but not too friendly.

"A chart?" one of my interviewers asked.

I pulled it out of my binder and handed it across the table.

The gentleman gave it a good once-over. Another man on the end of the lineup said, "Let me see it." It was passed around and got quite a few head nods. I could still feel my heartbeat, now devoid of nerves, and gathering excitement and satisfaction.

Judging from his appearance and demeanor, the man on the end looked like a member of the "good ol' boys" club. He set my chart aside and looked me square in the eyes.

"Does it intimidate you to sit across the table from this many years of experience?"

My inner self rolled her eyes, yet I remained impassive. Two of my other interviewers gave each other glances that seemed supportive of me. "Seriously, Dale?" one said, implying that his question had crossed a line.

Rather than ignore or defer the question, I met Dale's gaze squarely. "Actually, no, it doesn't intimidate me. I feel excited and honored to be here in the presence of this much experience."

The others chuckled with approval. Mic drop. Thank you very much, Dale!

When the interview concluded – well past its scheduled time -- a representative from Human Resources walked into the room to collect me. My panel of interviewers was still there, milling around. She smiled at me, then glanced at my binder quizzically. "Is that a binder?"

"Yes," I responded.

"Did we give that to you?"

"No," I said, "I built it to prepare for this interview."

The HR woman looked more closely. "It has tabs," she said, impressed. "I've never seen anyone take that much time and effort to prepare for an interview."

I loved that she said that out loud in front of the whole group. "Well, now you know how much I want this job," I smiled.

In summary, the stakes were high – for me, anyway. I knew the audience would be tough. Through immense, diligent, comprehensive preparation, I won my round of High-Stakes Communication. The Brave-ah-na felt euphoric!

I was offered the job, despite my rival who had a history with the company, inside-track affection, and all the industry expertise. My lack of industry knowledge was dismissed after my live demonstration of what well-crafted p reparation and unwavering confidence can do.

Job interviews are special cases of High-Stakes Communication. They don't usually pop out at you without warning. In cases other than interviews, you won't always have the option to prepare. They can arise without much notice, especially in the case of conflict resolution. Getting in the habit of using the Situation-People-Organization-Conversation preparation system, however, might surprise you in how it will condition you. The preparation you do for one high-stakes meeting will carry over into another. You'll spot trends in how your conversations went, what went well, and what you'd do differently next time. Through experience, you'll gain confidence – knowing how to navigate communication and achieve shared success even faster.

Whatever High-Stakes Communication you face, preparation is your BFF. Use these ideas to become a Communication Crusher! Celebrate as you rack up your success stories!

What's at Stake?

As our friend Benjamin Franklin taught us, "Failing to prepare is preparing to fail." Your success rate in High-Stakes Communication is closely dependent upon the meticulousness of your preparation!

Key Points

- Evaluate the Situation, the People, the Organization, and the Conversation itself to prepare thoroughly for High-Stakes Communication.
- Reduce risk of having your confidence rattled by familiarizing the unfamiliar and erring on the side of over-preparation.
- Interviews, negotiations, sales pitches, conflict resolution, and even change management are all examples of High-Stakes Communication.
- Preparation allows you to gather details, organize thoughts, and build confidence through information and practice.

Confidence Challenge Checklist

- ❏ That high-stakes conversation you keep postponing? Time to schedule it and get to prepping!
- ❏ Review an example of High-Stakes Communication from your past by recalling the questions that came up and how either side handled them. Is there anything you'll do differently next time?
- ❏ Gather your teammates to prepare together for a big meeting.
- ❏ Prepare for your next professional interview or promotion by creating a binder of information. What is most helpful and relevant for your research?
- ❏ Grab a friend or colleague and role-play a case of High-Stakes Communication in your workplace.

To condition and claim my confidence, one action I commit to is:

_____

_____

_____

Call to Action
It's Time to Speak Up, Step Up, and Lift Up!

As I sit typing these final pages, the evening news is on in the background. Like many of you, I'm working from home, socially distancing and never leaving home without my mask. When the initial manuscript for this project was completed, COVID19 had not yet begun. Since then, we've experienced cancellations and countless disruptions to our lives. It's unfamiliar, high stakes circumstances for us all.

Thankfully, in the midst of this unprecedented time, other things are becoming contagious too. People supporting people has reached new levels. Conversations that would never have taken place, now are. The Black Lives Matter movement has a louder voice than it's ever had, as do initiatives for women's empowerment. Incredibly courageous voices are **speaking up** so as to finally be heard.

I love that we're seeing countless examples of how individual performance is further enhanced by support from our friends and our communities. Also known as the people in our squad, our personal and professional squad, whose support helps assist in transforming one's mere survival into thrival.

The lessons laid out in this book are simple in concept. Yet putting them into action for the first time might be challenging. Some take practice. Success rates may fluctuate, but what won't ever waver is the value of a strong support system. It's the people in your support system, on your designated squad, your MACs and beyond, who help you see the gifts and talents within you, even – perhaps especially – when you cannot see them yourself. They believe in you, cheer for you, celebrate your victories and lift you up should you stumble. They offer support to you just like you do for others.

So now it's time. To call on your courage. To reach for the Brave-ah-na. To step up to the plate. And to take that first swing. That's all it takes to get your confidence in motion. Take a swing, even a tiny step, in the direction you want to go.

Flip back through the challenges and commit to completing the ones that speak to you most. Justify the time you've invested in reading this book by applying the ideas, implementing new habits, growing your confidence, and achieving transformation. And know that you don't have to go it alone. There is strength in numbers. Remember Derek Jeter saying with confidence, "Hit it to me"? Jeter, like all team athletes, had people who supported him. A squad whose strengths complemented his weaknesses, and who encouraged him when he'd made an error.

Ask yourself: who's on *your* squad? Who are the men and women you can go to when you need a hand, or when you deserve a high five for a big win? Who are the people who on a day-to-day basis will lend a helping hand and be a voice to support and challenge yours. To root you on as you stretch your confidence muscles, to celebrate your successes, to help you learn from failures, and to remind you to keep moving forward.

Prioritize and cherish those people. Hold them in high regard. Review the chapter on Mentors, Allies, and Champions to be reminded how to find them! As Bette Midler sang, they are the wind beneath your wings and we can all use that boost from time to time!

To find your squad members, be that squad member. Be the friend, supporter, manager, subordinate, colleague, and woman whom you want others to be for you. In times of abundance as well as times of crisis, there will be people who challenge you, or are threatened by your efforts to succeed. They may attempt to thwart your efforts. As I hope you now know, down to the very core of your soul, those people do not have power over you. They are not your people… and they deserve none of your energy other than as catalysts to rise above the obstacles and break through the barriers they try to impose! Standing up for yourself, speaking up for yourself, staying true to yourself, and finding support for yourself: those are the keys to surviving and thriving, each and every time.

I'll leave you with a final inspirational story. Recall that one of the gifts of confidence is its contagious nature. One way to grow our confidence is by boosting another's. And the favor may be easily returned. There's a power in the transferable energy of confidence, and one that even aerodynamics has recognized.

Envision a flock of birds flying in V-formation, a site frequently seen as you look up into the sky. Do you know why birds do that? Why they fly in that specific shape? They do it for one single reason. *To lift each other up.* The bird in front provides uplift to the one trailing behind it and then that one pays it forward (or backwards in this case) with the one behind it and so on. Beyond its simplistic collaborative nature, here's the really cool part: their *combined* efforts allow the flock to increase its range by up to 71 percent. Seventy-one percent!

They fly significantly farther and faster together than they can manage alone.

Ladies, it gets even better. This same concept is ours to implement.

When you're in a meeting and see another woman struggling, flailing her wings as it were, because she's too afraid to speak up and share her brilliant insight, you be the lead bird for a moment and extend her some uplift. "You know, Michelle and I were talking about this earlier," you can say. "Michelle, will you share with the group what you told me? Your idea was brilliant. Everyone would benefit from hearing it." Michelle gets the floor to share her genius and you both just increased your range and visibility on the leadership radar.

In another meeting, another moment, a soft-spoken woman might contribute something good, but louder voices talk over her and miss it. Contribute your uplift by piping up, "Jill, please say that again. Everyone didn't hear you the first time." What a gift when you speak up to catalyze someone else to speak up too! Be sure to celebrate with a high five and a victory dance in your office later!

And when it's your own turn, if solo courage isn't igniting your voice, picture that woman whose confidence inspires you. What would she do? And make her proud by emulating her leadership as you SPEAK UP.

As women, we are better together, stronger together, more confident together, and more successful together. Sure, we can fly on our own. But together, Sheroes? Together we soar.

Soaring takes confidence. It proves confidence. And confidence, pure and simple, is the message of this book. Cultivating it, owning it, and living it to empower the highest and best version of you.

Here's to soaring, lifting each other up, and carrying ourselves with the confidence we all possess. May your skies be blue, your wings spread widely, and your confidence shine brightly!

May you always stand strong in your power to
Speak Up, Sister!

I'd love to hear your success stories! Or help with any challenges. I invite you to explore options to implement what you learned here, as well as to further develop your Confidence and Leadership skills and enhance your career! Please visit www.jamieempowers.com, where you'll find resources and information for groups and individuals. Or tell me what's on your mind by contacting me directly at www.jamieempowers.com/contact. I'd love to hear from you!

About the Author

Jamie Dandar McKinney, MBA, is a professional coach, keynote speaker, certified virtual presenter, and author. The President and Founder of Jamie Empowers, Inc., she launched her business in 2019 and is fully immersed in her mission to empower women to ditch doubts, speak up and achieve the careers they deserve and desire.

Leaning on lessons learned over the course of 20 years while working her way up in heavily male-dominated industries, Jamie ignites action in her clients to advance their careers. Combining neuroscience with real-life experience, she discovered the formula for building confidence and demonstrating effective leadership. She was recognized by the Denver Business Journal as a Top 40 Woman in Energy and jokes that her stilettos have steel-toes.

Jamie lives in Denver, CO with her husband, Rob and their dog, Penny. Glitter is her favorite color and she calls on Supreme Court Justice Ruth Bader Ginsberg as her spirit animal.

Talk with Jamie

Social media offers a great opportunity for you to connect and interact with Jamie. She continues to share her wisdom and experiences on her social channels.

 Jamie Dandar McKinney

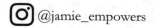 @jamie_empowers

Snap a selfie while holding the book and tag us on Instagram @Jamie_Empowers!

One Last Thing...

If this book had an impact on how you think about your confidence and has given you any nuggets of wisdom on how to find success, please take a moment to write a review. Please visit any **online bookstore** or **GoodReads.com**, search for this book and leave a review. It would also be an honor if you share this resource on any of your social media pages.

Your review does make a difference in helping others find this resource.